Sunday, Sabbath, and the Weekend

Sunday, Sabbath, and the Weekend

Managing Time in a Global Culture

Edited by

Edward O'Flaherty, S.J., & Rodney L. Petersen,
with Timothy A. Norton

William B. Eerdmans Publishing Company
Grand Rapids, Michigan / Cambridge, U.K.

© 2010 Wm. B. Eerdmans Publishing Co.

Published 2010 by
Wm. B. Eerdmans Publishing Co.
2140 Oak Industrial Drive N.E., Grand Rapids, Michigan 49505 /
P.O. Box 163, Cambridge CB3 9PU U.K.

Printed in the United States of America

16 15 14 13 12 11 10   7 6 5 4 3 2 1

Library of Congress Cataloging-in-Publication Data

Sunday, sabbath, and the weekend: managing time in a global culture /
   edited by Edward O'Flaherty & Rodney L. Petersen; with Timothy A. Norton.
     p.   cm.
   ISBN 978-0-8028-6583-0 (pbk.: alk. paper)
   1. Sunday. 2. Sabbath. 3. Rest — Religious aspects — Christianity.
   4. Time management — Religious aspects — Christianity.   I. O'Flaherty, Edward.
   II. Petersen, Rodney Lawrence.   III. Norton, Timothy A.

BV111.3.S87   2010
263'.3 — dc22

                         2010022388

www.eerdmans.com

To Roger A. Kvam

Contents

Contents

Preface

Why do we have Sunday, or Sabbath — or even the weekend for that matter? Is it release from the serious time given over to work and vocation? Is it a period marked by youth and professional sports? Does such a day, or period of time, provide opportunity for or escape from commercial pursuits? Our contemporary culture presses for a 24/7 engagement with life, but still we have Sunday, Sabbath, and the weekend to factor into the management of our time. Is the maintenance of Sunday, Sabbath, and the weekend a holdover from a previous culture or do these periods of time reflect a different view of the management of time from that of the 24/7 culture in which we find ourselves, a view that is important for our well-being? The argument of this book is that such is the case.

Abraham Heschel, in *The Sabbath: Its Meaning for Modern Man*, a book on the nature and celebration of Shabbat, the Jewish Sabbath, writes that the idea of Sabbath is rooted in the thesis that Judaism is a religion of time, not space, that the Sabbath symbolizes the sanctification of time. How we use our time says something about us and what we would like to be. The Sabbath, as opened up by Judaism in the Hebrew Bible, or Old Testament, says at least three things about time and, therefore, about us. First, it is said to be for our well-being. Second, keeping Sabbath gives us a certain lens through which to view life. Finally, how we practice Sabbath says something about how we understand ourselves to be made in the divine image.

Christians keep Sabbath and call it Sunday. In some essays in this book, the historical change of observing the Lord's Day, the day of Christ's resurrection, as the day of worship is recounted, as well as the theological reasons justifying the change. The Christian Day of the Lord lost nothing of the values which Sabbath inculcates: mercy, service, liberation, healing, and rest. The forces affecting early Christian worship on the Lord's Day (persecution, minority status preventing taking time from work obligations, etc.) prevented initially a full observance of a "new" day of rest, a "new" Sabbath. Only gradually did the Lord's Day become Sunday and provided opportunity for the full living out of Sabbath values in the context of celebrating Christ's resurrection.

EDWARD O'FLAHERTY AND
RODNEY L. PETERSEN

Dedication and Acknowledgment

The volume you hold in your hands is the result of many hours of volunteer labor by The Rev. Dr. Edward O'Flaherty, S.J., and my colleague and co-director of the Lord's Day Alliance, Rev. Dr. Rodney L. Petersen. These two men, along with all who contributed to this work, are due our most heartfelt thanks and hearty congratulations for a work well done.

In its 2005 Annual Meeting, the Board of Managers of the Lord's Day Alliance of the U.S. heard a proposal to honor one of their own, Roger A. Kvam, for his many years of service as a member, officer, president, and president emeritus of the Board. This book is dedicated to him.

As a point of personal privilege, having served alongside LDA Presidents Dr. Paul J. Craven, Dr. Roger A. Kvam, Dr. W. David Sapp, and Mr. Brian C. Hanse over my tenure as executive director of the Lord's Day Alliance, I would like to thank each for their leadership.

And I'd like to especially thank Roger Kvam, a mentor, counselor, and friend, for his friendship, pastoral care in times of need, and willingness to go "above and beyond" in his service of the God we serve.

TIMOTHY A. NORTON

Relational Presence

Is Sunday a time to be alone or to be with others? Posed starkly, this question seems to admit only a "yes" or a "no," but in reality it introduces us to the complexities of trying to define, that is, put limits on, the reality of Sabbath rest. For some people Sunday provides a retreat from a heavy schedule, or being available to a cohort of business friends, clients, or the public in general. "I want to be alone," we sometimes cry in despair. And yet do we?

Perhaps we are looking really for relatedness on a deeper, less utilitarian level, a connection with God, self, and the other that does not exhaust but enlivens us. Gloria White-Hammond, MD, reflects on this desire and need. Pediatrician, mother, and co-pastor, she has been convinced by her personal experience, her religious work, and her professional work of the need for this deeper level of relatedness among those with whom we are closest. Relationships cannot be quantified, only experienced, and that requires time. And time points to the Sabbath.

Our relationships obviously extend beyond family to the neighborhood, city and town, and to the nation itself. These relationships too need to be deepened no less than those with our intimates, but first they need to be recognized and embraced as requiring special attention. Rodney Petersen gives the theological underpinnings for such realistic acceptance of those with whom we interact, but do not see face to face. The world of global citizenship contends for attention. This global world is structural in such a way that what happens in Beijing reverberates in Boston, as well as in Berlin. We are not an archipelago of individual nations, but one continuous continent in upheaval. Thus the question: Is Sabbath rest a need or gift only for us? What about the others? Contemporary events show us the line between a national "we" and an international "them" is blurring.

Surely Christian faith, weak as it may be, does link men and women throughout the world, and this unity finds expression in our common Sunday. But what of those with whom we share no common faith? What Christians do share with the Jewish people and Muslims is a desire to keep holy the Lord's Day or Sabbath. Each religious group names a different day as their day of observance, but the principle is the same: keep the day holy. Marva Dawn explores this need for the Sabbath and shows us how a true understanding of Sabbath keeping leads to peace-making and peace makers thirst for justice without which lasting peace is impossible. The name "Sabbath" is understood in these three traditions quite clearly, but the notion of Sabbath is not confined to them. The day of rest, of peace-making and justice promotion, finds allies elsewhere, that is, men and women with whom Christians can make common cause in trying to eliminate violence as a tactic for peace. Marva Dawn's essay shows us how we can recognize and strengthen these links.

CHAPTER ONE

Home Alone — Seeking Sabbath

Gloria White-Hammond

My life is like yours, a very full life. I wear several different hats, and the days that are really toughest are the days I have to wear all the hats at once. I am the co-pastor and the pediatrician and the doctor and the mom and the wife, and my husband and I have had the privilege of taking care of his mother who has been living with us, and she has had middle stage Alzheimer's disease. At the end of the day, it has been a full day for me as I am sure it is for you most days.

As I think about "seeking Sabbath" in my life, or about Sunday as Sabbath, my thoughts turn to the Gospel of Luke in the second chapter. Here we read of the account of the boy Jesus at the Temple. It begins:

> Every year his parents went to Jerusalem for the Feast of the Passover. When He was twelve years old they went up to the feast according to the custom. After the feast was over, while his parents were returning home, the boy Jesus stayed behind in Jerusalem, but they were unaware of it. Thinking he was in their company they traveled on for a day, then they began looking for him among their relatives and friends. When they did not find Him they went back to Jerusalem to look for Him.

Now I'm especially interested in verse 44: "Thinking he was in their company, they traveled on for a day." And I'm going to ask you to very quickly think with me on the topic of "Home Alone." Home alone. I was especially excited to take up this topic. I must confess that when I first received a request to think about "Seeking Sabbath," I had awakened early in the morning and, going through the mail (and in our house mail can sit for a couple of weeks before we actually get to it — thank you, Jesus!) I opened up this

3

mail and the invitation — and I still had sleep in my eyes — and the first thing I read was "*Sneaking* Sabbath." And I thought, oh my gosh! Isn't this a really deep kind of thought, that we are *sneaking* Sabbath. It was only after I looked again that I realized in fact the title was "*Seeking* Sabbath."

The reality is, the reason so many of us might have had the same reaction is because for too many of us we do in fact have to *"sneak"* Sabbath. When we make room for it at all, we have to sneak that time of rest. I come to you through the medium of this opening chapter in a book on "Seeking Sabbath" in this culture, or on Sunday as Sabbath in a global culture, recognizing the difficulty of what this may mean for each of us. And I come not only as clergy, but as a pediatrician who is very concerned about the impact of the fact that we as a culture do not seek the Sabbath and in fact many times do not even *"sneak"* the Sabbath. And so my title in these opening remarks is "Home Alone — Seeking Sabbath."

Many of you may recall the title *Home Alone.* It was the name of a very popular box office hit several years ago. The movie takes place during Christmas time when the family is preparing to go abroad to celebrate Christmas. They are so frantically going through all of their packing and preparations to get to the airport and onto the plane that it is not until they are well in the air and well on their way that they discover that one of their children is in fact not with them. Instead, he has been left home alone. He is home alone, there to fend for himself — and to fend off some bumbling burglars! Much of the movie is focused on this little boy who is home alone and on his efforts to be rid of the intruding burglars. It is a delightful comedy, but also one that drew me to the text of Luke 2:44 as we are drawn to the topic of Sabbath — and of Sunday as Sabbath — in contemporary culture.

In this particular text in the Gospel of Luke we come upon the parents of Jesus as they too have set out on a journey, not realizing, unaware, ignorant, incognizant, unmindful, and not "with it" — caught tripping, not hip-to-the-fact that their boy Jesus was not with them. Thinking that he was with their company, assuming that he was with them, they traveled on. However, like with the little boy Kevin in the movie *Home Alone,* Jesus' parents were well on their way before they realized that in fact their child was not with them. He was, in fact, making his own way and doing his own thing. In the business of organizing and reorganizing, making lists and "checking them twice," they had assumed that the boy was with them when in fact he was not.

This is a phenomenon that is probably familiar to those of you who like me come from large families. There were eight in my family. In fact there were five of us who were one year apart. And so I can remember some occasions when someone got left behind. There was one occasion when my father took us to the beach. The eight of us used to pile into our old blue Studebaker and he'd stack us into the car in the days before mandatory seatbelts. We grew up in an Air Force family and lived on Guam at the time. Every Sunday afternoon he would take us to the beach. I remember looking out of that car and seeing my mom on the porch waving goodbye. I thought she was so brave because she was smiling even though there was no room in the car for her. I thought of her as making a sacrifice of love so that we could go to the beach; she would have to stay at home, alone. It wasn't until I grew up and had children of my own (by the way, although my mother had eight I have only two — and I call one *alpha* for the beginning and the other *omega* for the end) that I realized that in fact she wasn't making a sacrifice of love, she was *sneaking* Sabbath.

I come to this conversation of finding what Sabbath means in our society with a sense of urgency. As a pediatrician I have devoted over twenty-five years to a professional career ministering to the health and wholeness of children and of their families. Among my greatest rewards as a practitioner is seeing many of my children grow and develop and mobilize their strengths and marshal their resources to successfully negotiate the increasingly daunting package called life in the twenty-first century. Most of these children will do well, but a few will not. Because God desires that none should be lost, a few is a few too many.

From wealthy suburban neighborhoods to impoverished urban communities, too many of our children are experiencing the painfully slow but steady process of going under. Life is killing them softly as our best and brightest gradually succumb to the risky behaviors that attract them toward death at an early age. We are in a crisis. According to the recent publications of the state of America's children, published by the Children's Defense Fund, at the end of every day, including this day, six children and youths under twenty will commit suicide and ten children and youth under the age of twenty will be homicide victims. At the end of this day 186 children will be arrested for violent crime, and 1,354 babies will be born to teenage mothers. Almost 8,000 children will be reported as being abused and neglected, and over 17,000 public school students will have been suspended at the end of this day. These are the victims of a not-too-silent holocaust that characterizes your community and mine. It invades our communities, our churches, and even our homes. Too many of America's children are home alone.[1]

I often receive referrals from the School Department requesting me to evaluate children for attention deficit disorders. And I often find that the problem is less with the child, who is naturally curious and active in his or her own way, with his or her own way of learning, and more an issue with the school which does not want to take the time to discover this particular child's learning style and to set up a structure that will adapt accordingly. Occasionally I do see a kid who is high impact, nonstop energy, who cannot be focused on drawing a nice picture for the doctor and will not be distracted from destroying every nook and cranny of my office. Now that is an attention deficit hyperactivity disorder.

A couple of weeks ago I took the bus in to work and there was this one little girl I was watching on the bus. She was just a pure wiggle worm. She moved back and forth in the seat, and then she started singing at the top of her voice, "A B C D E F G. . . ." And she would just turn around and around. She was just a busy little girl. And I thought, "My goodness, what a handful she is!" Only soon did I discover, as we both got off at the same stop and went to the second floor of my office building, that she was my first patient for the day. Indeed, she had attention deficit hyperactivity disorder.

I fear that our culture has developed a malignant case of ADHD, and that it is destroying the integrity of the village that needs to raise the children. It's been said that in order to locate one's heart you must look at one's calendar and one's checkbook. If we look at our collective calendar and checkbook, my fear is that it may reveal a set of priorities in this culture that functionally regards our children as readily dispensable and easily disposable. Too many of our children are home alone.

For many of us the pull to be here and the push to go there, the drive to buy some of this and purchase more of that finds us busy, and in fact too busy to minister effectively to our families. Every day over 351 children are arrested for drug abuse and over 2,000 babies are born to mothers who are not high school graduates. Too many of America's children are home alone. Of course, I realize to a large extent that I am preaching to the choir. I suspect that that is why many of you may be interested in a book like this, because you know all of this to be true. We need to find that Sabbath in our

---

1. See the Annual Reports of the Children's Defense Fund (CDF), a non-profit advocacy organization for all children: 25 E Street NW, Washington, DC 20001.

lives that enables us to be present to one another and, in particular, to our children. Many of you, like me, are on the front lines, and we do not have the luxury of simply reading the statistics or simply hearing about the stories. Sabbath has something to do not only with our relation to God but also to one another. We are daily reminded of this as we are challenged to look beyond the matter of facts of the numbers and peer at the strained faces of boys and girls trapped beneath a load of overwhelming cares, for too many of our children are home alone.

My own need for Sabbath comes firsthand, up close and personal. Some time ago my husband talked with the CEO of TJX Companies, which owns TJMaxx Corporation. The company lost several of its buyers on Flight 11 out of Logan in the 9/11 tragedy. He said the most salient aspect of the crisis was not helping people to work through their anxieties about flying again but processing their concerns about the busyness of their lives, and the extent to which their lifestyle takes them away from their families.

He said that many of the people with whom he met were trying to come to grips with the reality that nobody on their deathbed ever regrets not making just one more meeting. They regret the breakdown or loss of relationships. I know that especially on this side of September 11, 2001, God is calling you and me to be examples of behavior that manifests the good use of time, to wade through the rubble of life and to begin to rebuild from the ruins that characterize too much of our spiritual lives. We must raise up the solid foundations of our homes that have been chipped away at by the worries of this life, the deceitfulness of wealth, and the desire for other things; repair the broken walls of our fractured churches which, because they have been divided against themselves, have not been able to stand; and restore the streets of our neighborhoods with dwellings that signify life, real life, rested life, for us and our children, and that is the life that is more abundant. It takes Sabbath space — and many of us ground this in Sunday as Sabbath.

I write this opening chapter not only as a pediatrician, and not simply as a fellow choir member, but as someone who urgently understands the need for rest. Our family has emerged from what was for us a low point in our life. The wounds are fresh, too fresh to share a lot of the details. Suffice it to say that some time ago, after I had injured my back and slowed down for a half minute, I got busier than ever. Then followed a jolting pain, but I did not stop because I was too busy. Next, I found myself stretched out on the floor in excruciating pain, but the physical pain that I experienced paled to the emotional pain that my other family members were experiencing. It was a terrible, horrible, no good very bad day, extending for several days and then several weeks. As the psalmist declares, my tears were my food day and night. And as I lay on my back at Brigham and Women's Hospital the Lord reminded me that He had been trying to get my attention for several months and in fact in some areas for several years, but I was too busy with the Work of the Kingdom to address some things. He had warned me that either I would slow down or I would break down. I did not slow down, and so. . . .

Sometimes the trauma is obvious. Sometimes the way that we are unavailable for our children is obvious, but sometimes it is more subtle. It is "the little foxes that destroy the vine." It's the short fits of anger and rage and the small seed of bitterness and the teeny tiny unforgiveness which over time, because of our lack of time, according to the Epistle of James becomes full grown and gives birth to the death of hope and vision and leads to a breakdown. And so depression and discouragement and disillusionment had moved into our home, and I had been too busy to address them — and our own family experienced "home alone."

And I felt I was being told that the back injury was not about me toting and lifting. Rather, it was about the Lord talking to me and me not taking the time to listen. It was a breakdown, not a trick of the enemy. It was God trying to get my attention, and it was not about new stuff but about the very old in my life. Stuff that with time and lack of attention had become old and smelly and rotten, and it had not been addressed and it was time to clean house. It was not a test; it was a true emergency.

I come at this opening chapter with the intent of encouraging you to take to heart the notion of seeking Sabbath in your life, and to know that Psalm 34:18 is true: the Lord is close to the brokenhearted and He does save those who are crushed in spirit, and God says that if you will stay still long enough, if you will listen and be quiet long enough, He will take you from a breakdown to a breakthrough. The word of encouragement for us as a family is that we made more progress in our life together following the crisis than we had in many years previous to it. I am writing this to let you know that God is faithful and that if you will slow down long enough you can proclaim to the enemy for your family and for the families in your congregation and for the families in your community and for the families in this culture that they shall not die but live and proclaim what the Lord has done.

And so you must be present. You must take the time to be present.

Studies show that the average father spends thirty-seven seconds a day in significant interaction with his children. That is unacceptable. We must demonstrate better by the lives that we live, by the sermons that we preach, by the relationships that we establish in society and among our congregations a different standard. The psychologist David Elkind from Tufts University has written about the "hurried child" and about his own anxiety that our culture is in too much of a hurry.[2] Writing about a day when he visited his son in the classroom, he tells of his observation of a group of boys, including his own, who sat in a circle nearby. The conversation went like this: One little boy said, "My Daddy is a doctor and he makes a lot of money and we have a swimming pool." And another child said, "My Daddy is a lawyer and he flies to Washington and he talks to the President." And then the third child said, "My Daddy owns a company and we have our own airplane." At which point Elkind's own son, with a proud look in his father's direction, declared, "My Daddy isn't any of these things but my Daddy is *here.*"

My Daddy is here. And so we must take the time to be here, and when you leave wherever you may be, and think about home, if you're not there, and you will go to wherever that might be, whether Boston, New York, Charlotte, or some other place or town, and you will go to all kinds of cities and places, then you must go home, and you must be present with the children whom you love and the families who love you back, and you must be there physically and you must be there emotionally.

When my father died I looked in the casket and realized that I did not know that man. I did not know what his hopes were, his dreams or his disappointments. I didn't know what his favorite color was or favorite food. He was functionally present and emotionally absent. You can't be present when you spend thirty-seven seconds a day with your children. You must be there emotionally, and especially you must be there spiritually. Much of what we struggle with is not about flesh and blood; it's about spiritual battles that are being waged in very high places. And so I have learned to fight my battles on my knees and to be present — to be present on my faith before the Lord. This, to me, is what seeking Sabbath is all about, about presence.

Go home, go home, go home, and make a difference, and be present.

---

2. David Elkind, *The Hurried Child: Growing Up Too Fast Too Soon.* The 25th anniversary edition is a parenting classic (New York: Da Capo Press, 2006).

CHAPTER TWO

Seeking Sabbath:
Keeping the Lord's Day in a Global Culture

Rodney L. Petersen

When the film *Chariots of Fire* was released in 1981, based upon the story of British athletes preparing for and competing in the 1924 Summer Olympics, many warmed to the winsome story of Eric Liddell, the "flying Scotsman," who viewed running as a way of glorifying God before traveling to China to work as a missionary. His adherence to Christian Sabbath principles was a part of the strength of commitment shown in the film that paralleled his athletic prowess and perseverance. The title of the film, making reference to the line, "Bring me my chariot of fire," from William Blake's poem adapted into the hymn "Jerusalem," regarding Elijah being taken up to heaven in a chariot of fire (2 Kings 2:11), adds resonance to connections between athleticism, religious perseverance, and the mystical idea that inherent in Sabbath practice is the possibility of fostering a heaven on earth.

The film makes for a good introduction to the question of what difference Sabbath practice might make to our contemporary urban and global world. Much has been written about the social reality we experience; that it is characterized by the compression of time and space. This comes through in the opening chapter of this volume as Gloria White-Hammond wrestles with the "home alone" syndrome in our busy world. We refer to the temporal dimension of this as "24/7" and, with the technology at our fingertips, allow that press of time to shape our lives. Our cell phones, iPods, Blackberries, and iPhones dominate both our business and "down" time. Yet we often have the feeling that we are doing more but accomplishing less.

The spatial dimension of this temporal experience is often urban and global. In May 2007 the population of the world became more than 50 percent urban. Spatial compression has been an accelerating phenomenon. Apart from ancient Rome, London was the first city to reach a million residents by 1820; by 2020 the world will have 500 cities with more than a million residents. The compression of space into that of an urban experience for most people has yet to be fully considered in terms of its impact upon our lives and upon the caring professions, such as ministry, that help to define us and to carry us through the stages of life. According to theologians Bryan Stone and Claire Wolfteich, this experience is characterized by the multiple transitions through which people move in today's fast-paced world and by a comprehensive social need made more evident in urban life. Negotiating identity in the face of more proximate difference often contributes to subsequent alienation and division. Diversity and immigration and the scarcity of resources for many are but a few of the pressing issues.[1] In an urban world characterized by globalization these six issues are also global issues and will shape global ministry into the future.

The interpenetration of our urban world with globalization, then, is synonymous. Many of the same factors that have contributed to the concentration of population have also been defining aspects of globalization — commerce, technology, the widespread dissemination of contemporary culture shaped by the movement of population and by social issues that cross borders and shape wide bodies of people. Christian faith is one of these cross-cultural realities. It is African, Asian, European, North and South American, and Aboriginal — and it may be each of these in a local congregation in an urban context.[2] But what is true for Christianity is not uniquely true. It bears comparison with the experience of other faith traditions, most notably with Islam. These factors indicative of globalization affect how we keep Sabbath in ways that are only more complex since Eric Liddell ran his race in the 1924 Olympics.

Can Sabbath practice offer some solace and light to everyday existence in the midst of contemporary social reality? Does it promise a glimmer of that portended heaven on earth, perhaps implied in Blake's poem and in Eric Liddell's effort? The argument of this chapter is that it can. As many of our societies are awash with the movement of population throughout the

---

1. Bryan P. Stone and Claire E. Wolfteich, *Sabbath in the City: Sustaining Urban Pastoral Excellence* (Philadelphia: Westminster John Knox Press, 2008). Information on the urban character of our world and its implications for ministry is drawn from their book.

2. Philip Jenkins draws attention to the global spread of Christianity while Andrew Walls does so with respect to the cultural implications of the transmission of Christian faith. See Philip Jenkins, *The Next Christendom: The Coming of Global Christianity* (New York: Oxford University Press, 2007), and Andrew Walls, *The Cross-Cultural Process in Christian History: Studies in the Transmission and Appropriation of Faith* (Maryknoll: Orbis Books, 2002).

world, this becomes an important question for globalization. Sabbath is tied to a worldview. It is related to the basic structure of creation and to the argument that humanity is made in God's image (Exod. 20:8-11). Sabbath is central to a biblical worldview and to the freedom from bondage to which we have been called (Deut. 5:12-15). It is an explicit component of personal, religious, and political life (Exod. 23:10-13). In *Halakha*, the collective body of Jewish religious law, it is a path to follow more than a legal prescription. The community of Israel was to make room for the stranger and the alien who may not be a worshipper of Yahweh, to make room for their Sabbath "rights" (Exod. 23:12), already portending the fact of the universal validity of Sabbath (Isa. 66:22-23; cf. Heb. 4:9-11 and Rev. 22:3-6).

If Sabbath is for all people, what does it mean to keep Sabbath in a global culture — and in a way that underscores the value of this idea for all peoples? What does it mean for those following the path of *Halakha* or for those for whom Friday prayers are paramount for their weekly ritual life? What about others who understand Sabbath as the Lord's Day (Acts 20:7; 1 Cor. 16:2; Rev. 1:10)? And what of others who also might be encompassed by the term "strangers and aliens" (Exod. 23:12)? Can we allow for Sabbath for all, even though it may be practiced differently among different groups? What does it mean to keep Sabbath in the face of a 24/7 culture that is driven by technology and production? These and other questions are the ones that lie before us in the twenty-first century. However, they are not new. The challenges of industrialization and globalization that came at the end of the nineteenth century raised similar questions for societies undergoing rapid social change at that time. In order to face those challenges, the idea of the weekend was the creative response on the part of a coalition of religious groups, labor unions, and political interests in order to make room for the Sabbath understanding of all.[3] Once again, the challenges to Sabbath or Sunday practice are ones that will make or break the nature of our religious communities, their value to persons, and the very idea of a civic culture with soul.

Sabbath and Globalization

We would do well to consider Sabbath today in light of urban globalization. Globalization is not a distant reality. We are enmeshed in it and know it as a

---

3. Alexis McCrossen, *Holy Day, Holiday: The American Sunday* (Ithaca: Cornell University Press, 2000).

local reality. Urban evangelist Ralph Kee refers to globalization as "glocalization."[4] Globalization affects local labor practices as well as consumer opportunities. According to the International Monetary Fund, over the past two decades labor has become increasingly globalized. The integration of China, India, and the former Eastern bloc into the world economy, together with population growth, has led to an estimated fourfold increase in the effective global labor force, which could more than double again by 2050. The location of production has become much more responsive to relative labor costs across countries. This has led to increasing flows of migrants across borders, through both legal and informal routes. This ongoing globalization of the labor market has drawn increasing attention from policymakers and the media, particularly in the advanced economies.

While it is important for countries to maximize the benefits from labor globalization and technological change, while at the same time also working to address the distributional impact of labor, basic social safety nets and policies should be put in place to improve the functioning of labor markets. A few of these issues include strengthening access to education and training. A part of this social safety net to cushion the impact on those adversely affected, without obstructing the process of labor adjustment, is provision for Sabbath practice. Sabbath is an integral part of that social safety net for all labor. According to labor historian Robert Haynes, the campaign for the weekend (and Sabbath) was a part of an effort to enable wage earners to have the time to be mothers and fathers for their children and to cultivate themselves to be citizens of a democracy.[5] In giving shape to social order after Egyptian tyranny, Israel was counseled not to work 24/7. Sabbath was given, according to Karen Burton Mains, as a gift of mercy following years of servitude. It was a space of time in which to focus on relationships — between themselves and their work, their families, their community, and their God.[6]

Globalization affects consumer opportunities. It is moving us together throughout the world. Some of the reasons for this are as simple as technology and infrastructure. Our economies are more closely intermeshed. The Internet means that New York banks can hire clerks in India to bal-

---

4. Ralph Kee, "Globalization and Successive Church Planting," *Boston Theological Institute Newsletter* 31, no. 5 (October 10, 2001).

5. Robert Haynes, "Organized Labor and Organized Rest," *Labor and Leisure: A Look at Contemporary Values* (Boston: Massachusetts Council of Churches, 1994), pp. 35-38.

6. Karen Burton Mains, *Making Sunday Special* (Bel Air, CA: Star Song Communications Group, 1987).

ance their books overnight. Technological innovations like this link separate national economies in ways that would not be possible if relying on air mail. Marketplace choice has expanded, and with it our own consumptive desires and opportunities, such that Harvard University economist Juliet B. Schor argues that many people too easily become drawn into a "work and spend" cycle, trapped into longer hours of work in a cycle of rising material expectations.[7]

Our understanding of globalization and ways by which we are caught up in it arises not only from the interpenetration of labor and capital in today's world but also from our awareness of the social experience of many throughout the world, thanks to technology and the global media. For example, when we are talking about issues like foreign aid, CNN can get a camera crew into someplace where there is poverty or a famine and we can see in our living rooms the images of what is happening instantly. This makes a difference in how we feel about being one world and one community.

In other words, globalization is not just being pushed by the interests of labor and production, but also by a global moral consciousness. There is a moral core that sustains the work of global humanitarians that are often involved in human rights work around the world, building up the fabric of humanitarian concern that is transnational and often trans-religion, but not necessarily trans-values or ethics. Often the same ethical concerns cross the boundaries of religions and nations in a world in which we are all susceptible to the realities of migration. A Jewish person and a Muslim and a Christian may be struggling together to end the devastation of AIDS in Uganda and so are in a sense representing globalization from below fighting injustice, which is very different but equally transnational as the global movement of labor and products. Since the beginning of the twenty-first century, under the work of Kofi Annan and then Ban Ki-moon (successive General Secretaries of the United Nations), there has been a concerted effort to take the ethical voice of the world's religions more seriously and more systematically into account.[8]

We tend to think of ethics as national, but the pressures of labor, mar-

---

7. Juliet B. Schor, *Overworked American: The Unexpected Decline of Leisure* (New York: Basic Books, 1993).

8. Julia Berger, "Religious Nongovernmental Organizations: An Exploratory Analysis," *International Journal of Voluntary and Nonprofit Organizations* 14, no. 1 (2003): 15-39; cf. The Secretary-General's Panel of Eminent Persons on Relations with Civil Society, "UN System and Civil Society — an Inventory and Analysis of Practices," http://www.ngocongo.org.

kets, and global ethics remind us that we are a part of a larger and global community. For example, the best-known book on justice since the Second World War, John Rawls's *A Theory of Justice,* focuses on justice within our own national community. In a subsequent book, *The Law of Peoples,* Rawls begins to address the concept of international justice, but still remains focused on justice in societies, and the obligations of societies to each other are seen as much more limited than the obligations of justice within society.[9] But can we continue to think of justice only on a national basis? If we buy and sell internationally, should we not press to practice Sabbath internationally? Sabbath in a global culture pushes us to consider the most pressing questions of justice in the world today along with the innate sense of global ethical consciousness. The concept of Sabbath adds to the recognition that we are a part of a larger and global community. If we take this globalization seriously, what should we be thinking from a Sabbath point of view?

The idea of Sabbath does not arise as an argument just to help specify the nature of the ethical challenge; it also poses a counter-challenge to the very nature of the globalization that we experience and the ways by which we work to manage it. Globalization, the compression of time-space relationships and planetary integration creates a human reality that contributes to the construction and deconstruction of local life worlds as social transitions occur in local societies, the kinds of issues raised by Stone and Wolfteich. Globalization is pushing a social reality that's conducive to a sense of global ethics and at the same time challenges the way in which that ethical sensitivity takes social form. *Sunday, Sabbath and the Weekend* time argues for the importance of the kind of social safety net that makes possible a life of civic duty and responsibility outlined in the biblical vision and its perspective on human nature.

In other words, issues of religion and religious understanding are interrelated with the issues of globalization. Globalization is not an abstract question, nor does it come at us with neutrality. It challenges us and makes possible new definitions and ways of being human that are enhanced when we maintain Sabbath. Religions may embrace, alter, or even resist globalization, but the religions of the world are not unaffected by the changing social realities such forces bring about. But principles of Sabbath reality can alter the way in which globalization takes shape. In other words, if

---

9. John Rawls, *A Theory of Justice* (Cambridge, MA: Belknap Press, 2005); and see *The Law of Peoples* (Cambridge, MA: Harvard University Press, 2001).

globalization is shaping religious discourse and ritual views on space-time rhythms, the idea of Sabbath, or Sunday, poses a way of counter-influencing globalization.

Global Citizenship and the Religious Other

Globalization implies an encounter with religious difference. The idea of Sabbath can provide a positive and leavening force in such settings. If we remember the six issues raised by Stone and Wolfteich as shaping urban ministry, which are also shaping ministry as it confronts globalization — the experience of multiple transitions, comprehensive social need, negotiating identity, alienation and division, diversity and immigration, and ·scarcity of resources — Sabbath reminds us that all humanity is made in the image of God. Yet, while we may believe this, we often divide ourselves into identity groups. The demands of living in such tribes, races, nations, and religious or linguistic groups is such that we easily define our own identity group as "safe" while the other is threatening. This "drive to dichotomize" may be a natural and even autonomous survival mechanism, but it is countered by the universal implications in Sabbath.[10] Political theorist Joseph Montville has taken this idea and applied it to religion and peacemaking insofar as such a tendency to place ourselves in groups becomes foundational to conflict.[11] The Sabbath idea helps us to move in a different direction and to find here a basis for common human identity.

Using September 11, 2001, as an emblematic date, we might consider how the destruction of that day has stimulated persons in the U.S. and elsewhere to think more intensively about the religious other. This has involved the necessity of thinking in a more nuanced perspective on religious difference, a more multilateral approach in recognizing the religious other. Persons met in today's world are always persons substantially like us. Central to liberal political thinking and to Christian theology is the point that we are all made in the image of God, *B'Tselem Elohim*. This is something about which we are reminded by Jessica Montel, Director of the Israeli human rights organization B'Tselem, as she and her organization ad-

---

10. See Charles A. Pinderhughes, "Differential Bonding: Toward a Psychophysiological Theory of Stereotyping," *American Journal of Psychiatry* 136, no. 1 (1979): 33-47.

11. Joseph Montville, "Religion and Peacemaking," in *Forgiveness and Reconciliation: Religion, Public Policy and Conflict Transformation*, ed. Raymond Helmick, S.J., and Rodney Petersen (Philadelphia: Templeton Press, 2001), pp. 97-116.

dress issues of abuse in the Palestinian Occupied Territories, bringing rights violations to light in the spiraling violence in the Middle East. She reminds us that we are "*made* in the image of God," sharing in a common humanity. This draws us to a third point handed down in Jewish tradition, that we are made in the image of God — and, as such, made for relationships. The phrase, "Let us make man in our image" (Gen. 1:26), central to the creation story, is a phrase that implies relationship. God in God's internal triune nature celebrates creation. We, in our relationships, do the same. We "image" the creator in whose image we were made. Sabbath reminds us of our equal human rights (Isaiah 58).

Among the challenges for nation-states in the twenty-first century is the degree to which human rights are affirmed. Such are bound up with the allegiance citizens give to local, national, and international political bodies. The concept and practice of citizenship emerged out of what it meant to be part of a tribe, to be a "subject," or even to be a "national."[12] The aftermath of the American and French revolutions in the eighteenth century saw the emergence of *civil* citizenship. The idea of *political* citizenship can be seen to have arisen in the nineteenth century, and that of *social* citizenship in the twentieth century. Following this sense of evolution from narrowly defined tribal loyalty to greater civic tolerance, the idea of an emergent global citizenship with religious rights and responsibilities has arisen as a growing social reality. The social reality of people migrating around the world and an increasing tendency to standardize citizenship has promoted a sense of global citizenship which bears upon how we practice Sabbath in a global culture. In other words, persons from the West who travel to the Middle East might expect to be accorded religious freedom to worship as they will, but such expectations need to be matched with civic reciprocity.

Emergent global citizenship, the pursuit of corporate public responsibility amidst the constant transitions of globalization, requires a theoretical religious framework and practical ethic apart from a spiritualized sense of religion. Religious ritual requires forms of practical engagement that take on social form. This social form, and the sense of citizenship which it takes on, is also shaped by issues of identical lifestyle and global needs and

12. Anthony W. Marx, *Faith in Nation: Exclusionary Origins of Nationalism* (New York: Oxford University Press, 2003), argues that European nationalism emerged in the early modern era as a form of mass political engagement based on religious conflict, intolerance, and exclusion.

networks. The very technology that makes global citizenship possible is a factor shaping a growing sense across the globe that rights and obligations pertain alike to all people, including religious rites and practices. This has been particularly the case since World War II, as embodied in the *Universal Declaration of Human Rights* set forth by the United Nations in 1948. This sense of rights was given further significance for religious consciences and liberties in the UN's declaration on the elimination of all forms of intolerance and discrimination based on religion or belief (1981). Globalization has promoted a sense of the value and importance of inter-religious dialogue and relationships, often seen in the value placed upon inter-religious prayer services that are challenging for persons of all religious persuasions.

Many of the challenges to religion in the emerging world order are parallel to the challenges faced by nation-states as exemplified in inter-religious dialogue, a kind of religious multilateralism. A global Sabbath set in the context of globalization promotes religious multilateralism. When we take Sabbath seriously, we are taking community life seriously, and that implies a meaningful consideration of social reality. In fact, the failure to take Sabbath seriously may imply a failure to take community seriously, whether informal social communities or the more formal forms of civic life. Sabbath touches upon and drives these issues.

Recognition of the religious other drives us to engage another person, but also the social reality of which that person is a part. It is not an obstacle to community, but should be seen as an opportunity for deeper and more meaningful community together with an enhanced sense of theological identity in the context of the right to the free expression of religion. Related here is the question of how personal development, threatened by the realities of conflict and civil strife, is short-circuited, warped, or deferred. Our development is often understood as a process of increasing equilibrium between the self and the environment. While this process can face limits as to the amount of new information that one can take in, identity formation under conditions of conflict is made more complex. With threat, identity formation shuts down; humiliation fuels an impulse for revenge and violence. It fosters rigidity.[13] Religious identity in a world of globalization must be shaped by dialogue and engagement. Making space for Sabbath is making space for meaningful dialogue and the growth of community.

---

13. Donna Hicks, "The Role of Identity Reconstruction in Promoting Reconciliation," in Helmick and Petersen, eds., *Forgiveness and Reconciliation*, pp. 129-50.

Celebration and the Lord's Day

We have seen the importance of Sabbath benefits. Sabbath makes possible a more sure social safety net in the workplace and promotes opportunities for meaningful family and communal life. Taking Sabbath seriously means taking humanity seriously and the consequent human rights that emerge from a sense of equal global citizenship. Christian public theology and practice take place today in a public square characterized by a multi-religious context. It is within this social framework that we must argue for our conception of Sabbath. To be sure, nothing has been said so far about the connection between the Christian Sunday and Sabbath, despite the case that can be made for it.[14] There are hints in the New Testament that the first day of the week was set aside for worship, including the Lord's Supper (Acts 20:7; 1 Cor. 16:2) — and Revelation 1:10 refers to "the Lord's Day." But the entire debate over Sabbath and the Lord's Day is set within the context of theological discussion over such issues as whether the "first day" replaced the "Sabbath day," whether there is a transfer of Sabbath theology to Sunday worship, whether one is a day of rest and the other a day of celebration, and how one is to measure the seven-day week.

In the context of such debate, which only becomes enlarged when we move beyond the Jewish and Christian worlds, defining Sabbath in an age of globalization may imply not only a recommitment to the weekend as we know it but further flexibility in making room for Sabbath for all. This might necessitate new civic rituals that recognize the diversity that exists so as to permit new covenanted relationships with all persons in society. Such might promote a deeper commitment to inter-religious dialogue and essential cooperation toward a more humane world.

A recognition of the religious other in such a way as to grant equal religious citizenship to the other means acknowledging civic space rituals that promote social inclusivity. The value of such rituals is underscored by the scholar Marc Gopin in relation to rituals that promote an attitude conducive to reconciliation. For example, might Thanksgiving evolve into a national day of thanksgiving for reconciliation on analogy with the transposition of the Day of the Vow in South Africa to the Day of Reconciliation?[15]

---

14. D. A. Carson, ed., *From Sabbath to Lord's Day: A Biblical, Historical, and Theological Investigation* (Grand Rapids: Baker Books, 1982).

15. Donald Shriver, *Honest Patriots: Loving a Country Enough to Remember Its Misdeeds* (New York: Oxford University Press, 2005).

Once connected with the commemoration of a famous Boer victory over the Zulu, the anniversary and its celebration are now more broadly tied to South African reconciliation since the end of Apartheid. Might the American Fourth of July be seen as a day that not only celebrates the independence of the U.S. but also expresses our hope that all people throughout the world might be invited into the same liberties that we enjoy? Civic and religious holidays in the sense described above might represent a momentum toward global citizenship and full religious rights granted to all people.

What of Sunday, the Christian Sabbath? Could this day, already a part of an acknowledged weekend, be enlarged upon to recognize the American Islamic population? Getatchew Haile from Ethiopia is developing ideas in this connection at the ecumenical center from his homeland based on a forty-nine-hour Sabbath.[16] This is in an orthodox Ethiopian Christian tradition that might be appropriated in American culture. It is a Sabbath that begins on Friday at sundown and extends until Sunday around sundown. A modest enlargement on this would be to recognize Friday prayers of the Islamic community and then the beginning of the Jewish Shabbat.[17] Maintaining the weekend as it stands would take us through Saturday and into Sunday evening, making room for varying interpretations of Sabbath as well as for the Christian celebration of the resurrection of Jesus Christ on Sunday as the "eighth" day in liturgical conception.

It is of the order of our world that one direction religious rituals can move is in the direction of privatization. Technology can promote private Sabbaths.[18] We all take private Sabbaths — and there may be places and

16. Getatchew Haile, "The Forty-Nine Hour Sabbath of the Ethiopian Church," *Journal of Semitic Studies* 33, no. 2 (Autumn 1988): 233-54. Noting the long debate within the Ethiopian Church as to whether Saturday or Sunday should be recognized as Sabbath, and the continuing tradition of recognizing both days as Sabbath, Getatchew Haile cites the *Sinodos* with the following quotation: "He [God] ordered that one should not work on it [Saturday Sabbath] and he made it the end of days and, similarly, of the creation of the world. And the rest on Sunday is in order that we may know that God started on it making and creating all creations, and that he is omnipotent. He made it the first and the beginning, as (it is) said in the Scripture [cf. Gen 1:1] whose fulfillment is Our Lord Christ, and he fulfilled it. He is also the beginning of the Gospel [cf. Mark 1:1] the new spirituality (f. 76b) for the new nation."

17. Christopher D. Ringwald, *A Day Apart: How Jews, Christians, and Muslims Find Faith, Freedom, and Joy on the Sabbath* (New York: Oxford University Press, 2007).

18. Albert Borgmann, *Power Failure: Christianity in the Culture of Technology* (Grand Rapids: Brazos, 2003). Borgmann argues that technology conspires against the gospel in that it promises something totally different. While shown to be a moral issue with implications

times for such. Nevertheless, following what was said about Sabbath in the first part of this paper, there is also something valuable about a public Sabbath, about the way in which we celebrate and acknowledge our Sabbath. Religion has a corporate character that carries us beyond a private spiritualized meaning and affects the meaning of community. Philosopher Albert Borgmann argues that there is an increasing tendency for Americans to live in a virtual world and that doing this undermines our very understanding of ethical responsibility. In a dangerous world and an often unhappy society we need to face reality (or "get real" as current jargon would put it) if we are to do the right thing.[19]

The social importance of acknowledging such public celebration is that it affirms the fact that society is not just united around work, but that it finds that work set in a larger context of meaning defined by celebration. One of the chief ends of religion is that of celebrating life's transitions. An effect of the marginalization of religious life, even its privatization, in secular America is that of the marginalization of places of common community celebration. A part of the quest for religious authenticity in America today is a quest for meaningful community celebration — and genuine community in the midst of the distrust in or hollowing out of many other institutions. Our religious institutions will continue to play a role in social experience; understanding them is important to an understanding of our corporate culture.

Of equal importance is the fact that religious meaning is easily co-opted by the state when the state and its holidays become the only socially unifying force in the life of the nation. The implications of this for the separation of church and state and a misplaced civil religion are significant. By taking themselves seriously, and by taking inter-faith dialogue seriously, religious institutions can help to promote the freedom of expression and vibrancy of the prophetic office for the well-being of all other institutions

---

of disengagement and loss of meaning, technology, in Borgmann's opinion, also bears possibilities of contributing to a rich public life of celebration and personal life of focal practices. The use of technology continues to promise many innovations in Sabbath practice and worship life, although some may also find this very technology subversive of genuine community. Further, the commodification that accompanies technology makes a promise of liberation that it is unable to keep or around which there is much debate as Borgmann outlines contingent aspects of social and political life that remain open to fundamental choices, which can lead us to a more full engagement with social reality.

19. Albert Borgmann, *Real American Ethics: Taking Responsibility for Our Country* (Chicago: University of Chicago Press, 2007), p. 20.

in society. Hence, we are drawn back to the importance of the connection between Sabbath and social justice (Isaiah 58).

The challenges we face as societies in the twenty-first century are daunting. Those that are derivative of globalization and its urban character — the experience of multiple transitions, comprehensive social need, negotiating identity, alienation and division, diversity and immigration, and scarcity of resources — drive us to consider how the systematic practice of Sabbath, keeping the Lord's day in a global culture, might provide the space for dealing with these. Can Sabbath practice offer some solace and light to everyday existence in the midst of contemporary social reality? Does it promise a glimmer of that portended heaven on earth, perhaps implied in Blake's poem and in Eric Liddell's effort? The argument of this chapter is that it can.

CHAPTER THREE

Sabbath Keeping and Social Justice

Marva J. Dawn

Whenever I speak about matters related to God, I begin with three things. The first will be a brief moment of silence. In that time I encourage you to pray to God for openness to whatever God purposes for you now. I do not know what's most important for me to say, so the silence is critical as a time for us to listen to God.

After the silence I will welcome you with the ancient greeting that comes from the Book of Ruth. When Boaz comes to the harvest field, he says, "The LORD be with you," and the reapers respond, "And the LORD bless you." Tonight I ask you to respond as many of you do in your congregation's worship services, "And also with you." But first, let's remember why we do this.

When I say, "The LORD be with you," I am reminding us all that the Great "I Am," YHWH, the Covenant God, the Promise Keeper, is in our midst. With these words I am praying for your ears, so that you hear better in this community of saints; I am praying for your mind, your life, your ministry — that what we do this evening will cause your whole self and your work to be transformed. When you answer, "And also with you," you are praying for my mouth and mind — that I would speak the Word of God and not my own, that I would bring to you what God intends.

Thereby we make a commitment to each other. We know the presence of God in the midst of us in our common concern for a holy day. Even though we may have different perspectives and persuasions, we desire to learn all we can, so we will help each other to speak and listen better. To that end, the third thing that we will do is pray.

Let's begin with silence, then, and wait upon the LORD.

(silence)

The LORD be with you.

(audience: And also with you)

Let us pray: God of all goodness, mercy, and truth; God, the Creator and Sustainer of the world; God who rescues us from ourselves and our sins: We offer our lives into your hands. We offer our communities into your safekeeping. We beg of you that you would unite us to each other so that we may together value the Holy Day, that we might know this day as a day of rest to form us afresh. May we be a people who love our neighbors, a people who reach out to the world for the sake of justice and peace, reconciliation and hope. We thank you for the privilege of being gathered here, for each person who is part of this community, for the fellowship we have enjoyed, for the beautiful harp music we have heard, for the way you play your music into our lives. Now as we consider together the meaning of the Sabbath day and how it leads us to justice building, we pray for your Spirit's guidance and the opening of our hearts, that we might move our hearing into life. We ask this, confident of your goodness and your care for us. Amen.

The question of this chapter is, How can we counteract the violence of the world around us by building social justice? This question stands whether we consider the violence of assault, of destructive behavior, or of distant conflicts with which we are familiar. Everywhere we turn we encounter brutality and destructiveness. How can we move from such a milieu of violence towards a world of justice building and peace making? Does the Sabbath have anything to do with that?

One of the problems that prevents our becoming peacemakers and justice builders is that we are afflicted with what Neil Postman calls a "low information-action ratio" or the L.I.A.R. syndrome. As you all are aware, we are bombarded with much too much information, with the result that we do not act on what we know. This is a question that has bothered ethicists for ages: Why do people not act on what they know? Why do we not keep our promises? Why do we talk endlessly about the proliferation of violence and yet not take any actions or modify our own behavior to establish more peace? Why do not people of faith gather together to persuade the U.S. Congress, for example, to appropriate more money for feeding the hungry, digging wells in areas of contaminated water, fighting AIDS, and engaging in other ways to support life, rather than spending our tax dollars to destroy people in a senseless war? These are questions with which we should continue wrestling, but they can be summarized in the perpetual puzzle: Why do most of us have such a low ratio of action to information?

More than twenty years ago, Eerdmans Publishing Company produced Joyce Hanks's translation of Jacques Ellul's *The Humiliation of the Word,* and I've been noticing ever since how helpful that phrase is. It enables us to see how loosely people treat their words as they throw them around. No wonder promises are not kept! That has been especially noticeable in politicians during significant campaigns for government offices, but one can't miss how very true the phrase is of advertisements. When you have to use the word *stupendous* or *extraordinary* for laundry soap, you hardly have any vocabulary left to speak about God! I've never met one detergent that was that good! That, however, is the way we've become accustomed to employing words in our society, and, as a result, we don't practice applying words rightly.

The "humiliation of the word" is aggravated by our technological tools and gadgets, which multiply words and make accessible such a diversity of "facts" and "opinions" that we are not sure what or whom to believe. When there are so many words in the air, which ones do we trust and act upon? In consideration of this L.I.A.R. problem, where do we find hope? Is it possible that we can actually be assisted by Sabbath keeping? Three preliminary observations can give us hope along the way.

Homo Reparans

The first one comes from Elizabeth Spelman's book called *Repair,* as reported by Carol Zaleski in the *Christian Century.*[1] Spelman, according to Zaleski, believes that human beings are happier as re-creators than as innovators. She calls us *homo reparans.* This description of our being emphasizes that we, too, are damaged goods, so we need to be reformed after the image of the God who made us. As a mixed group in our culture, we recognize that this includes, for example, the design of the Triune God if

---

1. Elizabeth Spelman, *Repair: The Impulse to Restore in a Fragile World* (Boston: Beacon Press, 2003).

you are Christian, the tetragrammaton *YHWH* if you are Jewish, and Allah if you are a Muslim.

When I speak for pastors' conferences, people often say, "I knew that, but didn't know how to articulate it." That is so true. As servants of God, we basically try to restore what is originally good; we don't create something that is new. As the prophet Qoheleth so clearly announced, "There is nothing new under the sun."

When we work for authentic renewal in society, we don't jettison the past, but rather reclaim it. Fragile institutions need to be remade in fidelity to tradition. That is the point of the whole liturgy at the beginning of Genesis 1. We all believe in a God who is the Creator. Since we acknowledge that equally, we also would agree that since God is the only Creator we need only to restore what God has already made for the sake of the renewal of society.

This gives us hope. The wonderful liturgical pattern of Genesis 1 — with its continual repetition of "God said," "it was so," God called it "good," and "the evening and the morning were the day" — displays the unity and harmony and orderliness of the entire cosmos. We are heartened in our trust that God will work through us to bring about renewal in that cosmos. We read that liturgy as a faith proclamation about the character of God and can, therefore, rely on that God to inspire and empower us. Repairing of society will not be our own invention, but is the process in which God is always involved. God invites us to participate in that process, so when we get on the right track we are enabled to reestablish God's own purposes and bring to fruition what God has designed. This is the source of tremendous hope.

Rituals and Practices

A second observation that gives us hope for the reformation of society is that we are fashioned by the rituals and practices in which we engage. If young people in our synagogues and churches, for example, grow up being repeatedly engaged in the practice of hearing, "The LORD be with you," they learn more and more to recognize the LORD's presence in their midst. Some students of mine began the practice of using the ancient greeting at their high school — and were thereby encouraged to realize how many fellow students were believers in God. After all, the biblical precedent is Boaz going to the field and greeting the reapers. This is not "synagogue" talk; it is street talk — or rather barley-field talk. We can use the greeting and the response, "and also with you," in daily life to acknowledge that the Covenant God is in our midst, creating peace between us. If we physically or spiritually grow up saying this, that peace becomes a way of life.

Such formation by ritual is emphasized in Tom Porter's book, *Conflict and Communion*. Writing for Christians, Porter asserts that our coming to the Lord's Table immerses us in the Eucharistic communion.[2] Again, ritual is important for human formation and reformation. We saw the effects of this most clearly in the reaction of the Amish people as a whole to the lamentable shooting of several of their children a few years ago. They have been formed to be a people whose God-created response is forgiveness and restoration. Thus, they reached out to the attacker's widow and to her children, recognizing that they, too, were victims of tragedy.[3]

Similarly, the Maori people of New Zealand (Aotearoa) who are Christian are formed by their culture to be peacemakers. I have chosen to wear tonight a pendant designed by the Maori to demonstrate reconciliation or *Whakahoanga*. Notice that the symbol develops out of the cross. God's work of forgiveness in Christ is the basis out of which our ability to reconcile emerges.

Underneath the cross is a triple symbol that evolves from a common image for New Zealand. Perhaps you have seen the fern coil painted on the tail of Air New Zealand planes. The coil is called a koru. When the koru opens, we see inside a large number of little coils. When these all open out, the fern leaf is formed. A koru can be as large as almost a foot across in the case of large, tree-like fern plants whose fronds can be up to twelve feet long. Their unfolding is truly a magnificent sight.

The pendant displays two of these koru opposite each other beginning to unfold. The emphasis of the symbol is that true reconciliation cannot take place unless both koru open out into their full potential. Peace cannot be achieved unless both sides find wholeness. So the Maori people acknowledge in their search for tribal rights that they cannot be whole unless the "Second people," the "Whites" who came to New Zealand after they did, attain wholeness too.

This was the genius also of Martin Luther King, Jr. He understood that

2. Thomas Porter, ed., *Conflict and Communion: Reconciliation and Restorative Justice at Christ's Table* (Nashville: Discipleship Resources, 2006).

3. Donald B. Kraybill, Steven M. Nolt, and David L. Weaver-Zercher, *Amish Grace: How Forgiveness Transcended Tragedy* (New York: Jossey-Bass, 2007).

genuine reconciliation does not mean compromise, in which one or both parties have to give up something. When we are aiming for the higher goal of reconciliation and justice in the world, no one should be deprived. King taught that the black folk would not find true freedom unless they, in turn, freed the whites from their prejudices.

As we look at the task of reconciliation in the world today, we recognize that the U.S. has a major job to do, for we in our wealth will not find virtuous wholeness unless other parts of the world achieve freedom from necessity. This says much about the effort that lies before us, for we will want to feed the hungry, clothe the naked, house the homeless, provide medical care for the afflicted, and so forth. How great the challenge is, for the world is deeply flawed! But that God works through us to accomplish divine purposes gives us hope.

The Maori symbol is so well carved that, on closer look, we discern that the two fern coils are also two people holding hands with bowed heads. In typical Maori custom, the two hands are blocked in shape and proportionally larger to emphasize the importance of relationship. The fingers are interlocked in genuine friendship and thereby invite us to a reconciliation that leads to deeper partnership.

This touches on the meaning of the Hebrew word *shalom*. It does not signify simply "peace." It is not only that people can claim peace for themselves with God and within themselves. The word emphasizes that we all have a responsibility because God has originated peace. Out of our own sense of peace, we offer to those we encounter whatever they need to be at peace also. This is the lesson, of course, when James writes, "How can you say 'peace, peace' to someone and then send that person off without lunch?" (That's my loose paraphrase of James.) "Peace" doesn't mean anything if it is just empty words. The word calls us to a literal incarnation, so that peace is made whole for us both.

That requires humility, as is symbolized by the reverently bowed heads on the Maori carving. Of course, that is a trait noticeably lacking in U.S. culture today. And even as we blame our society for being horribly arrogant, we are forced to recognize such conceit or narcissism in ourselves and to repent.

Let's take the idea of ritual practices one step further. When we talk about the formation that practices nurture, we perceive that engaging in the action leads to comprehending more profoundly the meaning of the action. Our data-overloaded society usually tends to function the other way by thinking that a person must understand something in order to engage in it. But that shift from the Enlightenment does not characterize all the cultures of the world. Some have avoided the modern notion that wisdom is merely a mental activity and not an embodied discipline. We have much to learn from African, Asian, and Latin American cultures which more deeply embody their wisdom and believe that what is best understood is that which is actually moved and lived. Biblical formation results in movement in participation with God's purposes.

We are prepared for such formation when we immerse ourselves in the Scriptures. That is why in Deuteronomy Moses can say, "When the LORD led you over the Red Sea," though none of the people listening had been alive at the time. He meant, "You are part of the community of the people of Israel. This is a component of your history."

This is true for all of us. To become more faithful to Islam, one must immerse oneself more thoroughly in the Koran and its instructions. A Jew must be bathed in the Hebrew Scriptures, and Christians ought to be implanted in both the Hebrew and New Testament Scriptures. We become part of the entire community of our tradition in order to get its way of life into our bones. When *shalom* becomes a part of our way of being — in all three of our traditions — we will have been formed to be genuine peacemakers.

One person who was a great mentor to me was the late John Howard Yoder. I had gone to the University of Notre Dame to study pacifism with him, but far more important than what I learned intellectually was what I discovered about embodiment. John was a reconciler through and through. I had become convinced about the urgent need for nonviolence in our world, but I still hadn't developed habits for living it in myself. I was the sort that wanted to cream other people cerebrally, since I couldn't do it physically. I saw illustrations of such behavior constantly. However, John Yoder was different. He was a magisterial model of reconciliation. At conferences in the department or at the American Academy of Religion he consistently exhibited conciliating behavior. Though I once heard a woman critiquing him in ways that completely missed his point, he responded to her with gentleness and gradually helped her to understand his work more thoroughly without battering her self-esteem. It was a phenomenal performance, some would say, except that it wasn't a performance. This behavior was a habit, a way of life, the character of a peacemaker. I'm forever indebted to Yoder for displaying the genuine heart of pacifism.

If we look carefully at the Hebrew Scriptures which are at the core of the faiths of all of us, we discover that the entire narrative of God moves Israel away from the violence that surrounded them, beginning with the

Akedah, as Jews call the story of Abraham's intended offering of Isaac. The point of the story is not how terrible it was that God asked for such a sacrifice, nor that Abraham made a great leap of faith.

Instead, the account shows that God revealed to Abraham a deeper insight into the divine character. At the foot of the mountain, when Isaac asks his father where the offering is — since they have wood and fire — Abraham answers, "God will provide." But when they see the ram in the bushes and present that instead, the mountain is named "The LORD will provide," and the narrator, by repeating the issue of that name, stresses that this isn't any old god of the countryside who demanded child sacrifice. This is *YHWH,* the LORD, the Covenant God, who does not want such violence.

Many other narratives in the Hebrew Scriptures continue this trajectory to transform Israel from the violence of the cultures that surrounded it. King David was not permitted to build the temple because he was a warrior. Instead, it was given to Shalom-man (Solomon) to construct it in the capital city, Jeru-Shalom (Jerusalem). The prophets warned Israel that the people would be taken into captivity if they ignored the Torah (instructions or law) of God. They were indeed put in bondage because they had become greedy instead of abiding in God's clear directions for economic justice and genuine *shalom.*

These stories are in the roots of all Abrahamic faiths. We are all encouraged to be part of a peacemaking community, formed by our Scriptures, in contrast to the surrounding societies. Those of us gathered here tonight — Muslims, Jews, and Christians — are called away from the violence of our milieu to be harmonizers instead. When we contemplate the specifics of a holy day, the Sabbath of God's gifting, that will contribute the very core around which we can be formed to be reconcilers.

"Scripture Reasoning"

That leads me to our third initial sign of hope as we prepare to look at our Sabbath core. Some of you reading this are, no doubt, familiar with the movement called "Scripture Reasoning." There have been sessions for scriptural reasoning at the American Academy of Religion. Such prominent persons as David Ford of Cambridge, the Jewish scholar Peter Ochs, Archbishop of Canterbury Rowan Williams, and Bishop of Durham N. T. Wright have engaged in these sessions. The purpose of their gatherings is to bring Muslims, Jews, and Christians together to read and compare similar passages in their particular scriptures. As a result, participants discover that we all have much in common. By highlighting our traditions in their universal elements, we remove barriers to understanding each other.

I experienced the same unity when I was lecturing at the Johns Hopkins University Medical School a few years ago. A Jewish rabbi, a Muslim imam, a Hindu, and a Buddhist would add perspectives from their traditions that were similar to mine as I lectured about Sabbath keeping from a Christian vision. We all agreed on the fundamental importance of Sabbath ceasing and resting, of celebration and embracing our mutually acclaimed traditions.

I always like to kid that if we really paid attention to our Scriptures in the Middle East there would be no fighting on Friday, Saturday, and Sunday. In honor of each other's holy days, we would refrain from warfare on three days out of the week and would only need to add the other half.

Sabbath Keeping

Indeed, Sabbath keeping is a widespread practice that most religions share. It is also the hinge between our efforts to love God and our efforts to love the neighbor. As you are able, enter into the following activity with at least one other person or a group of people. Print out two sets of texts, one from Exodus 20:8-11 and the other from Deuteronomy 5:12-15. Those using the former will be called the "Exodus people," and those using the latter will be called the "Deuteronomy people." Read antiphonally, an important practice in churches and synagogues. (The angels sing antiphonally in Isaiah 6.) Reading the texts in this way will enable us to see the differences in the two traditions of the Sabbath command in the Hebrew Scriptures.

> Exod. 20:8 Remember the Sabbath day, and keep it holy.
> Deut. 5:12 Observe the Sabbath day and keep it holy, as the LORD your God commanded you.
> Exod. 20:9 Six days you shall labor and do all your work.
> Deut. 5:13 Six days you shall labor and do all your work.
> Exod. 20:10 But the seventh day is a Sabbath to the LORD your God; you shall not do any work — you, your son or your daughter, your male or female slave, your livestock, or the alien resident in your towns.

Deut. 5:14 But the seventh day is a Sabbath to the Lᴏʀᴅ your God; you shall not do any work — you, or your son or your daughter, or your male or female slave, or your ox or your donkey, or any of your livestock, or the resident alien in your towns, so that your male and female slave may rest as well as you.

Exod. 20:11 For in six days the Lᴏʀᴅ made heaven and earth, the sea, and all that is in them, but rested the seventh day; therefore the Lᴏʀᴅ blessed the Sabbath day and consecrated it.

Deut. 5:15 Remember that you were a slave in the land of Egypt, and the Lᴏʀᴅ your God brought you out from there with a mighty hand and an outstretched arm; therefore the Lᴏʀᴅ your God commanded you to keep the Sabbath day.

Hear what God's Spirit is saying to God's people. Thanks be to God!

As you read these texts, you are able to specify the vast differences between the two texts. Those variations are all the more striking because for the rest of the Ten Commandments the texts in Exodus and Deuteronomy are almost exactly identical. Our discoveries of alterations highlight the hinging work of the Sabbath, drawing together our relationship with God to that with our neighbor. We will now look more closely at these relationships.

First Version of the Sabbath Command: Imitating God

We might begin by looking at more details of the Exodus text. First of all, you probably remember that the Exodus version of the commandments begins with "I am *YHWH* who brought you out of Egypt. . . ." It is essential that we start with that because there is a terrible misunderstanding of commandments in our society today. Somehow the word *obedience* has gotten a bad press. The idea of obedience is treated as if God were sternly saying, "Shape up or ship out" — which is, of course, not the way God speaks to us. Rather, God proclaims, "I am the Lᴏʀᴅ" who rescued you. In response to that deliverance, this is the best way to live!

Ponder the Ten Commandments. What would it be like, in Boston, if you never had to lock your car or your house? Wouldn't that be extraordinarily delightful? It would save a lot of time and worry and energy if nobody ever stole. So do you think that the commandment not to steal is a good idea? Similarly, wouldn't it be wonderful, women, if we never had to worry about being assaulted? For that matter, all of us — women and men alike — would rejoice if we never had to fear violence against ourselves. Then isn't the commandment not to kill a great notion?

It is refreshing to contemplate the commandments this way. Our culture is desperate for the good sense of "Thou shalt not commit adultery." The loneliness and despair of so many in our society are due to all the havoc that is initiated when one party breaks the marriage covenant which God has designed. Furthermore, God's extra gift is the social sexuality that frees us to establish deep friendships with one another in both genders. That we are able to have profound friends across all barriers shows the brilliance of God's creating purposes.

And so it is with the Sabbath command. God has not told us, "Keep this Sabbath day or else. . . ." Rather, God offers us a great gift and urges us to ascertain how this treasure will change our lives — and our world! I really love it that Muslims, Jews, and Christians all share the practice of keeping a holy day. If we really paid attention to what that holy day connotes, think of the difference it would make in the *shalom* or the *salaam* between us, the peace between our peoples. Ruminate on the contrast it could make in our world in these terrible times!

Let's continue reflecting closely on the transformation made possible by the Exodus version of the Sabbath command. This version is inaugurated with the verb, *Remember.* English speakers run into trouble because we think of remembering as only a mental act, but that is not the way in which the Hebrew language understands it. In Hebrew culture, to remember is to act upon that remembrance.

You remember something by proclaiming it, by remaining faithful to it, by acting upon it. There is a typical connection between word and action in the Hebrew language. For example, the term *dabar,* which is translated "word" in early literature, later came to be understood as "event." This is especially true of God because *YHWH* is the Promise Keeper, the Fulfiller of the Covenant made with the Lord's people. I don't mean this in the simplistic sense that I saw once in a play in which the characters continually repeated, "God said it. I believe it. That settles it." The biblical record is much more nuanced. But the point the play made was true: what God has promised will be fulfilled, so we don't need to "sweat the small stuff." In fact, we don't need to sweat the big stuff either. We remember that the "Word of the Lord" carries within it its own fulfillment.

Again, wouldn't it be tremendous if we took words seriously in this way — knowing that what we say becomes an event, for good or for ill. As we thought about the Amish community earlier, we realized that their community demonstrates another trait that we might emulate. If Amish people make an agreement, it is not necessary to sign some sort of document in triplicate. If an Amish person says, "I give you my word," you can trust that what is promised will be fulfilled.

Could we all — Jews, Christians, and Muslims in this group tonight — become known as people who live our words? What if we said only what we really mean and will surely act upon? That is the invitation of the words *remember* the Sabbath day and *keep it holy.* This does not mean merely that we are not to forget to practice it. We are instead called to recollect all that the Sabbath connotes and to reestablish its holiness in our lives, too.

The name *Shabbat* does not denote the day of the week, but its root actually means "to stop," "to cease." My Jewish Study Bible emphasizes that this refers to a complete cessation of all kinds of activity. When connected with the command to keep it holy, this suggests that we withdraw the Sabbath day from any "common" uses. Whatever endeavors characterize our normal work days are prohibited. Especially anything contrary to God's designs for the universe is forbidden. That is why we refrain from violence on that day — and, hopefully, such discontinuance will become more of a way of life throughout the week. Imagine the possibilities if we could share this observance more deeply among our fellowships!

The next verse in the Exodus text, "Six days you shall labor and do all your work," is the only verse that occurs exactly the same in the two versions. It is also the easiest to follow. We only need to warn ourselves neither to slouch nor to overwork on the other six days of the week that are meant for labor. However, the full thrust of the Jewish idea of Sabbath includes extra enjoyment for those days of toil, too, because a Sabbath way of life actually frees us for a different understanding of time.

Our typical perception of time does not free us for reconciliation. In our Western culture, we think we have to work like crazy and then deserve a holiday. Instead, Jews know that the Sabbath is the focus of the week. One begins with Sabbath rest, and out of the joy of that rest one does one's work. It makes a big difference whether we do our work out of duty and burden or if we do it out of elation!

This sense of time is suggested by the liturgy of Genesis 1:1–2:3. Human beings were created at the end of the week, just before God hallowed the Sabbath. So the first things they did were rest and celebrate. They got around to tilling the garden on their second day. The same idea is implied by the fact that the days begin with evening and then follows morning. We sleep first, and then we arise to join in the work that God is already doing.

"Rest and then labor" is a superb prescription for better attitudes. We all serve better if we do it as a response to the gift of rest, rather than as a burdensome obligation.

Visualize, for example, how it would change the tone of academia if everyone worked out of the enjoyment of their rest and celebration rather than out of the frenzy of competition to secure a more honored place in the institution. We would be much less violent in our dealings with each other. We could become more a community of learning than a place of rivalry and discord.

Now explore with me Exodus 20:10. Notice that the holy day is a Sabbath to the LORD our God — I can't accentuate that enough. There are quite a few books on Sabbath these days that merely discuss ways to refresh oneself. The Hebrew command, in contrast, features ceasing for the sake of God. When we keep the Sabbath, we cease our regular work in order to learn more about God, for if we know who God is and what God's character is like we will be formed in God's image. That is why the major emphasis in this commandment in the Exodus version is that Sabbath keeping is done in imitation of God. Remember again that Genesis liturgy from which we learned that we are created in the image of God so that we can participate in God's mission to restore order and harmony in the world. We want by God's grace to bring back the beauty and unity of God's great designs. The more we imitate God in Sabbath keeping, the more our reforming and renewing work on the other six days will contribute to the rebuilding of the cosmos according to God's purposes. How urgent is the mandate in the first version of the Sabbath commandment: imitate God!

Second Version of the Sabbath Command: Performative Observance

Now let's delve briefly into the Deuteronomy version. Its listing of the Ten Commandments begins differently. Instead of God saying, "I am YHWH who brought you out of Egypt," Moses convenes an assembly and declares, "Hear, O Israel, the statutes and ordinances that I am addressing to you today; you shall learn them and observe them diligently. The LORD our God made a covenant with us at Horeb." Evidently by the time of Deuteronomy Moses has realized that Israel is not very good at obeying zealously. He's had plenty of experience with their whining and complaining, their idolatries and iniquities. He seems to be saying, "Wait a minute, you guys! You have forgotten what life is all about." Then he reminds Israel of the great grace of the LORD before reiterating the Ten Commandments.

Thus we commence with this reminder that what we hear about God's grace is not to be taken for granted. Instead, in response to that grace emanates a way of life. Again, notice the close connection in Hebrew literature between a word and a way of life. Grace isn't fully received until it is enacted.

When we read the first word of the Sabbath commandment, once again our English language fails us. The verb *observe* in English seems simply to mean "watch closely." But the Hebrew connotes more than that. The "watching closely" leads to "guarding carefully." This is what the Lord's Day Alliance promotes: trying not to lose the greatness of the Holy Day even though our culture doesn't support that at all any more. The Hebrew understanding of "observing" moves even further beyond guarding carefully into "performing it diligently." It is a performative word.

The best way I could illustrate that is with "performance art." I have a friend who is a brilliant and socially concerned artist. Once he was asked to design a teepee village for a global ministries conference so that visitors could explore the way of life of native peoples. At first he refused, because the committee had not asked the native folk themselves to do it. Why invite an artist to construct a deceitful replica of what native people do by habit? After discussing the issue with a local tribe, he came up with the perfect solution to the problem. With their permission, he assembled a burned-out teepee village. Then he made signs to resemble federal park signs, only he reversed the colors so that he wouldn't be arrested by the law. The signs told the history of this particular village, how it had been burned out by marauding soldiers, and so forth. But as visitors drew nearer to the center of the village the notices were decreasingly in English and increasingly in Lakota. At the central display of the largest teepee, completely incinerated, the placard was entirely in Lakota.

The art had a similar response each time it was displayed. The performative exhibit evoked tremendous admiration because its viewers finally understood how often we leave other people out — of our conversations, of our society, of our possessions. We haven't experienced that much because we're not usually left out of English, are we? In most places in the world, we can find others to speak our language with us. But to be prevented from understanding the climactic display by the Lakota sign was an entirely new ordeal for almost everyone.

The showing was so effective that my friend was invited by the Art Museum in Denver to bring it there, and some local tribespeople agreed to come and help with the enormous task of setting it up. For some reason, however, they were not able to get to Denver in time, so my friend gathered all kinds of people who were coming out of the nearby government offices to help erect the village. The artist commented that it was truly amazing to see the very people whose ancestors might have burned out the tribal people helping to set up the display. They were thereby being reminded of the violence that had been done in their name.

This is how we can best understand these Hebrew verbs *remember* and *observe* — as performance art. We can't just read the commands. It is not enough to understand those verbs in the English sense of them. They lead to a way of life. This first major difference between the Exodus and the Deuteronomy versions in the use of these two verbs causes the Jewish people in history and today to light two candles or a candle with two intertwined wicks when they begin their Sabbath evenings with the ritual of *Kiddush*.

Deuteronomy 5:12 also includes the phrase, "as the LORD your God commanded you." We don't keep the Sabbath day out of our own whims and fancies. Rather, to do so is part of our responsibility as God's people. Such a requirement we relish if we are truly paying attention to our God. Therefore, it is such a tragedy that many of us have lost the treasure of the Sabbath, even though it is a major part of our heritage.

Though Deuteronomy 5:13 is exactly the same as verse 9 in the Exodus 20 text, verse 14 of the Deuteronomy version adds more creatures to the list and the significant line, "so that your male and female slave may rest as well as you." It is an enormously significant statement to declare that on this day, the Sabbath Day, we are all equal. On this holy day that envisions God's paradise all people are of the same worth.

The apostle Paul perhaps had this commandment in mind when he wrote to Philemon to treat Onesimus as his brother, rather than as his slave. Why does the world still not understand the equality of all human beings? The most remarkable difference between the two versions of the Sabbath commandment is that Deuteronomy gives an entirely unrelated reason for the mandate. When we remember that we were slaves in the land of Egypt (or wherever we have been in bondage to fears or doubts, confusions or sins) and that the LORD our God "brought [us] out from there with a mighty hand and an outstretched arm," the strong implication is that we would never, ever want to be the source of anyone else's oppression. Having experienced our own set of woes, we could never do such terrible things to other people.

Thus, the two versions of the Sabbath command show us why Sabbath keeping is the hinge of the Ten Commandments. The first version calls us to love God by imitating the LORD. The second urges us to love our neighbors by refraining from causing them any harm. The first version is turned toward the commandments that preceded it in the First Table of the Law — the ordinances to have no other gods besides the LORD, to make no idols, to make no wrongful use of the LORD's name. The second version is turned toward the commandments that follow it in the Second Table of the Law — the mandates to honor our parents, to refrain from murdering, committing adultery, stealing, bearing false witness, and coveting. The First Table of the Law is summarized by the first and greatest commandment, "You shall love the LORD your God with all your heart and with all your soul and with all your mind." The Second Table can be condensed into "Love your neighbor as yourself."

Our imitating of God naturally — rather, by God's grace — leads to all the ways to build justice and make peace that are positive alternatives to the actions prohibited by the other commandments. This is the hinge that Christian churches (I don't know about the Jews and Muslims) have not understood thoroughly enough. Sabbath keeping might involve showing up now and then for a worship service in a congregation, but this has not led consistently to imitating God in all of life, especially by loving the neighbor.

The Deuteronomy version of the Sabbath commandment widens out in the Hebrew Scriptures to numerous passages that give specific guidance as to how we can live out the freedom and faith granted us by the LORD's deliverance from bondage. For example, Deuteronomy 15 proclaims that every seven years there will be a restoration and a reparation of goods for people who are in debt. Leviticus 25 introduces us to the Jubilee, when everyone's property will be restored so that the rich do not get richer and the poor recover their equity. My favorite text of all is Isaiah 58, which reproaches Israel for its wrongful keeping of the Sabbath.

Isaiah 58, as you might remember, begins with the lofty cry, "Shout out, do not hold back!/Lift up your voice like a trumpet!/And declare to My people their transgression,/And to the house of Jacob their sins./Yet they seek Me day by day, and delight to know My ways;/As if they were a nation that practiced righteousness. . . ." Israel pretended to keep the Sabbath, as if they were a community that did what God had asked. They complained (in a childish falsetto), "WHY have we fasted, but YOU do not see?/WHY have we humbled ourselves and YOU do not notice?" (You have to act like a three-year-old to read that text rightly.) But the point of God's rebuke is set out in verses 6 and 7: "Is this not the fast which I choose,/To loosen the bonds of injustice,/To undo the bands of the yoke,/And to let the oppressed go free,/And break every yoke?/Is it not to divide your bread with the hungry,/And bring the homeless poor into your house;/When you see the naked, to cover him;/And not to hide yourself from your own flesh?"

Those sentences challenge us to get to the root of systemic evil in order to set the oppressed free and to divide our own bread with the hungry — that is, not to give simply the leftovers or extras, but to share our own bread. When we truly love our neighbors in these ways, "Then your light shall break forth like the dawn,/And your healing shall spring up quickly;/And your righteousness shall go before you;/The glory of the LORD shall be your rear guard." The first line of this verse 8 is the source for my pen-name Dawn, which I chose in order to remind me and you that our calling is always to feed the hungry and never to turn away from any human being. Its second line surprises us with the truth that we ourselves receive healing when we care for our neighbors by working against injustice. The last two lines utilize images from the Exodus and display the LORD's powerful protection as God led Israel with the pillar of fire and cloud.

Conclusion

We could continue to cite passages that guide us in genuine Sabbath keeping — in loving our neighbor because we once were slaves in Egypt. But let us instead track how far we have come by summarizing what we have been given by God.

After recognizing both more blatant and more subtle forms of violence that plague our culture, we were given hope with three treasures. The first was Elizabeth Spelman's notion of *homo reparans,* that we are all characterized by a longing to be rebuilt and a desire to contribute to restoration. Her emphasis that authentic renewal doesn't jettison the past, but reclaims it leads us to a greater appreciation for fidelity to the tradition of Sabbath keeping.

Second, we were given hope by the present theological emphasis on formation by practices and rituals and especially by our Scriptures. We have participated in a few rituals together this evening, and we have recognized the importance of immersing ourselves in our scriptural traditions so that the way of life they present can get "into our bones."

39

The third element of hope we were given came from the movement called Scriptural Reasoning. Scholars in this movement are bringing together Jews, Muslims, and Christians to share readings in our traditions in order to see what bonds us. Of course, Sabbath keeping is a major practice that unites us, for we all have a heritage of keeping a holy day.

When we antiphonally read the two versions of the Sabbath command in Exodus and Deuteronomy, it became obvious to us that the Abrahamic tradition which unites us also is the hinge bringing together the two Tables of the Law. The point of the Exodus version is that we imitate God in keeping a holy day, while the Deuteronomic version urges us to enable everyone to have a holy day for we were slaves in Egypt and know how terrible it is to be oppressed. Thus, the ritual of keeping the Sabbath intermingles loving God as the motivation and loving our neighbor as our response to the tremendous grace of the LORD who brought us out of Egypt and created a covenant with us. We saw in several texts that the Hebrew Scriptures provide ample resources for us to rebuild social justice as part of our Sabbath way of life. As in the Ten Commandments, Sabbath keeping is the hinge between what we know about God's power and grace and how we live, between the love of God and the love of the neighbor.

Let us remember and observe the Sabbath, for it is holy to the LORD. Keeping it will also form that holiness in us, so that we can live what we know in justice and peace to contribute to eradicating the violence of our world. Imitate God! And remember that you were slaves in Egypt. . . . Let us free others from their need for justice as we ourselves have been freed by *YHWH*, the Covenant God, the Promise Keeper, the LORD of the Sabbath!

Spiritual Coherence

The Lord's Day Alliance is a Christian group organized to encourage all people to recognize and observe a day of Sabbath rest and to worship the risen Lord Jesus Christ on the Lord's Day, Sunday. For many years the Alliance has encouraged the development of coherent presentations on the benefits of the Lord's Day through lectures, papers, newsletters, and sermons. Those benefits are not limited to one particular aspect of Sabbath observance (for example, rest from labor). It is true that for many years the Alliance joined with other Christian groups to maintain laws to regulate Sunday activities, but the evolution of American society, especially since World War II, saw the erosion of those regulations. Yet Sunday/Sabbath, while providing a healthy rhythm to a cycle of what otherwise would be a deadening pace of life without it, offers something more fundamental still: a rhythm of life for the spirit.

Numerous authors have taken up the theme of spiritual health and studied it from various angles, especially from the point of view of Protestant, Orthodox, and Catholic churches. The starting point for such studies is, of course, the Hebrew Bible or Christian Old Testament. Here in Part II, Dennis Olson offers a detailed exposition of Sabbath in the Hebrew text and shows that its observance is fundamental to Jewish faith since it shapes the Jews' understanding of God, creation, the cosmos, and individuals' relationships among themselves. Sabbath observance is not simply an obligation to be carried out, a duty whose fulfillment gives one an identity, but the principle which gives coherence to one's faith. How easy it is to understand the New Testament Gospel passages where Jesus was believed to disrespect Sabbath regulations; He was not seen as failing to fulfill the law, but attacking one of the bases for belief. Olson's essay reveals the rich complex of meanings that will echo through all the subsequent traditions.

Alkiviadis Calivas, Edward O'Flaherty, and Horace Allen deal with the Orthodox, Catholic, and Reformed Protestant churches' experience. The liturgy, to be sure, takes center stage in all their observances. Reflecting on these three essays, however, the reader will become aware that liturgy itself engages its participants in time and space more expansive than the hour or two that the worship ceremonies occupy those participants in a particular church building. The order of service reflects an order of the week and year; the readings can take us from the beginning of time to its end; the homily or sermon highlights the present moment of grace and opens to the worshipers that mystery, that plan which God "set forth in Christ . . . for the fullness of time to unite all things in Him" (Eph. 1:9-10). Sunday observance, these essays show, occurs in the here and now but does not leave us there.

Darrell Guder expands our horizon to let us see how the Lord's Day in non-Western cultures is incorporated into the lives of people. Their inculturation of the Lord's Day opens up our own theological treasures which routine and repetition have hidden away. It is not just theological dialogue, important as it is, that opens the horizon, but the actual Lord's Day observance, incarnated in a living tradition that produces the opening to grace.

CHAPTER FOUR

Sacred Time: The Sabbath and Christian Worship

Dennis T. Olson

Remember the Sabbath day, and keep it holy.

EXODUS 20:8

Some Salient Questions on Sabbath

Does the Old Testament commandment for Sabbath rest on the seventh day of the week (Saturday) apply to Christians who typically gather for worship on Sundays? Or does the Sabbath command apply only to Jews? Is the Christian Sunday properly called a Sabbath, or is it something entirely different from the Jewish day of rest? If Sunday is a Sabbath day, does that mean that we are not supposed to do any work on Sunday at all? What constitutes work? Should people in school do homework on the Sabbath? Should doctors and nurses work on the Sabbath? Can you cook food, clean the house, or go to the movies? Should stores be open on Sundays?

Christians today don't seem to take the Sabbath as seriously as the Old Testament itself, which prescribes that "Whoever does any work on the Sabbath day shall be put to death" (Exod. 31:15). The question is, Why don't we? Is the command to rest every seven days meant only for religious people, or is it built into us as a basic need for all human beings? Why are there

This chapter, delivered at an annual meeting of the Lord's Day Alliance, was first published in *Touching the Altar: The Old Testament for Christian Worship*, edited by Carol M. Bechtel (Grand Rapids: Eerdmans, 2008), pp. 1-34. Permission has been granted by Eerdmans Publishing Co., Inc., to reprint herein.

Dennis T. Olson

two different versions of the same Sabbath — Exodus 20 and Deuteronomy 5? What indeed is the meaning of this commandment for us today?

As we begin to explore these questions, we will discover many and varied biblical traditions associated with the Sabbath commandment in the Old Testament. The biblical theme of the Sabbath offers rich resources for fundamentally reshaping our view of time as it integrates and balances the way we relate to all our primary connections in life — our relationship with God, with other humans, with nonhuman creation, and even with ourselves. The Sabbath provides a window into the biblical view of time and all the meanings associated with it.

In his book entitled *A Geography of Time,* Robert Levine notes that modern Western industrialized societies tend to be ruled by the clock — fast-paced, punctual, and highly efficient. Instant messages, fast food, being on call "24/7," impatience with delay, and insistence on "being on time" characterize our society's time values. We are defined and valued by how efficiently we use our time. After all, we are told, time is money. Overfilled schedules and a fast-paced lifestyle somehow signify status, importance, and value. But not all human societies are like that. For some cultures, life is slower, interruptions are welcomed, and a balance of rest and work is the norm. Some societies don't even use clocks with minutes and hours, but instead mark time through the slow movement of the stars, the seasons of nature, the rhythms of the human body, or simply events as they occur.[1] In a study entitled *Time Wars,* Jeremy Rifkin writes, "Every culture has its own unique set of temporal fingerprints. To know a people is to know the time values they live by."[2] In many ways, the biblical Sabbath represents a set of time values at odds with contemporary culture.

Modern culture's time values often seem enslaving and oppressive. Bookstore shelves are lined with titles like *The Time Trap* and *Timeclock* and *The Time Bind.* Work time seems increasingly to expand and rob us of time with family and friends. Computers and the Internet bombard us with a constant flow of data, messages, and information. Hectic schedules and crowded calendars often restrict our options, sap our energies, and rob us of time for thoughtful reflection. Like circus performers desperately trying to keep multiple plates spinning on the ends of wobbly sticks, we rush back and forth from one function or activity to another. We some-

---

1. Robert Levine, *A Geography of Time* (New York: Basic Books/Perseus, 1997) p. xi.
2. Jeremy Rifkin, *Time Wars: The Primary Conflict in Human History* (New York: Henry Holt, 1987); quoted in Levine, *A Geography of Time,* p. xi.

times feel harried and hurried, out of balance, out of sync, not in rhythm. Sociologists tell us that the average American workday has gradually gotten longer, while the time we devote to sleep has grown shorter. We spend less time with family and friends and in voluntary organizations and service. For others in our society, time is out of balance and oppressive in other ways. Some people's lives are marked by having too much time on their hands, feeling bored and isolated, watching the hours pass by without a genuine sense of meaning and purpose. They are the lonely, the unemployed, the depressed, the imprisoned, the bored workers, the elderly in a nursing home, the children with no friends, the poor with few options for play or work.

The biblical vision of time is something quite different from all of this. Time is a gift intended to give human life a sense of balance, meaning, and purpose. God's eternity puts human time in perspective. At the beginning of the Bible in Genesis 1, we read, "In the beginning, God created." Creation happens with a God-given framework of time defined as the days of the week — six days of work and a Sabbath day of rest. At the end of the Bible in John's grand apocalyptic vision, God reaffirms the absorbing of all human time within the all-encompassing eternity of God: "I am the Alpha and the Omega, the beginning and the end" (Rev. 21:6). One of the most important features of this biblical vision of time is the Old Testament Sabbath. The Hebrew noun "Sabbath" is related to *shabat,* meaning "to cease, stop, interrupt." The Sabbath involves breaking into the routine, interrupting what is presumed normal, periodically stopping us in our tracks in order to return us to a healthy rhythm of worship and work, a balance between focusing on God and focusing on others, an equilibrium between caring for our own basic needs and caring for God's whole creation. Such interruptions open up space in time for us to remember, to redirect our lives to what is true and good, to regain perspective, to be broken and then freed, to be stopped and made new again.

Biblical scholars have sought to find parallels to the Old Testament Sabbath and the seven-day week in texts from other ancient Near Eastern cultures who were neighbors to ancient Israel, but no clear or direct parallels have emerged.[3] Regular Sabbath rest appears to be a fairly distinctive

---

3. Some proposals for parallels to the Israelite Sabbath have been made. For example, scholars have pointed to one ancient Babylonian text that seems to mark time in seven-day increments according to cycles of the moon. Other texts indicate that the Babylonians may have offered sacrifices to their gods on the day of each full moon, called a *sabbattu* (a word similar to the Hebrew word *Shabbat,* "Sabbath"). However, the general consensus is that

45

element of ancient Israel's own practice and reflection. The Sabbath and
the seven-day week were subsequently adapted and reshaped by the early
Christians (the earliest of whom were Jewish in background) and often
eventually implemented and enforced by Christian rulers and other political authorities as an agreed-upon and common way of reckoning time,
weeks, and months in a now widely shared system of marking time across
the globe. Although we may work within the seven-day framework of the
Sabbath, many of us have lost a basic understanding of the full and integrating meanings of the Sabbath in relationship to the worship of God,
human justice, the rejuvenation of the self, and concern for God's whole
creation.

We will begin our exploration of the Old Testament Sabbath by looking at the two versions of the Sabbath commandment as they appear in Exodus 20 and Deuteronomy 5.

The Sabbath Commandment in Exodus 20 and the Book of Exodus

> *Remember the* Sabbath *day, and keep it holy. Six days you shall labor
> and do all your work. But the seventh day is a* Sabbath *to the* LORD *your
> God; you shall not do any work — you, your son or your daughter, your
> male or female slave, your livestock, or the alien resident in your towns.
> For in six days the* LORD *made heaven and earth, the sea, and all that is
> in them, but rested the seventh day; therefore the* LORD *blessed the* Sab-
> bath *day and consecrated it.*

EXODUS 20:8-11

The book of Exodus tells the story of God's rescue of the enslaved people
of Israel, who are forced against their will to work for Pharaoh in ancient
Egypt. God's servant, Moses, leads Israel across the Red Sea and into the
wilderness on a journey toward the promised land of Canaan. Along the
way, Israel stops at the mountain of God called Mount Sinai, where God
makes a covenant with Israel as God's special people. At the heart of this
covenant are the Ten Commandments. Among the most important of

---

these alleged parallels do not stand up under scrutiny. The Babylonian texts in question
seem to apply quite narrowly to certain religious rites and do not signify a society-wide way
of marking time.

these ten imperatives is the command to "remember the Sabbath day, and keep it holy" (Exod. 20:8). The Sabbath commandment is the lengthiest of all the commandments, making up about a third of the text of the Decalogue. Moreover, the Sabbath commandment stands structurally at a central and integrative transition point between the first group of commandments, which articulate obligations to God (no other gods, no worship of images, careful use of the divine name), and the second group of commandments, which articulate obligations to other humans (honoring parents, not killing, not stealing, not committing adultery, not bearing false witness, not coveting). Between these two groups stands the Sabbath commandment, which ties together our obligations to God, to other humans, to our own well-being, and to nature (animals are also included in the Sabbath rest). All of these relationships come together in this one commandment.

The Sabbath and the Holy

The commandment in Exodus 20 begins, "Remember the Sabbath day, and keep it holy" (v. 8). To keep something holy means to set it apart from what is ordinary. The day is special and devoted to God, who is holy. Israelites periodically stop the normal routine of ordinary weekday work and set aside a day as an offering of time to God. What is holy is typically associated with worshiping God and coming together as a community around God's revealed and holy presence. Thus the Sabbath is holy "to the Lord" (Exod. 16:23; 20:10; 31:15; 35:2; Lev. 19:3; 23:3). But the Sabbath is also holy "to you," the people of God (Exod. 16:29; 31:14; Lev. 16:31). The holiness of the Sabbath binds together *God's* holiness with *Israel's* holiness as the beloved and chosen people of God. "You shall keep my Sabbaths, for this is a sign between me and you throughout your generations, given in order that you may know that I, the Lord, sanctify you. You shall keep the Sabbath, because it is holy for you" (Exod. 31:13-14). Israel rests on the Sabbath so that they might have the time to remember and know that it is the Lord who sanctifies or makes them holy. It is not their human work, not their frantic activity, not their human power or efforts that make them holy, special, and set apart from others. Rather, it is God who makes them whole and holy. The friendly commandment of weekly rest reminds the people of Israel of their reliance on God's gracious presence and activity to sustain their life, their freedom, their identity, and their hope.

47

The Sabbath and Work

Every seventh day is to be a day on which "you shall not do any work." Specific types of work are prohibited in the Old Testament. On the Sabbath, there is to be no kindling of fire or cooking (Exod. 35:3), no gathering of wood with the intention of starting a fire (Num. 15:32-36), no carrying of burdens (Jer. 17:21-22; 24:27), no trade or commerce (Neh. 10:32; see Amos 8:5), no treading of winepresses or loading of beasts (Neh. 13:15-22), and no traveling away from your home territory ("each of you stay where you are; do not leave your place on the seventh day" — Exod. 16:29). The literal Hebrew of Isaiah 58:13 even prohibits "speaking words" on the Sabbath. Some interpret this injunction as a requirement to maintain total silence during the Sabbath and others suggest it is a requirement simply not to speak about work matters on the Sabbath. Given the imprecision and ambiguities in the biblical Sabbath instructions, the Jewish rabbinic tradition developed a large number of clarifying interpretations about what one was and was not allowed to do on the Sabbath. But strict observance of Sabbath rest from all work was assumed, even in the busiest times of year: "even in plowing time and in harvest time you shall rest" (Exod. 34:21).

Within the larger literary context of the book of Exodus, the Sabbath commandment provides a thoughtful commentary on the nature of human work and vocation. The book of Exodus contrasts two major work projects. The one described in Exodus 1–13 is oppressive, enslaving, and dehumanizing. It is the Egyptian empire's enslavement of the Israelites, who are forced to do menial and hard labor against their will and without just compensation. The other work project in Exodus 25–31 and 35–40 is Israel's eager and willing building of the Tabernacle, the seat of God's presence in their midst, a portable shrine and sanctuary that is the visible sign of God's presence in their midst. It is only this — the divine presence, "God with us" — that makes Israel holy and set apart from every other people (Exod. 33:16). And so Israel willingly offers its resources, time, and energy to construct the Tabernacle. Concerning these two large work projects in Exodus, Ellen Davis makes this observation:

> Exodus is setting before us two lengthy, vivid pictures. In the first thirteen chapters, we see Israel enslaved in Egypt, trapped in "that iron furnace" (Deut. 4:20), the great industrial killing machine of Pharaonic Egypt. There Israel builds store cities for a king so deluded he thinks he is a god. Then at the other end of the book, thirteen chapters portray Is-

rael's first concerted activity in freedom. Israel's first "public work" is to build a sanctuary for her God, who is of course the real God. These two long narratives at beginning and end are a sort of unmatched pair, designed to contrast absolutely. They are, respectively, perverted work, designed by Pharaoh to destroy God's people, and divinely mandated work, designed to bring together God and God's people, in the closest proximity possible in this life. That is what worship is for.[4]

The instructions for the "divinely mandated work" of building the Tabernacle in Exodus 25–31 can be divided into six sections or speeches that correspond to the six days of creation in Genesis 1. And just as the Sabbath day comes at the end of six days of God's work in the creation story (Gen. 2:1-3), so the six sections of the Tabernacle instructions conclude with a seventh speech that repeats the Sabbath commandment (Exod. 31:12-17).[5] What is the significance of this correspondence between God's creating work in Genesis 1 and Israel's Tabernacle building in Exodus 25–31? It is important to note that God's creating in Genesis 1 works with the resources at hand and empowers intermediaries to participate with God in the creation and stewardship of the world. "Let the waters bring forth swarms of living creatures" (Gen. 1:20). "Let the earth bring forth living creatures" (Gen. 1:24). "God set [the sun and the moon] in the dome of the sky . . . to rule over the day and over the night" (Gen 1:17-18). "God said to [the humans], '. . . have dominion . . . over every living thing that moves upon the earth'" (Gen. 1:28).[6] Earth, water, sun, moon, and humans participate with God in co-creating the world in the midst of the watery primeval chaos with which Genesis 1 begins. God is the master architect and builder, but creation is less a one-God show and more an or-

---

4. Ellen F. Davis, "Slaves or Sabbath Keepers? A Biblical Perspective on Human Work," *Anglican Theological Review* 83 (2001): 30-31.

5. Peter Kearney, "Creation and Liturgy: The P Redaction of Ex 25–40," *Zeitschrift für die alttestamentliche Wissenschaft* 89 (1977): 374-87; Peter Weimar, "Sinai und Schöpfung, Komposition und Theologie der priesterschriftlichen Sinaigeschichte," *Revue Biblique* 95 (1988): 337-85; and Bernd Janowski, "Tempel und Schöpfung, Schöpfungstheologische Aspekte der priesterschriftlichen Heiligstumskonzeption," in *Schöpfung and Neuschöpfung, Jahrbuch für Biblische Theologie*, vol. 5, ed. Luis M. Alonso Schökel et al. (Neukirchen-Vluyn: Neukirchener Verlag, 1990), pp. 37-70.

6. Eric Flines, "Creation and Tabernacle: The Priestly Writer's 'Environmentalism,'" *Horizons in Biblical Theology* 16 (1994): 144-55; Terence Fretheim, "Creation and Co-Creation," in *Making All Things New: Essays in Honor of Roy Harrisville*, Word & World Supplement, Series 1 (St. Paul: Luther Seminary, 1992).

chestrated community effort in which the created order participates under God's direction.

Similarly, God's instructions to build the Tabernacle (the center of God's presence and Israel's worship) are ultimately God's work that at the same time invites human intermediaries to participate and cooperate in this new creation in the midst of the chaos of the wilderness. Both the creation of the world and the creation of the Tabernacle have as their culmination and goal the Sabbath day and its rest. Sabbath rest interrupts work time with time to enjoy, reflect, remember, and worship the God who rules over all creation and yet comes near and is present in the midst of God's people as they gather as a community in worship. Regular Sabbath rest and worship remind us that the work we do on the other days of the week should align itself in a cooperative way with God's continuing presence and creative activity in loving service to the world and its inhabitants, human and nonhuman alike.

The Sabbath and Worship

In its earliest stages of development in ancient Israel, the Sabbath, scholars believe, was simply a day of rest from work without any association with worship. The motivation for the earliest version of the Sabbath law in the Book of the Covenant in Exodus 23:12-13 is simply "so that your ox and your donkey may have relief, and your homeborn slave and the resident alien may be refreshed." But gradually the Sabbath became associated more and more with a time for the community of God's people to be gathered for worship. Some texts already before Judah's exile into Babylon (587 B.C.E.) associate the Sabbath with worship (Hos. 2:11; Isa. 1:13). However, it is in later exilic or post-exilic texts (after 587 B.C.E.) that we find a more frequent connection between the Sabbath day and acts of community worship (Leviticus; 2 Chronicles). Leviticus 23 defines the Sabbath as a day of convocation, festival, and the giving of offerings to God (vv. 2-3, 37-38; see also Lev. 24:8). The Sabbath is a day to "reverence the sanctuary" as the community gathers around the Tabernacle in its tent or in the temple as the seat of God's holy presence in the community (Lev. 26:2). The prophets condemn Sabbath worship and the bringing of offerings to God if justice for the poor and righteousness in everyday life are not maintained (Isa. 1:13-17; see also Amos 5:21-24). The post-exilic book of 2 Chronicles retells the earlier stories of 2 Kings and adds a reference to Sabbath worship and the giving of offerings at the temple when King Solomon builds the first temple in Jerusalem (2 Chron. 2:4; 8:12-13). These texts mention three categories of regular worship and assembly by post-exilic Jews: three "annual festivals"; twelve assemblies, one every month at the "new moon"; and weekly "Sabbaths." The role of priests in Sabbath worship with music, prayer, and the singing of the psalms is suggested by Psalm 92, which is entitled "A Song for the Sabbath Day." The psalm is a hymn of praise and begins with these words:

> It is good to give thanks to the LORD,
> to sing praises to your name, O Most High;
> to declare your steadfast love in the morning,
> and your faithfulness by night,
> to the music of the lute and the harp,
> to the melody of the lyre.
> For you, O LORD, have made me glad by your work;
> at the works of your hands I sing for joy.

Sabbath worship likely involved the use of the full range of psalms from lament to praise, from prayers of confession to songs of thanksgiving. One important biblical text brings together the Sabbath and worship as it offers an ideal and distant future vision of all humanity gathered together before God: "from Sabbath to Sabbath, all flesh shall come to worship before me, says the LORD" (Isa. 66:23).

The Sabbath and Food: Greed versus Trust

Another important story related to the Sabbath is Exodus 16 and the divine gift of manna. The manna is a special food that appears every morning to the Israelites during their wilderness journey. Remarkably, although on a given day some Israelites would gather more of the manna and some less, "those who gathered much had nothing over, and those who gathered little had no shortage; they gathered as much as each of them needed" (Exod. 16:18). Two important themes associated with the Sabbath and worship appear here for the first time: the theme of feasting and food as gifts of God, and the theme of basic equality of God's provision to all, regardless of effort, ability, or status. What is given is what is sufficient to meet one's basic needs — that is all that is required. When in the Lord's Prayer we pray

"Give us this day our daily bread," we are praying out the tradition of the manna story for only what we need for this particular day, no more and no less.

The Sabbath enters the story explicitly in God's instruction to Moses that the people are to gather twice as much as usual on the sixth day in order that they may rest on the Sabbath or seventh day from the work of gathering food. The people must learn to trust that God will provide what they need, even though they do not work on the Sabbath. There are those who went out on the Sabbath day looking to gather more manna, "but they found none" (Exod. 16:27). The greedy desire to hoard, to wring something more out of the gift of time given to us, to refuse to trust God and trust only one's own hard work and "efficient" use of time and energy — and all of these are put under critique and judgment in the story of the manna. As a constant reminder of the lessons of the manna, God commands Moses to take some of it, put it into a jar, and place the jar with the manna "before the Lord, to be kept throughout your generations" (Exod. 16:33). The jar of manna is a visible sign in worship "before the Lord" of God's gracious gift of food, the equality of all before God, the character of the Sabbath as a special day to lean back in trust into the comforting arms of God, and the trustworthiness of God to "give us this day our daily bread."

Sabbath Rest and Creation

One of the most central features of the Sabbath commandment in Exodus 20 is that the primary motivation and reason for resting on the Sabbath day is rooted in the model or example provided by God as Creator in Genesis 1–2: "For in six days the LORD made heaven and earth, the sea, and all that is in them, but rested the seventh day; therefore the LORD blessed the Sabbath day and consecrated it" (Exod. 20:11). This grounding in God's activity as Creator is the most distinctive element of the Exodus version of the Sabbath commandment in comparison with its alternate version in Deuteronomy 5. The commandment in Deuteronomy 5 grounds the Sabbath not in creation but in God's rescue of Israel from Egyptian slavery. The focus of Exodus 20 on God as a kind of teaching model, One who labors in creation for six days and then takes a rests (Gen. 2:1-3), raises some theological issues. Another version of the Sabbath commandment in Exodus 3:17 suggests that the Lord "rested" and indeed "was refreshed" on the seventh day of creation. But does God, the Lord of eternity and Creator of the world, really need to take a rest? Does the almighty God actually become tired and exhausted? Do not the Psalms confess that the God "who keeps Israel will neither slumber nor sleep" (Ps. 121:4)? Is not God always at work, always active, always awake?

Precisely here is an important insight into the meaning of the Sabbath. In Genesis 1:1–2:3 God creates time. The modern reader need not take the creation as a literal scientific description of the origins of the universe in order to appreciate the profound truth expressed in the creation story. God fashions the framework of the six days of creation and seventh day of rest in Genesis 1:1–2:3 with the alternation of light and darkness along with the sun, moon, and stars as markers of the passage of time. God is Alpha and Omega, beginning and end, sovereign over all human time. But by resting on the Sabbath, God willingly enters into and becomes subject to the created framework of human time that God had just created. The act of divine resting on the Sabbath day of creation is the first instance of God's gracious accommodation, God's self-limiting, the first step toward the eventual coming of God in human flesh in the person of Jesus. In the Gospel story of Jesus calming the storm on the sea, Jesus combines the power of the Creator God to still the raging waters of primeval chaos (see Gen. 1:2) with the human need for sleep:[7]

> And when [Jesus] got into the boat, his disciples followed him. A windstorm arose on the sea, so great that the boat was being swamped by the waves; but he was asleep. And they went and woke him up, saying, "Lord, save us! We are perishing!" And he said to them, "Why are you afraid, you of little faith?" Then he got up and rebuked the winds and the sea; and there was a dead calm. They were amazed, saying, "What sort of man is this, that even the winds and the sea obey him?" (Matt. 8:23-27; cf. also Mark 4:35-41; Luke 8:22-25)

The community of Jesus' disciples gathered in a boat was for the early church a common symbol of Christians gathered in community for worship. Even today the inside architecture of many church buildings represents an inverted boat or ship. The image also recalls the story of Noah and

---

7. On the interesting theme of God and sleep in the Old Testament and its ancient Near Eastern environment, see Thomas McAlpine, "Sleep, Human and Divine, in the Old Testament," *Journal for the Study of the Old Testament,* Supp. 28 (Sheffield: JSOT, 1987).

the ark, with Noah's family being saved from the raging floods of Genesis 6–9. The Noah narrative is the story of another new creation. This same divine power to create, tame chaos, and bring Sabbath rest is evident there in Jesus, who both rests and acts in power to save. Rest, peace, calm — creation's seventh day offers to worshipers a Sabbath refuge from the winds, storms, and waves that buffet our workdays and threaten to throw us off balance or even drown us in the waters of chaos. The Sabbath and Sabbath worship are first of all about God's coming down into our lives and communities to act, to create, to calm, and to give rest. Sabbath worship is an interruption in human time whereby God becomes revealed and present in power among a gathered community of faith.

This is why the Sabbath day is described as "blessed" by God (Exod. 20:11; Gen. 2:3). Sabbath time becomes an arena or sphere of God's blessing, a temporal space set aside to give life, well-being, and wholeness. In this way, the Sabbath holds together in some tension a more somber sense of holiness, obligation, and "solemn rest" (Exod. 16:23; 31:15; 35:2) and a more joyful sense of the Sabbath as a gracious gift that is received, embraced, and celebrated in an atmosphere of freedom and feasting. Thus the prophet in Isaiah 58 promises that "if you call the Sabbath a delight . . . then you shall take delight in the LORD, and I will make you ride upon the heights of the earth" (Isa. 58:13-14). There are echoes of this promise elsewhere in Isaiah. "Happy is the mortal . . . who keeps the Sabbath" (Isa. 56:2). "All who keep the Sabbath, and do not profane it . . . these I will bring to my holy mountain, and make them joyful in my house of prayer" (Isa. 56:6). The Sabbath is associated with festivals and feasts involving the sharing of food and celebration (Lev. 23:37-38; 2 Chron. 8:12-13). As with many of its facets, the Sabbath holds together a dialogical tension between holy, solemn obligation and joyful, gracious freedom.

The Sabbath and Caring for Others

We have seen that the Sabbath in Exodus 20 carries with it several important themes: the holiness of the seventh day, the primacy of God's gracious action, a balanced understanding of work and vocation, the experience of God's re-creating power and presence in worship, and the joyful receiving of the Sabbath as a blessing and a gift for oneself. The Exodus 20 version of the Sabbath imperative adds one more theme to this list: Sabbath rest is not just for us but, just as important, it is for others — for family members, for workers, and even for animals. Grounded in God's creating of the whole universe in Genesis 1–2, the need for periodic and regular Sabbath rest is built into every creature created by God, whether human or nonhuman. Humans are created in the image of God (Gen. 1:26) and thus have built into them a resonance to God's exemplary rhythm of working six days and resting on the seventh. The gift of the Sabbath is for all humans, even the non-Israelite "alien resident in your towns" (Exod. 20:10). Foreigners and strangers are welcomed into receiving the blessing of Sabbath rest.

In the creation story in Genesis 1, humans are given dominion over the animals (Gen. 1:26). But that dominion is to be exercised graciously "in the image of God," who limited and accommodated God's self in order to provide the blessing of the Sabbath to humans. Similarly, humans are to give rest not only to their human workers but also to their animals in benevolent oversight and stewardship of all of God's creatures. The Sabbath as rooted in God's creating activity readily enables connections among practices of rest, worship, justice, and the care of the earth. The Sabbath is about interrupting the routine of our daily work and lives not only so that *we* might be refreshed and restored but also so others, human and nonhuman alike, may rest and be reinvigorated and renewed. Indeed, what may be the oldest version of the Sabbath commandment, in Exodus 23:12, offers a singularly practical and humane justification for the commandment: the Sabbath is to be a day of rest "so that your ox and your donkey may have relief, and your homeborn slave and the resident alien may be refreshed." Isaiah 56:1-2 affirms this dimension of "keeping the Sabbath" as not just passive rest and not just worship of God but also the active concern to "maintain justice, and do what is right" for the sake of others. Doing justice for the sake of others properly flows out of gratitude for the gift of Sabbath rest and blessing that we receive along with God's transforming activity within us in Sabbath worship. This concern for active justice for the sake of the other is present in the Exodus 20 version of the Sabbath commandment, but it is highlighted even more in the version we find in Deuteronomy 5, to which we now turn.

The Sabbath Commandment in Deuteronomy 5 and the Book of Deuteronomy

Observe the Sabbath day and keep it holy, as the LORD your God commanded you. Six days you shall labor and do all your work. But the seventh day is a Sabbath to the LORD your God; you shall not do any work —

you or your son or your daughter, or your male or female slave, or your ox or donkey, or any of your livestock, or the resident alien in your towns, so that your male and female slave may rest as well as you. Remember that you were a slave in the land of Egypt, and the Lord *your God brought you out from there with a mighty hand and an outstretched arm; therefore the* Lord *your God commanded you to keep the Sabbath day.*

DEUTERONOMY 5:12-15

The alternate version of the Sabbath commandment appears in Deuteronomy 5 in the context of an elderly Moses who is at the end of his life and wishes to leave a legacy for future generations. Moses has led a new generation of young Israelites through the wilderness to the edge of the promised land of Canaan. Moses is about to die and will not enter Canaan with them. But in the words of Deuteronomy 5, Moses repeats the Ten Commandments (found first in Exodus 20) with some variation, especially in the Sabbath commandment. It is important to observe that the Ten Commandments are central to the structure of the whole book of Deuteronomy. All the laws that follow in Deuteronomy 6–28 are laid out roughly according to the sequence of the Ten Commandments in Deuteronomy 5. Thus, the many particular laws in chapters 6–28 function as commentary on the Ten Commandments. In this way, the Sabbath commandment in Deuteronomy 5:12-15 is expanded and interpreted by a group of laws related to the Sabbath in Deuteronomy 14:22–16:17.[8]

The Sabbath: A Practice That Generates Memory

One interesting change in the Sabbath commandment in its Deuteronomic version is a shift in the verbs. Exodus 20:8 begins, "*Remember* the Sabbath day, and keep it holy." Deuteronomy 5:12 begins, "*Observe* [Hebrew *shamar* — 'to keep, watch, observe, guard'] the Sabbath day and keep it holy." In the Deuteronomic version, the emphasis is on being careful to preserve the doing of the Sabbath. Watch that you do the Sabbath regularly and maintain its practice. The notion of "remembering" that begins the commandment in Exodus 20 is not lost in Deuteronomy's version, but a different dynamic is set up that is instructive for understanding the practice of the Sabbath.

8. Dennis T. Olson, *Deuteronomy and the Death of Moses,* Overtures to Biblical Theology (Minneapolis: Fortress, 1994), pp. 14-17, 73-78.

The verb "remember" comes later in the Deuteronomic Sabbath commandment so that the logic is now this: "Observe the Sabbath day" (v. 12) in order that you may do the following: "Remember that you were a slave in the land of Egypt, and the LORD your God brought you out from there with a mighty hand and an outstretched arm; therefore the LORD your God commanded you to keep the Sabbath day" (v. 15). In other words, "observing" the Sabbath, actually doing the practice of resting from work every seventh day and gathering in worship, serves to generate memory. We remember who we were and who we are: we were slaves, and now we are free. We remember what God did for us: the Lord brought us out of slavery. We remember our core identity: we are God's own people.

But the Deuteronomic version knows that the people of God often suffer from a kind of spiritual amnesia. We are prone to forget who we truly are and whose we truly are. Thus, the practice of the Sabbath serves regularly to jog our memories back to the truth of our authentic identity and purpose as the people of God. This has implications for understanding the role of liturgy and practice within worship. Liturgy creates and shapes memory, which in turn shapes our core commitments, actions, and beliefs.

The Sabbath: A Memory That Generates Compassion

Exodus 20 grounded the Sabbath in a focus on God as Creator. Deuteronomy 5 grounds the Sabbath in God as liberator of those enslaved to work. The Deuteronomic version adds as a motivation for observing the Sabbath, "so that your male and female slave may rest as well as you" (v. 14). The command seeks to protect the well-being of those who have relatively less power in the community and who may more easily be exploited, abused, and overworked. The commandment appeals to a memory of Israel's foundation story of its own slavery, abuse, and exploitation at the hand of Pharaoh in Egypt. "Remember that you were once a slave in Egypt." Being a slave in Egypt was an identity that was not literally true for many later generations who read the Bible as their book. Nevertheless, the Exodus story was a primal narrative that each new generation adopted as their own life story and core identity. In the annual celebration of Passover, each new generation was to confess, "By strength of hand the LORD brought us out of Egypt" (Exod. 13:14). When each new generation of Israelites would bring its offering to the Lord's sanctuary, they were to reclaim the ancient story as their own: "When the Egyptians treated us harshly and afflicted us . . . the LORD brought us out of Egypt with a mighty hand and an outstretched arm" (Deut. 26:6-8). These Sabbath memories that interrupt our normal routine of business and work serve to generate empathy, compassion, acts of justice, and humane concern for workers, children, animals, and other vulnerable members of the community. These concerns are present as well in the laws that expand upon the Sabbath commandment in Deuteronomy 14–16.

Sabbath Interruptions and the Integration of Justice and Worship

The statutes and ordinances in Deuteronomy 14:22–16:17 all specify in some way regular interruptions in time, work, and ambition. In the cycle of years and annual harvests, the laws' interruptions include structured time to remember the gifts that God has given, time to give offerings back to God, time for worship, time for celebration, time for sharing with those in need, and time for periodically canceling debts and releasing slaves to ease the burdens of others. The many laws in this section speak of regular cycles of days, weeks, and years, in which offerings, festivals, and releases are to occur: "yearly" (14:22), "every third year" (14:28), "every seventh year" (15:1), "in the seventh year" (15:12), "year by year" (15:20), "the month of Abib" (16:1), "for seven days" (16:3), "on the seventh day" (16:8), "seven weeks" (16:9), "seven days" (16:13, 15), and "three times a year" (16:16). Time is punctuated by interruptions that call the members of the community back to remember their vocation as the people of God. These interruptions are structured, routinized, and institutionalized rather than left merely to the voluntary charity, decisions, and whims of the individual. The Sabbath day is to be observed every seven days. The tithe is to be given yearly. The canceling of all debts and the freeing of slaves is to occur every seventh year. The Passover, the Festival of Weeks, and the Feast of Booths are to be celebrated annually. Such discipline and planned interruptions are a form of teaching and shaping human minds and hearts to remember who they were, who they are, and who their true God is.

The Sabbath laws in Deuteronomy 15:22–16:17 break down into three groups of laws:

1. The laws in 14:22-29 treat the offering of tithes and crops and the first-born of animals to God. The purpose of such offerings is educational: "so that you may learn to fear the LORD your God always" (14:23).

Giving a portion back to God reminds us that all we have is a gift from God that rightly belongs to God, a truth which should lead to fear, love, and trust in God alone above all other allegiances. When the offering is given to God, it does not just disappear into the temple. Rather, the offering is immediately shared with others in the community who are in need: the landless Levites, the resident aliens, the widows, the orphans, and the poor, so that they "may come and eat their fill" (Deut. 14:29). Gathering for worship and offerings to God are intimately tied to compassionate acts of justice and sharing with those in need.

2. The laws in Deuteronomy 15:1-10 reach into areas of social and economic life within the community or society. They keep an important connection with the themes of the Sabbath centered on the so-called sabbatical year or year of release that is to be observed every seventh year. In 15:1-6, all debts are to be forgiven and canceled every seventh year. The goal is that there will "be no one in need among you" (15:4). In 15:7-11, the laws encourage generous sharing with the poor in case the ideal set out in verse 4 is not realized. In 15:12-18, the laws mandate the release of slaves every seventh year (see Jer. 34:8-22). In all of these laws, the periodic interruption in the holding of debts or slaves serves to prevent those who are rich or in power from abusing the poor or other vulnerable members of the community. The Sabbath puts limits on human greed and power.

3. The laws in 15:19-23 return to the theme of making offerings to God. The firstborn animal that is given as an offering to God at the sanctuary or place of worship is immediately slaughtered. The meat is eaten by the worshiper but also shared with others in need in a joyous feast.

What is striking about all of these Sabbath laws is the way in which worship and the giving of offerings are intimately connected with acts of justice, compassion, and concern. Such acts of justice and sharing are grounded again and again in the memory of who the Israelites were and what God had done for them: "Remember that you were a slave in Egypt" (15:15; 16:12).

The Sabbath, the Jubilee Year, and an Ethic for Land Use

The Sabbath theme that links worship and justice encompasses another important dimension — namely, the care and distribution of land among the various families and communities of Israel. In Leviticus 25:23, God reminds Israel of the fundamental divine ownership of all land: "the land is mine; with me you are but aliens and tenants." The land is to be worked for six years and then allowed to lie fallow and rest so that it may regenerate itself in the seventh year. The Sabbath commandment's concern for the human treatment of animals embodies a larger ecological concern that extends beyond animals to the land itself. The so-called Year of Jubilee occurs after seven cycles of seven years (thus every fiftieth year). In every Jubilee or fiftieth year, any land sold during the previous cycle of forty-nine years was to be returned to the family who originally owned the land at the beginning of the cycle. Thus, land could be freely bought and sold over the years. But this cycle of buying and selling was to be interrupted every fifty years with a land redistribution program so that all families would start over with what they originally had as their family's land inheritance. No one family or group could permanently amass unduly large tracts of land for itself on the one hand, or be forced into permanent poverty on the other. Every family was periodically to gain access again to their fair portion of the economic pie.

We have no evidence that the Year of Jubilee was ever actually implemented in ancient Israel. But it remained a vision and an ideal that eventually came to define a future hope of what God would one day bring. Thus the prophets pick up the theme of the Jubilee year or "the year of the LORD's favor" as an eschatological vision of what God's chosen servant will bring:

> The spirit of the LORD is upon me,
> because the LORD has anointed me;
> he has sent me to bring good news to the oppressed,
> to bind up the brokenhearted,
> to proclaim liberty to the captives,
> and release to the prisoners;
> to proclaim the year of the LORD's favor.

It was this text from Isaiah 61 with its promise of the sabbatical release of slaves and debts and the Jubilee year of the land redistribution that Jesus used in his first inaugural sermon at his home synagogue in Nazareth (Luke 4:16-19). The Sabbath and its integration of worship and justice evident in the laws of Deuteronomy 14–16 continued as a powerful theme in the Old Testament prophets and on into the New Testament.

From Saturday to Sunday: The Sabbath Day and the Lord's Day

In what ways were the practice and the themes of the Sabbath in the Old Testament continued or changed in the New Testament and the early church? The Gospels portray Jesus and his disciples as devout Jews who regularly attend synagogue worship on the Sabbath (Mark 1:21; Luke 13:10; John 6:59). However, the Gospels do portray Jesus and his disciples in some conflict with the Jewish Pharisees and scribes concerning the proper observance of the Sabbath. On one Sabbath, Jesus' disciples pluck some grain from the fields, something that might be construed as work (Mark 2:23-28). When the Pharisees object that the disciples are thus disobeying the Sabbath, Jesus replies with a principle that was also well known in other Jewish rabbinic traditions: "The Sabbath was made for humankind, and not humankind for the Sabbath" (Mark 2:27). Exceptions could be made for doing work on the Sabbath when it served human life or when emergency conditions demanded it. (See also Jesus healing the sick on the Sabbath — Matt. 12:9-14; Mark 3:1-6; John 5:1-24; 9:1-41). But then Jesus adds a second and more radical claim that goes beyond any previous discussions of the Sabbath: "so the Son of Man is Lord even of the Sabbath" (Mark 2:28). Jesus here claims for himself the role of arbiter and ruler over the practice of the Sabbath law instituted by God at creation (Gen. 2:1-3). Jesus as the Son of God has the power to release his followers from the obligations of the Sabbath.

According to the book of Acts, the earliest Jewish Christians after the death and resurrection of Jesus faithfully observed the Sabbath (Saturday) and attended synagogue worship services where they proclaimed the gospel message of Jesus the Christ (Acts 13:14-16; 17:1-3). But the early followers of Jesus also felt a need to gather together on Sunday, "The first day of the week" (Acts 20:7), to worship, break bread together, and collect offerings to help the poor of the community (1 Cor. 16:2). All the Gospels agree that Sunday was the day on which Jesus was resurrected from the dead (Matt. 28:3; Mark 16:2; Luke 24:1; John 20:1, 19). Accordingly, Sunday came to be called "the Lord's Day" by the earliest Christians (Rev. 1:10). While the early Jewish Christians continued to observe the Sabbath, the letters of Paul suggest that Gentile or non-Jewish converts to Christianity were not subject to the Jewish law of the Sabbath. In fact, Paul urged Gentile believers of Jesus not to impose upon themselves the yoke of the Jewish law, including the observing of festivals and other special days like the Sabbath (Gal. 4:8-11). Colossians 2:16-19 admonishes Gentile Christians, "Therefore do not let anyone condemn you in matters of food and drink [the Jewish dietary laws/or of observing festivals, new moons, or Sabbaths]." The general principle for Gentile Christians is stated in Galatians 5:1: "For freedom Christ has set us free. Stand firm, therefore, and do not submit again to a yoke of slavery." Clearly, Gentile Christians were free to disregard the obligation of the Sabbath.

As the Gentile Christian community grew and the Jewish Christian community diminished in size and influence, the early church more and more established Sunday, the first day of the week, as the primary day to gather for worship. For Christians, each Sunday commemorated the resurrection of Jesus on the first day of the week and could be celebrated as "a little Easter." The beginning day of the new week came to represent "the eighth day of creation," the dawn of a new creation in light of Jesus rising from the dead. Some early Christian writers rejected the Jewish Sabbath as in any way binding on Christians *(Letter of Barnabas 15)*. The church father Athanasius (296-373 C.E.) in his treatise *On the Sabbath and Circumcision* argued that Sunday was superior to the Sabbath — Saturday — because the Sabbath represented the end of the old creation while Sunday represented the beginning of the new creation in Christ. On the other hand, the so-called *Constitutions of the Holy Apostles* (380 C.E.) recommended that Christians observe both the Sabbath and the Lord's Day (Saturday and Sunday), since they both commemorated worthy fundamentals of the faith: creation (Sabbath) and resurrection (Sunday). Augustine (354-430 C.E.) reinterpreted the ongoing significance of the Old Testament Sabbath in two ways: eternal Sabbath rest in God as the goal of the history of the world (*City of God* 22.30), and eternal Sabbath rest in God as the goal of the individual soul of the believer (*Confessions* 13.35-36).

However, a significant development occurred in 321 C.E. when the Christian emperor Constantine decreed legislation that took the requirement of resting from work, a requirement applied only to the Sabbath or Saturday in the Bible, and applied it to Sunday. Whereas before the Sabbath and Sunday had been separate and distinct, the Sunday law of 321 merged them together as one concept. For Constantinian Christendom, Sunday took over as the Sabbath. The Sabbath commandment in the Old Testament became reinterpreted as requiring rest not on the seventh or last day of the week (Saturday) but on one day in every seven, whatever that day might be. Christians could then freely assign the Sabbath with all of its requirements to the first day of the week, Sunday.

This begins an ongoing debate and tension within the Christian tradition about the Sabbath. Was the Old Testament law, including the requirement of the Sabbath rest, applicable to Christians or not? The medieval theologian Thomas Aquinas interpreted Sabbath rest as a spiritual rest in God but rejected the need to observe a literal Sabbath day of no work. The sixteenth-century Reformer Martin Luther was suspicious about any imposition of the Old Testament law of the Sabbath as a legalistic requirement. Luther feared that making the Sabbath obligatory would rob the gospel of its freedom. Consequently, Luther reinterpreted the Sabbath commandment as a general admonition to stop work regularly and make time to hear and study God's Word. Following John Calvin, the Reformed tradition (Puritans, Presbyterians, Congregationalists, Methodists, and Baptists) tended to see the Sabbath as a continuing universal and binding law of creation for all humans, but Christianized in part, so that the Sabbath obligation was transferred to Sunday with more discipline and strictness than in the Lutheran tradition.[9] The debate and tension concerning the meaning of the Sabbath for Christians continue unresolved even to the present day. How then do we best understand the significance of the Old Testament Sabbath for Christian worship, life, and practice?

The Old Testament Sabbath and Christian Life and Worship

We conclude with a series of brief reflections on how the Sabbath commandment in its two versions in Exodus 20 and Deuteronomy 5 and their larger Old Testament contexts might inform and shape Christian faith and practice. In keeping with the number seven and its association with the Sabbath, let us consider seven concluding observations.

1. Creation and Exodus

The two different versions of the Sabbath commandment in Exodus and Deuteronomy (one rooted in the creation story and the other in the Exodus) imply an inner tension or dialogue in the understanding of the Sabbath, a fruitful tension that invites ongoing interpretation and resists legalistic precision. If we then add the larger context of other biblical laws and the sayings of the prophets, we soon see that the theme of the Sabbath is an

9. Samuele Bacchiocchi, "Remembering the Sabbath: The Creation-Sabbath in Jewish and Christian History," in *The Sabbath in Jewish and Christian Traditions*, ed. Tamara Eskenazi et al. (New York: Crossroad, 1991), pp. 78-86.

exceedingly rich but complex concept within the Old Testament. The Sabbath theme touches on numerous fundamental aspects of life: time, worship, work, creation, justice, compassion, ecology, economics, land use, future hope, memory, identity, and purpose. The biblical Sabbath is much more than simply not doing any work or worshiping on Saturday or Sunday. This rich meaning of the Sabbath may be expressed in a number of dialogical polarities or tensions that emerge from the full biblical witness to the theme of the Sabbath. Some of those polarities are noted below.

2. Holy to God, Holy to Humans

The Sabbath maintains a polarity of holiness to the Lord and to humans. The Sabbath is "holy to the LORD," but it is also "holy to the people of God." The Sabbath represents an obligation of time and attention set apart for God. But the Sabbath is also time and rest set apart for the benefit of human beings ("the Sabbath is made for humankind, and not humankind for the Sabbath").

3. Rest and Work

The Sabbath reflects a polarity between rest and labor. God has created humans for meaningful work. Even in the Garden of Eden, the human from the very beginning was called "to till it and keep it" (Gen. 2:15). But such work is to be balanced by regular periods of rest. We need time and activities that restore our energies, quiet our anxious minds, and regenerate our troubled spirits. Regular Sabbath rest enables our work and service to God and neighbor to continue in healthy and productive ways. Without the Sabbath, work can become an idol or an oppressor.

4. Anxiety and Trust

The Sabbath introduces a "test" in the struggle between worrisome fretting and confident trusting. God provided the miraculous food of manna to the Israelites during their wilderness journey from Egypt to Canaan. But they could gather only what they could use in one day, and they could not gather manna on the Sabbath. In this context, God says, "I will test them, whether they will follow my instruction or not" (Exod. 16:4). The Sabbath may be seen as an ongoing test of our willingness to trust God to provide or not. Do we know that not everything depends on what we accomplish? Have we learned the art of letting go and saying no? Have we focused our energies on gathering huge surpluses for a rainy day, or do we live simpler, leaner, and more trusting lives, confident that God will provide what we need for the day?

5. Somber Holiness and Joyful Delight

Several polarities revolve around the theme of the Sabbath and creation (Gen. 2:1-3). Sabbath rest is built into creation and so applies to all humans and all nonhuman creatures. And yet the Sabbath is also distinctive and unique, a "sign" of God's special covenant with Israel (Ezek. 20:12, 20). God's resting on the Sabbath after six days of creation invites reflection on the mystery of the eternal God who is beyond time and yet enters into time out of love for the world. Within human time, God models the practice of rest and refreshment for the sake and benefit of God's creatures. In the creation story, God both "hallows" or makes holy the Sabbath day and "blesses" the holy day. As both a holy day and a blessing, the Sabbath holds together the more somber traits of holiness, obligation, and "solemn rest" (Exod. 16:23) alongside the more positive characteristics of a gracious gift, a liberating freedom, and a generous blessing. If we emphasize too much the Sabbath as somber obligation, we lose its freeing delight and joy (Isa. 58:13-14). On the other hand, if we lose the discipline, respect, and importance implied in its holiness, we tend to neglect and drift away from the gifts and joy of regular Sabbath keeping.

6. For Us and for Others

The Sabbath carries within it a basic polarity between its benefits for us ourselves and its benefits for others: family members, workers, animals, and even the land that provides food. Indeed, the Sabbath commandment integrates all our relationships as none of the other Ten Commandments does: (a) our relationship to God, who is worshiped on the Sabbath as both Creator and Deliverer from bondage; (b) our relationship to other human beings as we give workers time off for Sabbath rest; (c) our relationship to nonhuman creation as we rest both animals and the land in order that they may be refreshed; and, finally, (d) even our relationship to ourselves as we benefit from the balance of work and Sabbath rest and regain our identity as we remember who we were (slaves in Egypt) and who at the core of our being we are (people saved and loved by God).

7. Worship and Justice

One final and crucial polarity that the Sabbath holds together in the Old Testament is an essential integration of and commitment to the worship of God *and* the doing of justice for the neighbor in need. The biblical Sabbath is the bridge which insists that both of these aspects of the life of faith must be held together. We began the essay by talking about cultures and the time values they display in their beliefs and practices. The Old Testament Sabbath may be one of the most strongly countercultural concepts in the Bible in relation to our modern society and its values. Our secular world tends to worship money, power, success, and fame. Our self-indulgent and individualistic culture asks "What's in it for me?" not "What would be just and good for my neighbor or for the community as a whole?"

Christians will likely continue to debate and disagree about how to implement and be faithful to these many polarities and tensions associated with the Sabbath. Many of the questions with which we opened this essay defy easy answers. Much will depend on the particular contexts and special issues for which we may be seeking guidance. Nevertheless, the biblical Sabbath has the capacity to speak a helpful and powerful word to us today. We live in the midst of worship wars, terrorist wars, battles of denominational unrest, the disestablishment of the church, increasing blindness toward the needs of the poor, human ravaging of the world's environment, and all manner of personal and community unrest and turmoil. The recovery of a full biblical understanding of the Sabbath will be an essential resource as the people of God navigate their way through the stormy and chaotic waters of our day, straining to hear the voice of the One who is the Lord even of the Sabbath saying, "Peace, be still!" In order to hear that voice, time must be broken, routines must be interrupted, business as usual must be stopped. Only then can the God of the Sabbath infiltrate our minds, integrate our spirits, and make us whole.

CHAPTER FIVE

The Lord's Day in Orthodox Liturgical Practice and Spirituality

Alkiviadis C. Calivas

> *Come, all you nations, learn the power of this awesome mystery; for Christ our Savior, the Word who was in the beginning, was crucified for us, and was buried of His own will, and arose from the dead, that He might save all things. Let us worship Him.*[1]

With an exceptional and extensive repertoire of hymns such as this one[2] and a recurring cycle of eleven Gospel lessons solemnly intoned at the Sunday Orthros,[3] each of which narrates an event related to the resurrection of Christ and His post-resurrection appearances and meals, the Orthodox Church marks the weekly celebration of the Paschal mystery, which commences with Vespers on Saturday evening and concludes with the Divine Liturgy — the rite by which the Orthodox Church celebrates the sacrament of the Eucharist — on Sunday morning.

In the Orthodox Church, the liturgical day is reckoned from one sunset to the next — a concept borrowed from Judaism that permeated the liturgical life of the Church from the earliest days.[4] Accordingly, the eve-

---

1. Sticheron of Saturday Vespers in Third time.

2. The large collection of hymns praising, explaining, and interpreting the Paschal mystery is codified essentially in the *Octoechos or Parakletike*, the liturgical book that contains the weekly cycle of feasts structured on a recurring cycle of eight weeks, one for each of the eight tones of Byzantine music, and in the *Pentecostarion*, the liturgical book of the Paschal season.

3. The Orthros is the morning service of the Orthodox Church. It is the longest and most elaborate of the several services (Vespers, Apodeipnon or Compline, Midnight, Orthros, and the First, Third, Sixth, and Ninth Hours) that comprise the Daily Office.

4. Under the influence of the Roman-Byzantine practice, the start of the day at mid-

ning, and therefore the service of Vespers, marks the beginning of each day. And Sunday — the Lord's Day — is the principal day, the αρχη of the Christian week because it is the day of the Lord's resurrection, which constitutes the fundamental truth and the absolute fact of the Christian faith (1 Cor. 15:1-28).

The Byzantine Liturgical Rite

As a result of her unity of life with the risen and glorified Christ, the Church is always oriented towards the eschaton, towards the end times, from which she draws her essential identity and self-understanding. The vision of God's Kingdom both orders and fuels her life and ministry, her existence in and her *diakonia* to the world. And this vision of the Kingdom is attained and experienced chiefly through liturgical celebration. Thus, any insight into the faith and practice of the Orthodox Church is not possible without an adequate knowledge and a proper understanding of Orthodox worship and liturgy.[5]

Worship, as I have noted elsewhere, is a fundamental and indispensable activity of the Church. Through her worship or liturgy the Church finds her fullest expression and realization.[6] The liturgy is the place where we meet the self-giving of God who draws us unto Himself. It is the place where we meet our own human lives in unforeseen and unexpected forms. We touch eternity and experience a reality that both transcends us and transforms us.

The liturgy is the Church's faith in motion, the unique setting in which she remembers and celebrates the revealed truths about God, creation, and humanity. "In the true Orthodox tradition," as Bishop Kallistos Ware notes, "there is no divorce between theology and worship, between private meditation and public prayer. All genuine worship, while embracing the emotions, must also be reflective, intelligent, and essentially theo-

---

night also entered into the life of the Church. Both notions, the Jewish and the Roman-Byzantine, coexist in the Orthodox Church, though the Hebraic tradition is the more dominant. A striking example that points to the coexistence of these two practices can be detected in the fasting rule of the Church. While the liturgical day begins at sunset, the prescribed fast for a particular day or in preparation for Holy Communion usually starts at some point before or at midnight.

5. See Mother Mary and Kallistos Ware, *The Festal Menaion* (London: Faber & Faber, 1969; South Canaan, PA: St. Tikhons Seminary Press, 1990), pp. 65-66.

6. See *The Festal Menaion*, pp. 65-66.

logical. . . . And at the same time all genuine theology must be a living theology — not an abstract exercise of the reasoning powers, but a vision of God's Kingdom."[7] Through prayer and dogma, the Church invites us to continually discover, experience, and realize our true and eternal mode of being, to become that which God has intended us to be.

The elements and structures of Orthodox worship constitute the venerable liturgical system known as the Byzantine Rite.[8] This Rite constitutes the final unification of liturgical practice in the Orthodox Church. The Rite takes its name indirectly from Constantinople, the great imperial city that was established in 324 by Constantine the Great, the first Christian emperor, and inaugurated in 330 as the new capital of the Roman Empire. Constantinople, named after its founder, was built on the small port city of Byzantion or Byzantium, an ancient Greek colony founded in the seventh century B.C. by Byzas of Megara, located strategically on the Bosporus, the strait between Europe and Asia Minor.

As the primary See of the Christian East, Constantinople developed into a renowned liturgical center. Its rite represents the intermingling of parochial and monastic practices and the reception, assimilation, synthesis, and development of the rich liturgical traditions of Eastern Christianity that were directly inherited from the praxis and the experiences of the apostolic and post-apostolic church.

Like all classical liturgical rites, the Byzantine Rite is composed of several basic components and by certain characteristic theological and ritual attributes that can be summarized best by the words of St. Germanos of Constantinople (ca. 730) in his commentary on the Divine Liturgy: "The church is an earthly heaven, in which the supernatural God dwells and walks about."[9] In and through the liturgy God is present to His people, taking them to Himself, unveiling His divine love, beauty, and holiness.

Each component of the liturgy has but one purpose: to bring us to the threshold of another world, to an encounter with the living God. Through each of its expressions — setting, word, sound, symbol, ritual, and interpretation — the liturgy seeks to grace the worshiper with the presence of

---

7. *The Festal Menaion,* p. 66.

8. For an excellent concise account of the development of the Byzantine Rite see Robert Taft, *The Byzantine Rite: A Short History* (Collegeville: Liturgical Press, 1992). See also A. Calivas, *Aspects of Orthodox Worship* (Brookline, MA: Holy Cross Orthodox Press, 2003), pp. 54-62 and 63-101.

9. Paul Meyendorff, *St. Germanus of Constantinople on the Divine Liturgy* (Crestwood, NY: St. Vladimir's Seminary Press, 1984), p. 57.

the inexpressible beauty, the searing truth, the boundless love, the inde-
scribable joy, and the deathless life of the Triune God.

The Festal Calendar, Sunday, and the Resurrection of Christ

One of the essential components[10] of the Byzantine Rite is its comprehensive calendar of feasts and fasts. The festal calendar is composed of an annual cycle of fixed and movable feasts and a weekly cycle of feasts that suc-
cinctly but ingeniously summarizes the annual festal cycle.[11] Both cycles,
the annual and the weekly, are centered on the Paschal mystery, which is at
the heart of Orthodox worship.

Annually, on the first Sunday after the first full moon of the spring
equinox, usually following Jewish Passover, when the solemnities of the
Great and Holy Week have been completed, the Church celebrates glori-

10. In addition to the calendar, the Byzantine Rite has a wide range of liturgical services, including three Eucharistic liturgies, sacramental rites, and other occasional services,
including burial rites and a variety of rites of blessing. It also has a daily office composed of
seven prayer hours with eight services, the chief of which are Vespers and Orthros. It also has
a system of biblical lessons and a variety of ritual symbols and ceremonials and an array of
distinctive gestures that include forms of blessing, various processions, and bodily prayer
postures. It also features highly developed and distinctive forms of the liturgical arts,
namely, architecture, iconography, hymnography, music, implements (vessels, thuribles,
etc.), and textiles (vestments, cloths, and veils).

11. The weekly festal cycle begins with Sunday, with celebration of the divine victory
over death and corruption. Monday or the Second Day is dedicated to the Angels. On Tuesday the Church honors St. John the Forerunner, Prophet, and Baptist and through him all
the prophets. Thursday is dedicated to the Holy Apostles and to St. Nicholas, who stands as
the model of all hierarchs, the successors to the Apostles and teachers of the Church. On Saturday the Church commemorates the martyrs, the ascetics, and those who have fallen asleep
in the hope of the resurrection. On Wednesday and Friday the Church brings into special focus the combined mystery of the Cross and the person of the Virgin Mary, the Theotokos.
Wednesday and Friday are also fast days when we contemplate the awful darkness of the
fallen world expressed in the betrayal of Judas (Wednesday) and the Crucifixion (Friday).
The liturgical year, with its succession of feasts and fasts, commemorates events in the life of
our Lord, His Mother the Theotokos, St. John the Baptist, the Holy Apostles, and the myri-
ads of saints, whose "sanctity is but a shining ray of the holiness of Christ." In accordance
with ancient custom, the liturgical year begins in September and ends in August. Its feasts
are divided into two categories, the movable and the fixed. The movable feasts are related to
the celebration of Pascha, a period of nineteen weeks that begins with the Pre-Lenten Season
and ends with the Sunday of All-Saints, the week after Pentecost. The fixed feasts, like
Christmas and Theophany and the feasts of the saints, occur on the same date each year.

ously and joyously "the chosen and holy day, the feast of feasts and the festival of festivals,"[12] the resurrection of our Lord, God, and Savior Jesus Christ. As the annual commemoration of the resurrection is celebrated on a given Sunday in the spring of each year, so the weekly commemoration of the resurrection also occurs on the first day of the week, Sunday, which by the end of the first century had acquired within the Christian community its own distinct and special title, Κυριακη Ημερα — the Lord's Day.[13]

The observance of Sunday — the Lord's Day — as a special day consecrated to the service of God is a Christian institution. It is a unique Christian festival. It is "the day the Lord has made" (Ps. 117[118]:24), the day, that is, on which God acted decisively to liberate the world from the tyranny of sin, death, and corruption by raising Jesus from the dead. The resurrection confirmed the authenticity of Christ's remarkable earthly life, vindicated the truth of His unique and compelling teachings, and sealed His extraordinary works and His redemptive life-creating death.[14]

The resurrection also constitutes the most radical and decisive deliverance of humankind. Christ has become the *Land of the Living*[15] for those on either side of death who believe in His name (John 20:31). We share in and experience the resurrection of Christ in two ways. It is the source for the continual mystical and spiritual regeneration of our dead souls; and it

12. From the hiermos of the 8th Ode of the Canon of Pascha.

13. The Lord's Day from the perspective of the Eastern Church has been treated by Robert Taft, "Sunday in the Eastern Tradition," in *Sunday Morning: A Time for Worship*, ed. Mark Searle (Collegeville: Liturgical Press, 1982), pp. 49-74, and Nikodemos Skrettas, "Κυριακη," in Το Χριστιανικου Εορτολογου (Athens, 2007).

14. For a brief examination of the theological implications of Christ's resurrection see A. Calivas, *Great Week and Pascha in the Greek Orthodox Church* (Brookline, MA: Holy Cross Orthodox Press, 1992), pp. 89-97.

15. The title *Land of the Living* is taken from the inscription on the fourteenth-century mosaic icon of Jesus Christ above the Beautiful Gate leading into the nave of the Church of the Monastery of Chora in Constantinople, now The Kariye (Chora) Museum. The Greek word *chora* means land or country as well as countryside. The monastery was founded in the fourth century outside the city walls built by Constantine and was thus named Chora because it lay outside the city.

It was destroyed and restored several times; the last restoration was undertaken by the scholar and humanitarian Theodore Metochites in 1312.

The resurrection is more than an event and a condition or state of being. It is, above all else, a Person, Jesus Christ: "I am the resurrection and the life . . ." (John 11:25). When Christ rose from the dead, He raised the whole race of Adam (1 Cor. 15:20-22). In Jesus Christ, risen and exalted in the flesh, God receives all flesh. See Christos Yannaras, *Elements of Faith* (Edinburgh: T&T Clark, 1995), pp. 114-18.

is the cause of our resurrection from the dead on the Last Day. Thus, for the Christian Sunday is always the special and unique day that sheds light upon the rest of the week inasmuch as it contains the "deeper messages about the history and meaning of our own personal lives."[16]

At every liturgical synaxis, and especially at every Eucharistic gathering on Sunday, the faithful are reminded of and empowered to pursue their high calling: to renounce daily the false values of the fallen world and to follow the risen and glorified Lord Jesus Christ, by thinking and doing, through grace, all those things that are true, honorable, just, pure, good, noble, natural, and sinless (Phil. 4:8).

The resurrection also made possible the miracle of the Church. The profound experience of the risen and glorified Lord enabled the Apostles to evangelize the world. That same unshakable belief in the resurrection empowers the Church in every age and place to proclaim and affirm with earnestness of purpose and steadfastness of faith God's plan for the cosmos, the ultimate theosis or divinization of humankind and the created order.

The Privileged Position of the Lord's Day

The primacy of the Lord's Day, to which the New Testament alludes (Acts 20:7-12; 1 Cor. 16:2; and Rev. 1:10), is affirmed by the liturgical praxis of the early church. For example, the *Didache* (chapter 14),[17] which some scholars believe is a composite document that developed in stages beginning as early as A.D. 50-70, includes this significant reference: "And on the Lord's Day, after you have come together, break bread and offer the Eucharist, having first confessed your offences, so that your sacrifice may be pure."

Another important witness on the significance of Sund ay for the Christian community is St. Justin the Martyr. Writing around A.D. 150, he notes:

> On the day named after the sun, all who live in city or countryside assemble in one place. The memoirs of the apostles or the writings of the prophets are read. . . . The president addresses us and exhorts us. . . . Then we

16. William C. McCready, "The Role of Sunday in American Society: Has It Changed?" in Searle, ed., *Sunday Morning: A Time for Worship*, p. 118.

17. See Kurt Niederwinner, *The Didache: A Commentary,* ed. Harold W. Attridge (Minneapolis: Augsburg Fortress, 1998), and Frank Hawkins, "The Didache," in *The Study of the Liturgy,* ed. Cheslyn Jones, Edward Yarnold, S.J., Geoffrey Wainwright, and Paul Bradshaw (New York: Oxford University Press, 1992), pp. 84-86. Recent views favor a later date, the middle or late second century, but based on the praxis of an earlier period.

stand and pray. . . . When we have finished praying, bread, wine, and water are brought up. . . . The president then prays and gives thanks . . . and the people give their assent with an 'Amen.' Next, the gifts over which the thanksgiving has been spoken are distributed and everyone shares in them. . . . It is on Sunday that we assemble, because Sunday is the first day: the day on which God transformed darkness and matter and created the world, and the day on which Jesus Christ our savior rose from the dead.[18]

Two centuries later, St. Basil the Great in his treatise *On the Holy Spirit* emphasizes the doctrinal implications and the spiritual value of the Lord's Day.

> Concerning the teachings of the Church, whether publicly proclaimed *(kerygma)* or reserved to members of the household of faith *(dogmas)*, we have received some from written sources, while others have been given to us secretly, through apostolic tradition. Both sources have equal force in true religion. No one would deny either source — no one, at any rate, who is even slightly familiar with the ordinances of the Church. If we attacked unwritten customs, claiming them to be of little importance, we would fatally mutilate the Gospel, no matter what our intentions — or rather, we would reduce the Gospel teaching to bare words. . . .
>
> We all stand for prayer on Sunday, but not everyone knows why. We stand for prayer on the day of the Resurrection to remind ourselves of the grace we have been given: not only because we have been raised with Christ and are obliged to seek the things that are above, but also because Sunday seems to be an image of the age to come. . . . This day foreshadows the state which is to follow the present age: a day without sunset, nightfall, or successor, an age which does not grow old or come to an end. It is therefore necessary for the Church to teach her newborn children to stand for prayer on this day, so that they will always be reminded of eternal life, and not neglect preparations for their journey.[19]

From these and other sources it is clear that Sunday — the Lord's Day — has always had a privileged position in the life of the Church as a special time for worship and celebration.

---

18. Justin the Martyr, *First Apology*, 67.
19. St. Basil, *On the Holy Spirit*, 27.66 (Crestwood, NY: St. Vladimir's Seminary Press, 1980), pp. 98, 100-101.

Sunday: The Time for Worship

Whoever is even remotely familiar with the Orthodox Church cannot help but notice that worship in general and the Sunday celebration of the Divine Liturgy in particular remains at the very heart of the Church's life. Whatever the level of knowledge or the intensity of faith Orthodox Christians may bring to the Divine Liturgy, it is their chief liturgical experience, the window onto the spiritual world, and the means by which the new life in Christ acquired through Baptism is continuously nourished and advanced.

Through the Eucharist, the Church calls her faithful people to share in the life of Christ, have communion with the Holy Spirit, enjoy a foretaste of the things to come, and enter into fellowship with one another as "fellow citizens of the saints and members of the household of God" (Eph. 2:19).

By setting forth the Church's living and authentic tradition, the liturgy communicates to people the meaning and purpose of life and helps them to see, understand, interpret, and internalize both the tragedy of the human condition in its fallen state as well as the limitless expanse and potential of the new life in Christ offered freely to all. The liturgy shapes the vision, the knowing, and the relationships of people. It is the Church's critical educative, formative, restorative, and transformative agent and environment.

Every Sunday the Church gathers to realize her eschatological fullness through the celebration of the Eucharist by which the Kingdom and the unending Day of the Lord — the hope and salvation of the world — are revealed in time. At the Eucharist, as Fr. Boris Bobrinskoy explains it, "the Holy Spirit actualizes the plenary and unique presence of Christ in His multiple dimensions: the creative Logos, the Jesus of history, the Christ of glory, the Lord of the Parousia and of the judgment."[20] The Eucharist recapitulates the Christ-event by which the comprehensive renovation and glorious transfiguration of the world has already begun. Through word, symbol, ritual action, and sacrament the faithful experience the fullness of Christ's presence and the fulfillment of His promise, "where two or three are gathered in my name, there am I in the midst of them" (Matt. 18:20).

The Eucharist is at the center of Orthodox worship as well as the source and summit of the Church's life. It is constitutive of the very exis-

---

20. Boris Bobrinskoy, *The Mystery of the Trinity* (Crestwood, NY: St. Vladimir's Seminary Press, 1999), p. 169.

tence of the Church and the condition of her growth. In and through the Eucharist the Church is continuously changed from a human community into the Body of Christ, the temple of the Holy Spirit, and the holy people of God. Hence, it is inconceivable to the Orthodox mind that, under normal circumstances, an observance of the Lord's Day is possible without the celebration of the Divine Liturgy.

Sunday: The Day of the Spirit

It is no coincidence but part of the divine plan of salvation that both the resurrection of Christ and the giving of the Holy Spirit took place on a Sunday. According to the Gospel of John, the Risen Lord gave the Spirit to His Apostles on the evening of the day of His resurrection (John 20:19-23). The book of Acts (2:1-4) tells us that Pentecost, the second oldest annual feast of the Church and the principal event marking the descent and outpouring of the Holy Spirit, also occurred on a Sunday, fifty days after the resurrection. H. B. Porter notes, "the powers which the Spirit bestows on the Church are in fact exhibited and set forth in a special way on Sunday."[21] Orthodox Christians experience this fact especially in and through the celebration of the Divine Liturgy.

We are reminded by the epiclesis portion of the Anaphora of both Eucharistic Liturgies — St. Basil the Great and St. John Chrysostom — that every Divine Liturgy constitutes a continuous Pentecost, a renewal and a confirmation of the constant coming of the Holy Spirit to the Church and her members. The epiclesis in the Liturgy of St. John Chrysostom, for example, states: "Once again we offer to You this spiritual worship without the shedding of blood, and we ask, pray, and entreat You, send down Your Holy Spirit upon us and upon these gifts here presented."[22]

---

21. H. B. Porter, *The Day of Light: The Biblical and Liturgical Meaning of Sunday* (Greenwich, CT, 1960), p. 44.

22. See *The Divine Liturgy of St. John Chrysostom* (Brookline, MA: Holy Cross Orthodox Press, 1985), p. 22. The epiclesis in the Liturgy of St. Basil is similar. It reads, in part, "We pray to You and call upon You, O Holy of Holies, that by the favor of Your goodness, Your Holy Spirit may come upon us and upon the gifts here presented. . . ." See *The Divine Liturgy of our Father among the Saints, Basil the Great* (Brookline, MA: Holy Cross Orthodox Press, 1988), p. 30. The Liturgy of St. John Chrysostom is celebrated every Sunday and feast day, except when the rubrics prescribe the use of the Liturgy of St. Basil or the Divine Liturgy of the Pre-Sanctified Gifts. See, for example, Hugh Wybrew, *The Orthodox Liturgy: The Develop-*

Through the whole action of the Divine Liturgy — from the gathering of the people, the hearing and explication of God's word, to the offering of the holy Gifts, the exchange of the Kiss of Peace, the profession of Faith, the consecration and communion of the Eucharistic elements, and the departure in peace to attend to the affairs of everyday life — the Holy Spirit acts to communicate to the faithful the gift of Christ's presence and thereby the gifts of the future age and Kingdom: forgiveness, purification, sanctification, koinonia, incorruptibility, and eternal life.

At the Divine Liturgy we come to experience and celebrate the inrush of eternal life into our perishable, mortal existence, accomplished through the presence of the Holy Spirit, who vivifies the Church and perfects each of her members.

Church, Eucharist, Sunday, and the Eschaton

In the theological, liturgical, and canonical tradition of the Orthodox Church it is clear that Church, Eucharist, Sunday, and the Eschaton are integrally related and inherently bound. Worship, witnessing, structures, and, above all, the sacraments constitute the face and the voice of the Church. The Eucharist in particular, as Metropolitan John Zizioulas notes, is "an event constitutive of the Church, enabling the Church to be."[23] And the Eucharist, through which the gifts of the future age are communicated to believers, is the principal activity of the faith community every single Sunday of the year.

So strong is the relationship between the Eucharist and Sunday that the canons deal strictly with those who willingly scorn the Sunday synaxis. Canon 80 of the Penthekte Synod of 691-692, for example, says the following:

> If any bishop, or presbyter, or deacon, or anyone else on the list of the clergy, or any layman, without any grave necessity or any particular difficulty compelling him to be absent from his own church for a very long time, fails to attend church on Sundays for three consecutive weeks,

---

ment of the Eucharistic Liturgy in the Byzantine Rite (Crestwood, NY: St. Vladimir's Seminary Press, 1990).

23. John D. Zizioulas, *Being as Communion: Studies in Personhood and the Church* (Crestwood, NY: St. Vladimir's Seminary Press, 1985), p. 21.

while living in the city, if he be a cleric let him be deposed from office; but if he be a layman, let him be removed from Communion.[24]

Attendance at and participation in the Divine Liturgy is an essential requirement of the Christian life not in fulfillment of a vague religious obligation but for "the inestimable privilege of glorifying God."[25] As St. Maximos the Confessor says, we come to the Eucharist that we may

> partake of the grace of the Holy Spirit which is always present there. . . . This grace transforms and changes each person who is found there and in fact remolds him in proportion to what is more divine in him and leads him to what is revealed through the mysteries which are celebrated, even if he does not himself feel this because he is still among those who are "children" in Christ, unable to see either the depths of the realities or the grace operating in it.[26]

Through the Divine Liturgy we remember and celebrate in joy and thanksgiving the whole mystery of the divine economy — God's household plan for the salvation of the world — from creation to the incarnation, and especially the passion, resurrection, glorification, and second coming of the Son and Word of God. "Remembering, therefore, the saving command ['do this . . .'], and all that came to pass for our sake, the cross, the tomb, the resurrection on the third day, the ascension into heaven, the enthronement at the right of the Father, and the second glorious coming, offering to You these gifts from Your own gifts, at all times and in all places, we praise You, we bless You, we give thanks to You, and we pray to You, Lord our God. . . ."[27]

By experiencing the presence of the risen and reigning Christ through the Eucharist, the Church lives the past, present, and future of the history of salvation as one reality. In the Eucharist time, history, and the people of

---

24. See the *Pedalion or Rudder,* an annotated collection of the holy canons compiled by Agapios and Nikodemos of the Holy Mountain, first published in 1800. Several editions followed, the latest of which was published in 1957. An English translation of the *Rudder* was published by D. Cummings.

25. Taft, "Sunday in the Eastern Tradition," p. 52.

26. St. Maximos the Confessor, *Mystagogy* 24 in *Maximus Confessor: Selected Writings,* trans. George C. Berthold, Classics of Western Spirituality (New York: Paulist, 1985), pp. 206-7.

27. From the Anaphora of the Divine Liturgy, in *The Divine Liturgy of St. John Chrysostom* (Brookline, MA: St. Vladimir's Seminary Press, 1985), pp. 21-22.

God encounter and enter into the eternal "present" of God. The Eucharist is always the messianic banquet, the meal of the Kingdom, the marriage supper of the Lamb (Rev. 19:9), through which all who have been baptized and chrismated are made continuously Christ-bearers and Spirit-bearers.

As a result of the celebration of the Eucharist the realities of the age to come break through in the assembly and Sunday acquires its identity as the Eighth Day, the successor of this earthly time, with its activities of birth and decay, which is destined to pass away. As the resurrection of Christ is the beginning of the new creation, so Sunday, the First Day of the week on which He was raised from the dead, is, in addition to all else, the Eighth Day. It is the day that reveals through worship the age to come, the unending day of the Kingdom, when death shall be no more, when mourning, crying, and pain shall be no more, when night shall be no more, when there will be no need of light, or lamp, or sun, for the glory of God will be the light and the lamp will be the Lamb (Rev. 21:4; 22:5).[28]

In the Scriptures light is a primary symbol of the Triune God — Father, Son, and Holy Spirit — and of Christians and of the Christian life. In the book of Genesis the creative activity of God on the "first day" begins with the creation of light. Light is also associated with the new creation, with the new life in Christ, with the beginning of another world.

Sunday, which is both the First and the Eighth Day, is also the Day of Light. It is dedicated not to the celestial sun, but to the Sun of Righteousness, Christ, who is the light of the world. "By claiming the First Day as their own," writes H. B. Porter, "Christians declare themselves as children of the Father of lights and fellow-heirs with Jesus Christ, a people whom He has delivered from the darkness."[29]

The motif of light runs through the prayers and hymns of the divine services of the Church, as, for example, the hymn which often concludes the rites of Holy Communion at the Divine Liturgy: "We have seen the true light; we have received the heavenly Spirit; we have found the true faith, worshipping the undivided Trinity, which has saved us."

28. See Roger T. Beckwith and Wilfrid Stott, *This Is the Day* (London: Marshall, Morgan & Scott, 1978), pp. 117-24.

29. Porter, *The Day of Light*, p. 33.

Sunday Is Everything: The Day of Sanctification, Rest, and Godly Action

For the Orthodox people, as Robert Taft observes, *Sunday is everything*, just as it was in the early Church.[30] Sunday was and continues to be, above all, a day for holy synaxis, a day for the celebration of the Divine Liturgy, in and through which the risen and reigning Lord is present to His people that He may grant to them His divine perfections, holiness (αγιοτης), incorruptibility (αφθαρσια), and immortality (αθανασια).

The idea of the sacredness and the splendor of the Lord's Day is so ingrained in the Orthodox conscience that no one, for example, attends the divine services dressed shabbily or casually. However deep or shallow one's inner awareness and sensitivities may be, everyone "knows" that you come before God as "a new creation" (2 Cor. 5:17), clothed in appropriate dignified apparel. "Church clothes," however plain or simple, are perceived as an extension of one's baptismal garment, the garment that signifies the newness of life in Christ. The Church is a Eucharistic community because she is first a baptismal community, God's own people called out of darkness into His marvelous light (1 Peter 2:9-10).

Sunday, as the weekly Pascha — the perpetual First Day of the new creation and the perpetual unending Eighth Day of the Kingdom — is a day of rejoicing. Hence, no one is permitted to fast or to kneel in sorrow or in penance. Moreover, since the Eucharist unites the members of the Church both to Christ and to one another, the Eucharistic assembly becomes the image of the new humanity gathered around the risen Lord, empowered, nourished, and perfected by His love and mercy. Thus Sunday, which is simultaneously the First and the Eighth Day and is differentiated from all the other days of the week by the celebration of the Eucharist, reminds us that the Church is the eschatological community of God, a community that experiences the new life in Christ and witnesses to the presence of God's Kingdom in history.

Christian existence is inherently corporate. Salvation comes through a community, the Church. Thus Sunday, which mirrors that corporality, is also a day for community feastings and family gatherings. It is the preeminent day for ordinations, baptisms, and marriages,[31] all of which are fun-

---

30. Taft, "Sunday in the Eastern Tradition," p. 51. See also Nikodemos Skrettas, "Κυριακη," p. 269.

31. See, for example, Porter, *The Day of Light*, pp. 65-77.

damentally ecclesial events inasmuch as all sacraments belong to the Church and are intrinsic to her life of grace.

It has been said, "according to some, the Sabbath of the Old Testament began as a day of rest and became a day of worship, whereas the Sunday of the New Testament began as a day of worship and, in the history of the Church, became a day of worship and rest."[32] As we know, Sunday was declared a day of rest — at least for segments of the populace — in 321 by Constantine, the first Christian emperor. Long before him, however, Christians were known to observe the day with special solemnity. The emperor's edict only served to enhance the festival by facilitating divine worship and providing more amply for the restful activity of godly service. Although the temptation exists, Christians must be careful not to confuse rest with idleness, inactivity, and purposeless leisure.[33]

While rest is an element of the Lord's Day, it is not the essential one. After all, during the first three centuries of the Church's life, Sunday was an ordinary workday. What gives Sunday its privileged status is the gathering of the people for the celebration of the Eucharist. Sunday is the Church's preeminent day of worship, the day the faith community gathers to celebrate the Kingdom of God already given as the very pledge of salvation. For a Christian who is in touch with the wellsprings of the faith, Sunday is, above all else, a day for corporate worship, for Christian fellowship, and for godly service through works of charity.

The Name "Lord's Day"

A small but compelling sign of the early Church's efforts to reshape the fabric of human life in accordance with the truths and the values of the Gospel were the names the Church chose to designate the days of the week. For the growing number of pagan converts, these names, rooted in the Church's Judaic past, constituted a dramatic shift in the way time was both conceived and lived.

The seven-day cycle — the week — by which time was measured gradually gained currency among the people of the ancient world. It was customary in ancient cultures to assign the names of their planet-gods to each

---

32. Thomas K. Carroll and Thomas Halton, *Liturgical Practice in the Fathers* (Wilmington, DE: Michael Glazier, 1988), p. 18.
33. See Skrettas, "Κυριακή," pp. 268-76.

day of the week. In fact, in the prevailing civil calendar, the days of the week in English are the Teutonic equivalents of the ancient Roman planetary names.[34]

In contrast, the early Christians — at least in the East — adopted a different system. They embraced the Jewish tradition and assigned numerical names to the days of the week based on the creation narrative in the book of Genesis. By adopting these names, the Church proclaimed her belief and trust in the sovereignty of the Triune God. Time, space, human life, and the entire cosmos are not under the control and influence of the false planet-gods but under the rule of the Triune God, the Author of life and the Lord of history, "the Creator of heaven and earth, and of all things visible and invisible."[35]

The tradition of the early Church lives in the native languages of the people in whose lands Orthodox Christianity prospered and flourished. The ecclesial as well as the civil calendars in most of these lands use numerical names for some days of the week and proper names for other days, replicating the Jewish names.[36] Monday, for example, the second day of the week, is called Second Day (Δευτερα),[37] followed by Τριτη, Τεταρτη, and Πεμπτη (Third, Fourth, and Fifth). The other days have proper names. The seventh day is called the Sabbath Day (Σαββατον) and the sixth day is called by its numerical equivalent, or more traditionally as the Day of Preparation (Παραστον).

The first day of the week — "η πρωτη" or "η μια των Σαββατων" (Mark 16:2), is known by its distinctly Christian name Κυριακη Ημερα, *the Lord's Day*, based on the book of Revelation (1:10). It is the day on which Christ the Lord — ο Κυριος — rose from the dead and appeared to His disciples. Russian Orthodox people and other Slavic peoples constitute an exception to the rule. They call Sunday "Resurrection Day."

34. See, for example, David Ewing Duncan, *Calendar: Humanity's Epic Struggle to Determine a True and Accurate Year* (New York: Harper Perennial, 2001).

35. The phrase is from the first article of the Nicene-Constantinopolitan Creed, the official Symbol of Faith (Creed) of the Orthodox Church.

36. In the language of the Romanians and the Albanians, the ancient pagan names prevail. In the Romanian language, however, Sunday is known as the Lord's Day.

37. In the Russian language, Monday is known as the Day after the Resurrection and Tuesday as the Second Day after the Resurrection.

A Reality Check

I have set before the reader an ideal understanding of the Lord's Day in the hope that it may help to increase and heighten one's awareness of its significance as a special day that shapes the personal, familial, and communal life of a Christian. It would be wrong, however, to assume that every Orthodox Christian experiences Sunday with the knowledge and the passion described above. Such an assumption fails to take into account the degrees and levels of the spiritual life and the inevitable fluctuations people experience in the pursuit of their Christian vocation. That said, it is also important to note that a correlation exists between the Lord's Day and Christian identity. The way one thinks of and spends the Lord's Day says much about the depth and breadth of one's Orthodox Christian identity.

The danger facing the Church and her members today is not so much the swings people experience in their spiritual pursuits but the blurring or the loss of the Orthodox vision of life, the loss or the absence of the sense of God, of His loving and transforming presence in the affairs of everyday life. As God ceases to be relevant in the lives of people, the need for worship diminishes and fades away. Occasional church attendance leads to casual church membership. It can even "lead to a movement away from the Church, not so much in a sense of renunciation or joining another body, but in the sense that Orthodox Christianity no longer is a prime definer of one's identity."[38]

Father Georges Florovsky was correct to state unequivocally that "the Church is ultimately real precisely as a worshipping community, a community or congregation of worshipping members-persons. She grows in her fullness in the process of worship."[39] Precisely because the Church is primarily a worshiping community, regular church attendance is crucial for the maintenance of a vibrant and living faith that upholds and nurtures Christian identity. As Mark Searle put it, "the identity of the Church and of the individual Christian is tied to the weekly assembly. Scripturally, theologically, and liturgically, there can be no Christians without Church, no Church without assembly."[40]

38. See the "Report to His Eminence Archbishop Iakovos — Commission: Archdiocesan Theological Agenda," in *The Greek Orthodox Theological Review* 34, no. 3 (1989): 301.

39. Georges Florovsky, "Worship and Everyday Life: An Eastern Orthodox View," in *Studia Liturgica* 2, no. 4 (1963): 272.

40. Mark Searle, "The Shape of the Future: A Liturgist's Vision," in Searle, ed., *Sunday Morning: A Time for Worship*, p. 139.

The Sunday assembly is so decisive and vital to the Church and her members that an ancient third-century Church Order, The Didascalia of the Twelve Apostles, considers intentional absence from the assembly a cause for great concern because it constitutes a kind of dismemberment of Christ's Body, the Church. Absence from the assembly deprives Christ, and by extension His Church, of one of His members.

> When you are teaching, command and exhort the people to be faithful to the assembly of the church. Let them not fail to attend, but let them gather faithfully together. Let no one deprive the Church by staying away; if they do, they deprive the body of Christ of one of its members! For you must not think only of others but of yourself as well, when you hear the words that our Lord spoke: "Who does not gather with me, scatters" (Matt. 12:30). Since you are the members of Christ, you must not scatter yourselves outside the Church by failing to assemble there. For we have Christ for our Head, as He Himself promised and announced, so that "you have become sharers with us" (2 Peter 1:4). Do not, then, make light of your own selves, do not deprive our Savior of His members, do not rend, do not scatter His Body.[41]

At the Eucharistic assembly we appropriate the saving grace of God and share in the life and the faith of the ecclesial community. There we learn and relearn, affirm and reaffirm who we are as persons and as community. There we are transformed to become servants of redemption, trained to recognize justice and injustice. There we hear the words of life and apprehend salvation. There is the place of our deification.

Unfortunately, however, for Christians who have fallen under the sway of the secular culture of our times Sunday has become less a day of worship and more a day for relaxation and private time; a day, that is, for sleeping in, for catching up on household chores, for the pursuit of hobbies and personal care, and for any number of recreational activities.[42] On top of this, Sunday has developed into a favored day for playing various team sports, claiming especially the attention of school age children and their parents. In addition, the creation of the "three-day weekend" has made Sunday worship less attractive and easier for people to "get away" for

---

41. *The Didascalia of the Twelve Apostles* (chapter 13), in Lucien Deiss, *Springtime of the Liturgy,* trans. Matthew J. O'Connell (Collegeville: Liturgical Press, 1979), pp. 176-77.

42. See McCready, "The Role of Sunday in American Society," pp. 104-10.

brief holidays. On the other hand, the abolition of the so-called "blue laws" has turned Sunday into another workday for many people and a shoppers' day for others. Thus, for large segments of the population Sunday is neither a day for worship nor a day for rest, at least in the traditional Christian sense.

From the Christian perspective rest is more than leisure, more than the suspension of the demands of the workplace, and more than an escape from the burdens and routines of daily life. To be true and edifying, rest must include more than self-indulging activities, more than fun and merriment. It must embrace opportunities for godly service and provide time for quiet reflection and for replenishment and perfection of one's energies — physical, intellectual, emotional, and spiritual. Such an inclusive and energizing rest is especially formed, informed, and vivified by personal prayer and communal worship.

Recreational activities, while they may lend themselves to casual and infrequent church attendance, are not the root cause of the problem. They are, after all, necessary ingredients of an authentic human life. Infrequent church attendance is due largely to the lack of motivation that springs from flawed priorities. When Sunday is reduced to a "day off," we rob it of its unique mystical quality. When we abandon the Eucharistic gathering for rest and recreation, we lose out on the regenerative powers that flow out of the liturgical assembly.

The liturgy is, after all, the gateway to heaven, a place of mystery, flooded by the presence of God. It is where we begin, develop, and nurture our intimate union with Christ and with His mystical body, the Church. The liturgy is the place in which God works to change the very core of our being, making us by grace what He is by nature.

At the heart of the Gospel is the truth of God's solidarity with His creatures, of the Presence of His rule, and of His gentle mercy and tender love. We have been made for worship. Our hearts, as St. Augustine observed, remain restless until they rest in the presence of God. The yearning for the wholly Other is deeply embedded in our soul. It cannot be eradicated. Therefore, we either learn to come before the true God in prayer and solemn feast or we delude ourselves with the worship of idols, the forms of which are many in our fallen and wounded world.

CHAPTER SIX

Pope John Paul II and *Dies Domini*

Edward O'Flaherty, S.J.

In Roman Catholicism the six commandments of the Church governing the practices of the faithful begin with "To assist at Mass and rest from servile work on all Sundays and Holy Days of obligation."[1] Reflection on this commandment traditionally focused on the details of the moral obligation that it entailed: What constituted a legitimate exception to the rule? What does servile work mean? In the popular mind there were no considerations of the mystagogical meaning of Sabbath; Sunday Mass attendance and refraining from work were an obligation and that was that.

With the Second Vatican Council, called by Blessed Pope John XXIII, the attention of Catholics was drawn beyond obligatory practice to deeper pastoral considerations. Currently in Roman Catholic circles, historians and theologians debate whether Vatican II was doctrinally innovative or simply bringing up to date traditional teaching. What is unquestioned is that Catholic practice of piety was profoundly influenced by the spirit of the council. Popular devotions, frequent reception of communion, decrease in the reception of the sacrament of penance, traditional abstinence on Friday — these and many other practices were noticeably affected. The obligation to attend Mass could be fulfilled by attending vigil Mass on Saturday. The conciliar call for renewal certainly produced change. What is debated now is whether that change is renewal. The renewal of liturgy with the vernacular being introduced had a profound effect on popular practice; Catholics' obligation to attend Mass on Sunday has been made easier by reason of the Mass being intelligible. But has the appreciation of

---

1. Donald Attwater, gen. ed., *A Catholic Dictionary* (New York: The Macmillan Company, 1941), p. 113.

Sunday as the central day of worship been enhanced? Pope John Paul II addressed this question in his apostolic letter *Dies Domini*.[2]

Pope John Paul II from the beginning of his pontificate focused his energies in writing and pastoral visits on preparing for the Great Jubilee of the year 2000. He wanted to remind the faithful of the rich traditions of the Church and have them rediscover new ways of living them out; he also wanted to renew — that is, increase in intensity — the practice of Christian life.

It is in the perspective of this preparation for the Great Jubilee that his 1998 apostolic letter *Dies Domini* should be read. It is the most complete treatment of Sunday observance that exists. It is not a reiteration of obligation but a profound and detailed reflection on the mystery, the celebration, and the significance of Sunday for Christian and human life. This theological reflection merits our close attention.

His starting point is the affirmation that Sunday is above all an Easter celebration, "wholly illumined by the glory of the Risen Christ" (p. 136, par. 8). The Pope, while he surely makes use of philosophical and psychological reflections on the use of Sabbath rest and the need for a rhythm to human life by means of a calendar, nonetheless makes it clear that he is directing his letter to Christians, for whom the resurrection of Jesus is the basis of faith. Christ is the center of our life, he is telling us; as we celebrate the Creator's work we do so from a Christocentric perspective. The theme of "God's rest" and the rest which he offered to the people of the Exodus when they entered the Promised Land is reread in the New Testament in the light of the definitive "Sabbath rest" (Heb. 4:9) into which Christ Himself has entered by His resurrection (p. 136, par. 8).

The story of creation contained in Genesis provides key elements which situate Sabbath in the history of God's creation: every element of the universe as it comes from God's hand is good; God's work and rest; man's activity viewed in the light of God's; the seventh day as holy; remembering by calendar God's work and rest. These core elements are expanded on in *Dies Domini*. Before doing so, John Paul II explains how the movement from Jewish Sabbath to Christian Sunday is to be understood. Observing the third commandment, "Keep Holy the Lord's Day," means

2. Pope John Paul II, *Dies Domini*, in *Origins* 28, 9 (CNS Documentary Service, Washington, D.C.), p. 136, par. 8. The text may also be found at the website: www.vatican.va/holy_father/john_paul_ii/apost_letters/documents/hf_jp-ii_apl_05071998_dies-domini_en.html. Hereafter, references to the text are cited parenthetically in the text by page number in *Origins* and paragraph number.

remembering God's saving works. Christians, the Pope says, saw the definitive time inaugurated by Christ as a new beginning, so "they made the first day after the Sabbath a festive day, for that was the day on which the Lord rose from the dead" (p. 138, par. 18). The Pascal mystery of Christ is the "full revelation of the mystery of the world's origin, the climax of the history of salvation and the eschatological fulfillment of the world" (p. 138, par. 18). In Christ the full meaning of Sabbath is realized. The letter continues: "We move from the 'Sabbath' to the first day after the Sabbath, from the seventh day to the first day: the *dies Domini becomes the dies Christi*" (p. 138, par. 18).

The letter examines this *Dies Christi* from four perspectives: (a) the day of the Risen Lord and the day of the Gift of the Holy Spirit; (b) the Eucharistic Assembly as the Heart of Sunday; (c) Sunday as the Day of Joy, Rest, and Solidarity; and (d) finally Sunday as the day of days, the primordial feast revealing the meaning of time.

Dies Christi: Sunday, the Day of the Risen Lord

The apostolic letter recalls the words of Pope Innocent I at the beginning of the fifth century: "We celebrate Sunday because of the venerable Resurrection of our Lord Jesus Christ, and we do so not only at Easter, but also at each turning of the week" (p. 138, par. 19). Fr. Calivas in his article (cf. above) gives the evidence for this early Christian understanding of the development of Sunday as the day of celebration. The Pope summarizes:

> According to the common witness of the Gospels, the Resurrection of Jesus Christ from the dead took place on "the first day after the Sabbath." On the same day, the Risen Lord appeared to the two disciples of Emmaus and to the eleven Apostles gathered together. . . . The day of Pentecost — the first day of the eighth week after the Jewish Passover — also fell on a Sunday. . . . From Apostolic times, "the first day after the Sabbath," the first day of the week, began to shape the rhythm of life for Christ's disciples. . . . In those early Christian times, the weekly rhythm of days was generally not part of life in the regions where the Gospel spread and the festive days of the Greek and Roman calendars did not coincide with Christian Sunday. For Christians, therefore, it was very difficult to observe the Lord's Day on a set day each week. . . . Yet fidelity to the weekly rhythm became the norm, since it was based

upon the New Testament and was tied to Old Testament revelation. (pp. 138-39, par. 20, 21, 22)

From the celebration of Christian Sunday early on the connection between the resurrection of Jesus and creation arose because the Christians saw a link between the resurrection taking place on the first day of the week with the first day of the cosmic week of creation. Sunday is a day for remembering and, broadly speaking, of making connections . . . remembering the creation, the salvation given, the eighth day (that day, St. Basil says, which will follow the present time, the day without end). (p. 139, par. 26)

In this connection, the Pope calls Sunday the day of Christ-Light, the day of the gift of the Spirit, the day of faith. What is clear from this abbreviated listing is that for the early Christians these spiritual associations and the impact of the social milieu moved the followers of Christ to accept the first day of the week in which to share worship. As *Dies Domini* puts it: "What began as a spontaneous practice became a juridically sanctioned norm." The Pope has tried to recover some of the spontaneity rooted in the realization of the early Christians that *dies Domini* is *dies Christi.*

The social pressures of today make the celebration of Sunday very difficult for some Christians, and the Vatican Council spoke of reforming the church's calendar to match different civil calendars but only under the condition of keeping a week of seven days with a Sunday.

Dies Ecclesiae: The Eucharistic Assembly as the Heart of Sunday

The insistence on the seven-day week and its irreplaceable Sunday does not reflect attachment to one particular calendar, for it is the core of Sunday, its very meaning, that John Paul is insisting on. Sunday is a celebration of the living presence of the Risen Lord in the midst of His own people and not just a celebration by individuals alone, but together, as Church, the mystical body of Christ. And each community becomes a place where the mystery of the Church is concretely made present and opens itself to communion with the universal Church. Early Christians defied Roman imperial regulations that forbade Christian worship, because they felt bound to celebrate the Lord's Day. Their worship on the Lord's Day is not a private affair. Over and over again it is emphasized that it is the whole community, not small groups that gather. It is the Church at prayer, not isolated individuals or a select gathering which assembles on Sunday.

"The *Dies Domini* is also the *dies Ecclesiae*" (p. 141, par. 35). By this statement the Pope stresses the community-forming function of Sunday liturgy. The faithful gather around the bishop, or the pastor of the parish who represents the bishop, to be nourished by word and sacrament. This gathering expresses the unity of the people who have been brought together in and by the unity of Father, Son, and Holy Spirit (p. 141, par. 36). Sunday worship becomes the privileged time and place where this unity is manifested. The community, for its part, does not manifest a unity which is perfect and complete; it has not received fully the gift God is giving. Because it is a pilgrim people, the community is "on the way"; the eschatological character of the gathering means its task is not complete, the community lives in hope. It anticipates the feast of the marriage of the Lamb (Rev. 19:9), but meanwhile it has not arrived at the fulfillment of God's promise. The Church is very much rooted in time with its imperfections, even as it looks forward to a timeless future.

The assembly makes use of the Lord's gifts to nourish those participating with the word and sacrament. The table of the word leads the faithful into the mystery of salvation history. The Paschal mystery is at the center of this history, and God's word should be proclaimed and explained in such a way that the Lord's actions can be celebrated and personally appropriated. This proclamation is a dialogue between God and His people, and from its richness the whole assembly receives challenge, understanding, encouragement, and hope. They are challenged to "conversion," a change of how we view the world and God in the world. They are encouraged and filled with hope in that the baptismal promises are strengthened; we have the opportunity to say "yes" or "Amen" to what we hear of God's fidelity and love, His *hesed.*

The table of the Body, too, makes the Lord's gift of Himself present and visible. This celebration of His presence in the midst of the assembly recalls all the saving work the Lord has done, especially His sacrifice on the cross.

Like the table of the word, the table of communion links us with brothers and sisters elsewhere in the world. It is an experience of solidarity and brotherhood and makes us aware of how much needs to be done so that solidarity can be complete. Sunday celebration may seem to be confined to one hour in church, but the participants are made aware of what awaits them in their ordinary life. Their mission is not completed either on

Sunday or in any particular day: it is a mission to which we are continually called.

The importance of this *Day of the Church,* the Eucharist, is seen for what it gives to the participants; at the same time the participants have a need to take part in the liturgical assembly (p. 143, par. 46). In the *Didascalia* (third-century text), it says:

> Leave everything on the Lord's Day and run diligently to your assembly because it is your praise of God. Otherwise, what excuse will they make to God, those who do not come together on the Lord's Day to hear the word of life and feed on divine nourishment which lasts forever.[3]

Pope John Paul II cites this early Christian text, which testifies to the importance of observing Sunday, the Lord's Day, with celebration and prayer (p. 143, par. 46). As time went on, the Church councils in the face of half-heartedness felt the need for prescriptions, but the underlying perspective was expressed by one martyr for the faith: "We cannot live without the Lord's Supper." If this need for the Lord's Supper was important then, it continues to be so today. Pope John Paul II, the pilgrim pope, traveled worldwide and was conscious of the difficult situations Christians find themselves in different parts today. He writes:

> They [the Christian faithful] live in surroundings which are some times decidedly hostile and at other times — more frequently in fact — indifferent and unresponsive to the Gospel message. If believers are not to be overwhelmed, they must be able to count on the support of the Christian community. This is why they must be convinced that it is crucially important for the life of faith that they should come together with others on Sunday to celebrate the Passover of the Lord in the sacrament of the New Covenant. (pp. 143-44, par. 48)

Dies Hominis: Sunday, a Day of Joy, Rest, and Solidarity

The celebration of Sunday is primarily a day of joy, for it is "an echo" of the first encounter with the Risen Lord. In the contemporary situation, the sense of obligation makes it difficult to remember the festive spirit with

3. *Didascalia,* 2.59.2-3.

which the first Christians celebrated the first day of the week. The disciples rejoiced to see the Risen Lord, and in our remembering the joy is repeated; it is a gift of the Spirit and much more lasting than feelings of satisfaction and pleasure which capture us for the moment and then disappear.

The Pope makes a point of asserting that there is no conflict between Christian joy and true human joys which find fulfillment in the joy of Christ glorified:

> This aspect of Christian Sunday shows in a special way how it is the fulfillment of the Old Testament Sabbath. On the Lord's Day which — as we have already said — the Old Testament links to the work of creation and the Exodus, the Christian is called to proclaim the new creation and the new covenant brought about in the Paschal mystery of Christ. (p. 145, par. 59)

Sunday is not so much a "replacement" for the Sabbath, says John Paul II; it is its fulfillment. The practices of the Jewish Sabbath are gone, but the underlying reasons for keeping the Lord's Day holy remain valid. What are some of these reasons? Sabbath is a day of rest, a fundamental and liberating moment, a day of solidarity. Since it is a day to keep holy (holy = something set apart) it should therefore be a day of rest. Intertwined with the character of rest is that of liberation from oppression. First and foremost is the very oppressive work by which, day in and day out, many men and women earn their daily bread under burdensome conditions. Rest is not merely a pause from work but a time to look anew upon the wonders of creation. Rest is not being idle but being able to enjoy God's gifts. "In order that rest might not degenerate into emptiness and boredom, it must offer spiritual enrichment, greater freedom, opportunities for contemplation and fraternal communion" (p. 147, par. 68).

Along with rest and liberation, Sunday is seen as a day of solidarity. Ever since St. Paul's injunction to the Corinthians, "On the first day of the week, each of you is to put aside and save whatever extra you earn" (1 Cor. 16:2), Christians have been attending to the needs of the poor. In St. Paul's instance it was a collection organized for the poor communities in Judea. In other places and times, the Sunday collection has become part of a culture of sharing with those less gifted in material blessings. The Eucharist itself links every recipient with the other. As John Paul says, "Lived this way, not only Sunday Eucharist but the whole of Sunday becomes a great school of charity, justice and peace" (p. 148, par. 73).

Dies Dierum: Sunday the Primordial Feast, Revealing the Meaning of Time

Finally, the Pope shows how the weekly celebration of Sunday opens up for Christians the rhythm of time in which we live. Christ is the center of time, at once Alpha and Omega. He brings a meaning to existence expressed in many, many ways, a meaning most naturally found in the gathering of Christians who commemorate His resurrection. The liturgical year helps us follow the mysteries of Christ's life, but at the center of them all is the resurrection which is commemorated each Sunday of the year.

At the conclusion, the Pope expresses his hope that Christians will recover the rich meaning of Sunday celebration as well as its practical consequences in rest, solidarity, joy, and freedom. Pope John Paul II proposed these reflections, as was stated at the beginning of this paper, for the Great Jubilee of 2000. Its specific purpose does not limit the use to which this document can be made. It is at once historical, theological, and mystical. Its manner is a far cry from the prescriptive tone with which Sunday obligations were understood, for example, in the commandments of the Church. It is a call to recapture the spontaneity and joy with which the early Christians celebrated Sunday: "We cannot live without the Lord's Supper."

CHAPTER SEVEN

The Lord's Day as Anticipation and Promise in Liturgy and Word

Horace T. Allen, Jr.

Fundamental for an appropriate understanding of the church's weekly calendar are two New Testament texts, namely Acts 20:7 and Revelation 1:10, with their references to the "first day of the week" and the "Lord's Day." Also relevant are the early references in Acts to the daily table fellowship and prayer life of the Jerusalem community, which seriously indicate an emergence of an eschatological daily and weekly calendar and perspective, contradictory as that may sound. That is to say, the one-day-in-seven of the Jewish calendar, the Sabbath, with its double historical references to creation and exodus, and its position in the week as the last and "seventh" day, was replaced with a "first" or anticipatory day.[1]

Reformation churches abandoned much of the pre-Reformation Western annual calendrical structure, together with the related Roman lectionary for the Lord's Day as the preeminent day of Christian celebration. As lectionary systems have slowly returned to use, there has been a tendency to select biblical materials for these feasts and festivals according to practices and pieties that are more late-medieval than ancient or patristic. As the Methodist liturgiologist James F. White puts it, "Many medieval pieties and practices remained intact in Protestantism because they were the only models available when reforming such items as daily public prayer."[2]

---

1. See John Calvin, *Institutes of the Christian Religion*, 2.8.33, n. 41. It is clear for Calvin that the Lord's Day, the Christian Sunday, is not simply a continuation of the Jewish Sabbath but a distinctively Christian institution as a means toward church order and spiritual health. See the note in the edition of the Library of Christian Classics, vol. XX, ed. John T. McNeill, trans. Ford Lewis Battles (Philadelphia: Westminster Press, 1960).

2. James F. White, *A Brief History of Christian Worship* (Nashville: Abingdon Press, 1993), p. 76.

At issue here are at least two historical developments.[3] One is the un-questioned fact that the Roman lectionary and calendar had become, by the sixteenth century, incredibly "cluttered up" by the intrusion into the Lord's Day worship of all manner of hagiographical commemorations ("saints' days") both local and universal, as well as by Marian festivals and theological emphases (Trinity, for instance). This was, of course, one of the issues the reformers addressed through their radical simplification of the calendar to reemphasize the classic Christological center as embodied in Christmas, Easter, and Pentecost. A part of this development relates to the decision of certain reformers, such as Zwingli and Calvin, to abandon the Roman lectionary in favor of "in course" or continuous reading week by week. Wise as this undoubtedly was in terms of a preaching and teaching agenda, it had the effect of dissociating "days" from lections such that in later centuries, when continuous reading gave way to pastoral selection, week by week, the principle of scriptural governance gave way — which in our present time of calendrical recovery has resulted in extraordinary dis-tortions. Suffice it to be said here by way of example that one of the most catastrophic instances of this is to be found in the displacement of the his-torical Advent emphasis on the so-called Second Coming of the Lord by a kind of "pre-Christmas preparation" with all of the consumerism our soci-ety proffers.

The second historical development to be mentioned is that the sixteenth-century reformers understood, both on biblical and patristic bases, the prior significance for all Christian worship of the weekly cycle with its "first day of the week." This was part of their response to the com-plex annual cycle of the Roman Rite, but also their reaffirmation of the primacy of a resurrection focus on that day. This nicely played into their revision of the annual calendar and may well have informed Calvin's litur-gical hermeneutic of preaching from the Old Testament at daily worship and from the New Testament on the Lord's Day (which day he understood not only in its Paschal character but also in its Eucharistic norm). The dif-ficulty our contemporary Reformed communities have run into at this point is the later development of a "Sabbath" definition and piety for the Lord's Day. (The use of the pagan name "Sunday" in English has not

---

3. For a fuller treatment of these developments and their implication for Reformed worship, see Horace T. Allen, Jr., "Calendar and Lectionary in Reformed Perspective and History," in *Christian Worship in Reformed Churches Past and Present*, ed. Lukas Vischer (Grand Rapids: Eerdmans, 2003), pp. 390-414.

helped!) Thus in our own day, without either a lectionary of paschal focus, weekly or annually, or a weekly Eucharistic norm, we are adrift in a highly non-biblical, a-historical, and extra-ecumenical definition of Lord's Day worship as something other than an essentially Christological celebration.

The Lord's Day as Anticipation of the Future

The Lord's Day carries an anticipatory relationship to the seven-day week. It is initiatory on the basis of the resurrection, and it opens up the weekly Messianic meal-fellowship of the community as a kind of realized eschatology which still awaits the return of Christ as Messiah and Lord of all creation, the true Jubilee in a sense. Karl Barth put this well in his description of "the time of the community" in his *Church Dogmatics:* "The time of the community is the time between the first *parousia* of Jesus Christ and the second. The community exists between His coming then as the risen One and this final coming."[4] Thus, the weekly temporal calendar is actually a matter of two trans-historical "times," the resurrection and the return of Messiah-Lord. Barth's theological student and friend, Paul Lehmann, puts this juxtaposition of past and future quite clearly in his book *The Transfiguration of Politics:*

> The word *story,* in this context (messianic) refers to the way in which one generation tells another how the future shapes the present out of the past; how destiny draws heritage into the human reality and meaning of experience, which is always a compound of happenings, hope and remembrance; how promise and disillusionment, celebration and suffering, joy and pain, forgiveness and guilt, renewal and failure, transfigure the human condition and are transfigured in it.[5]

Or in summary, "The past does not cross over the present into the future. The future draws the present toward itself from the past."[6] The Lord's Day therefore, unlike the Sabbath, does not complete or commemorate a "perfect" history, but rather inaugurates a future that is even more perfect,

---

4. Karl Barth, *Church Dogmatics*, IV/2: *The Doctrine of Reconciliation*, trans. G. W. Bromiley (Edinburgh: T. & T. Clark, 1958), p. 725.

5. Paul Lehmann, *The Transfiguration of Politics* (New York: Harper and Row, 1975), p. 7.

6. Lehmann, *The Transfiguration of Politics*, p. xi.

the *yom Yahweh*, the "Day of the Lord." Interestingly, the singular New Testament text which does refer to the liturgical "meetings of the community," Hebrews 10:19-25, explicitly alludes to "encouraging one another, and all the more as you see the Day [of the Lord] approaching."

Sunday as the Lord's Day becomes the chief "orienting" day of the week. Illustrating the way by which the Lord's Day shapes not only the week but also the year, Laurence Stookey writes:

> For Christians, Sunday is the chief festival of the faith. Many active Christians would say that Christmas is their chief festival. Closer to the mark but still missing it are those who say that Easter day is the principal feast of the church. What is amiss about such assessments? Simply this, no observance that occurs only once a year can connote the continuing work of God in daily life. Therefore, the chief festival occurs weekly and from it all else is derived, including those annual festivals that may be more visible and certainly are the more popular and cultural occasions.[7]

Fundamental for an appropriate understanding of the church's weekly calendar is to see it, as Stookey identifies it, as *the church's principal calendar*. This was one of the liturgical reforms of reshufflings by the sixteenth-century Reformation, and it came straight to Massachusetts via the Puritans, of course, who even rejected the annual church festivals. As we take into account the centrality of the weekly calendar in the Reformation moment as the cornerstone of daily, weekly, and annual calendar structures, we cannot but notice this basically eschatological, rather than historical, theological definition of what a calendar, the marking of time, is all about. "Contradictory" indeed: a futuristic calendar!

Hagiography

Sadly, the loss in our era of this daily-weekly pattern and theology of worship as practiced in Geneva (although uniquely in our time also by Korean Protestantism, which maintains a very serious tradition of daily prayer and preaching), and the concurrent replacement in our consciousness of the

7. Laurence Hull Stookey, *Calendar: Christ's Time for the Church* (Nashville: Abingdon Press, 1996).

"Lord's (resurrection) Day" by a kind of "Christian Sabbath" (which occurred around the sixth century), has fatally obscured this eschatological emphasis.[8] This has also taken its toll on our understanding especially of the Lord's Supper, whose symmetry with the Lord's Day has been lost.[9]

These reflections provide us with at least two lessons concerning what might be called the Reformed understanding of the weekly calendar.

First, the Lord's Day as celebration of death and resurrection must be recovered. This is no sixteenth-century innovation. It was for good reason that the Council of Nicaea determined that the annual Christian Paschal festival (which along with Sunday we denominate with a pagan term, "Easter") should fall on the Lord's Day, thus emphasizing as its primary liturgy *baptism,* as the beginning of the Christian's life by virtue of Christ's resurrection (Rom. 6:3-11; 1 Peter 3:21-22). (Christians are constantly using confusing pagan terminology: we do not worship that Nordic goddess Eostre, nor do we worship the Sun.)

This suggests something about our timing of the celebration of that sacrament. For as long as the first day of the week does not connote resurrection among our churches, then we should beware of the indiscriminate way we have of baptizing (often with little notice on any Sunday), and perhaps we should return to the early church's practice of relating that rite to Easter and Pentecost or such other Christological festivals as Epiphany, the Baptism of the Lord, First Lent, or All Saints'. I would like to point out in this connection that we easily destroy the Lord's Supper by celebrating it infrequently, and we destroy baptism by celebrating it *too* frequently.

You actually cannot have the Lord's Day without the Lord's Supper, nor can you have the Lord's Supper without the Lord's Day. This is an important connection.

Second, it is the daily-weekly calendar which provides the occasion for the great Reformed tradition of the continuous reading *lectio continua* of the Scriptures in public worship, now so emphatically embodied in the Roman system of 1969 and its progeny, the *Common Lectionary* of 1983 and its successor, the *Revised Common Lectionary* of 1992. The English-speaking Presbyterian foundational liturgical document, the *Westminster*

---

8. This is seen pointedly in the fact that Saints' Days are set in relation to the death of the saint, not their physical birth date.

9. The symmetry between the Lord's Supper and the Lord's Day has been magisterially expounded by Willy Rordorf, *Sunday: The History of the Day of Rest and of Worship in the Early Centuries of the Christian Church* (London: SCM Press, 1968), pp. 274-93.

Directory for Public Worship, at least suggests such a matter of weekly public proclamation of the Old and New Testaments (chapter 3).

The Lord's Day may be denominated a Sabbath, but its theology is one of resurrection and worship. Rordorf points out that it was actually a day of worship for centuries before it became a day of rest. That followed upon the Constantinian legislation. The irony of all this is that it became a day of rest because of legislation, whereas until that time it was simply the day the community met either at night or early in the morning for the Lord's Supper and, of course, for the reading of the Scriptures.

The Lord's Day and the Liturgy

Once we recognize the centrality of Sunday as the Lord's Day in the life of the Christian community, we might next consider how it shapes the rest of the week through the liturgy. The basic function of the weekly liturgical cycle is to provide for the continuous reading of Scripture in the context of worship as well as to provide the occasion for the weekly celebration of the Lord's resurrection and daily presence in the community. This daily-weekly pattern might well be considered in relation to the annual calendar, with its Easter cycle (Lent, Holy Week, Easter Day, the Fifty Days, and Pentecost) and the Christmas cycle (Advent, Christmas, the Twelve Days, Epiphany), but our focus here is on the Lord's Day as it gives shape to a weekly pattern.[10] This question might be considered in relation to the ongoing interests of The Consultation on Common Texts (CCT), a working group that emerged from ecumenical meetings held in the mid-1960s. It was formed by Catholic and Protestant liturgical scholars in response to the reforms in the liturgy mandated by the Second Vatican Council, especially in the area of English texts for the liturgy, and then in the dissemination of the 1969 Roman Lectionary *(Ordo Lectionum Missae).*

In 2005 the CCT published an integrated, thirty-year lectionary for both the Lord's Day and the surrounding weekdays. The strict definition of the word "lectionary" is simply a book in which are collected and printed the readings from canonical literature appointed by a given ecclesiastical authority for a cycle of liturgical occasions, be that the weekly Lord's Day service, a Daily Office pattern, or particular pastoral rites and

---

10. Cf. Thomas Talley, *The Origins of the Liturgical Year* (New York: Pueblo Publishing Co., 1986).

sacraments other than mass or Eucharist. While such books were in existence by the fifth century, at the time of the sixteenth-century Protestant Reformation and its technological ally, moveable type, it became practical to use publicly a whole Bible. This crystallized a theological distinction that roughly came to characterize Protestant and Catholic scriptural use and theology; the American lectionary scholar Fritz West has described this as a distinction between "Scripture" (the Protestant use of the whole Bible) and "memory" (the Catholic use of a lectionary book).[11]

The organizing center for understanding this system of the CCT daily lectionary of Scripture readings is the Lord's Day three-year table, first published in 1969 by the Holy See of the Roman Catholic Church, then revised for Protestant and Anglican use by the CCT, first in 1983 and then again, after nine years' use and revision, in 1992. Since this effort was widely and enthusiastically accepted, especially by Protestant pastors who had never before worked with a lectionary table, the Consultation undertook to provide a weekday supplement in 2005.

We will now emphasize the architecture, shape, and principles involved in this daily and weekly lectionary,[12] a pioneering attempt at integrating a weekly Lord's Day Eucharistic lectionary and a daily non-Eucharistic biblical system.

1. The Daily Readings (DR) provide for a three-year cycle (A-B-C) as in the Roman *Ordo* and Common Lectionary Readings (CLR). Its heart is the sequence of weekly Lord's Day Gospel Pericopes with their attendant Old Testament, Epistle, and Psalm selections.

2. The center of the Lord's Day effects a new "week" — Thursday, Friday, and Saturday being preparation and Monday, Tuesday, and Wednesday being reflective. Herein are two historic innovations: the Lord's Day is neither the beginning nor the end of the ecclesiastical week; it is the center. And, for the first time in recent church history, the Lord's Day cycle and the daily (weekday) cycle are integrated in terms of biblical themes and genres. Such lectionaries as have come down to us have been one or the other, with little integration other than occasional seasonal emphases.

11. Fritz West, *Scripture and Memory: The Ecumenical Hermeneutics of the Three-Year Lectionaries* (Collegeville: Liturgical Press, 1997).

12. *Revised Common Lectionary: Includes Complete List of Lections for Year A, B, and C* (Nashville: Abingdon Press, 1992).

3. Each weekly cycle forms a coherent mix of biblical material which may be used liturgically or catechetically, privately or corporately, but also on a daily basis. Thus the daily pattern:

Thursday	Old Testament — Epistle
Friday	Old Testament — Epistle
Saturday	Old Testament — Gospel
Sunday*or* **the Lord's Day**	
Monday	Old Testament — Epistle
Tuesday	Old Testament — Epistle
Wednesday	Old Testament — Gospel

Throughout, we used pericopes which had already been identified by Professor Gail Ramshaw (Lutheran) in her earlier, similar effort, *Between Sundays*.[13] The compilers of the CCT's work were Joseph Russell (Episcopalian), Fred Graham (United Church of Canada), Martin Seltz (Lutheran/Fortress Press), Arthur Clyde and Thomas Dipko (both United Church of Christ), and myself (Presbyterian Church USA). According to Thomas Dipko, this amounted to 2,000 pericopes covering virtually all of the New Testament and a substantial portion of the Old Testament.

The integrative character of Daily Readings (i.e., Lord's Day and weekdays surrounding the Lord's Day) assumes two significant but largely overlooked aspects of the Lord's Day itself.

The first is the central but unique theological meaning of that day. That was probably the rationale behind the early church's juxtaposition of the Christian week ("The first day") with the Jewish week ("The seventh/last day"). In our modern, secular world, that is not a problem. Our problem is that there is no "week"; there is only the weekend, which is devoted to sport, shopping, sleeping, or travel! This may be part of the reason that the misguided identification of the Lord's Day as the "Christian Sabbath" has never been evangelically very effective or convincing. So the Daily Readings provide a table of readings to accentuate the uniqueness of this day, the day of resurrection, the Lord's Day, around which *all* days and times revolve — and, incidentally, not "Sunday" which is a reference to another religion altogether.

The second and related aspect of Lord's Day theology which the Daily

---

13. Gail Ramshaw, *Between Sundays: Daily Bible Readings Based on the Revised Common Lectionary* (Minneapolis: Augsburg Fortress, 1997).

Readings raise is its sacramental significance. This may not seem obvious at first blush. Lectionaries are about the Word, not the sacrament, aren't they? Wrong, if Lord's Day worship is both Word and sacrament (read Luke 24 or Acts 20), the identity of Lord's Day and Lord's Supper, both linguistically (in Greek) and theologically, are increasingly affirmed by recent liturgical and New Testament scholarship. As I understand it, that is the *sine qua non* of Orthodoxy. Protestants have lost it by our normative, non-sacramental Sundays and (if I may say, along with many of my liturgical friends of the Roman persuasion) by the loss of the Catholic piety and practice of a daily Eucharistic celebration (for which there is a separate lectionary altogether). If, on the other hand, the Lord's Day requires the Lord's Supper, and the Lord's Supper is limited to the Lord's Day, with resurrection celebration as the linchpin, then any evangelical and catholic lectionary system must communicate and celebrate that. How might this be the case?

The answer in the Daily Readings is the balanced but clear focus on the canonical Gospels, whose very literary structure is resurrection-oriented. Thus, the Lord's Day Gospel pericope, with its other readings and praise, is the center around which the entire week is oriented ("East-ed"). And each of the three-day half-week sets also culminates in a Gospel reading (on Saturday and Wednesday).

Obviously, this issue raises the classic battle of canonical inspiration — that is, is there a "canon within the canon," namely the four Gospels? This we fought about at the CCT furiously, with, as one might expect, the so-called "liturgical churches" leaning in the direction of the uniqueness of the Gospels, and the "non-liturgical" churches leaning in the direction of "all Scripture is Gospel." This writer often found himself awkwardly in the middle. I like to think that the Daily Readings provide a middle ground that is a worthy ecumenical achievement in this matter, at least insofar as it shifts the focus of the argument away from the limited question of the inspiration of Holy Scripture and into a much wider context of Christian worship and formation. Thus we come to our third consideration, that there is a unique way of "receiving" Holy Scripture, namely, a *liturgical hermeneutic.*

Scripture and Liturgy

The whole lectionary undertaking rests on the assumption — fairly safe, I think — that the Church of Jesus Christ exists by reason of its dependence on a series of writings we call the Bible (*Ta Biblia,* or "the books"). Of course, this is a slippery expression at best. The very fact that it is a plural expression is suggestive enough. The controversy over the "apocryphal books" attests to this also. The process of translation certainly doesn't make the matter any easier.

The fact that no less than three Abrahamic communities embrace (some of) these documents is a complicating factor as well.

Then, too, there is the troublesome matter that these writings are all of human origin, except in the estimation of literal inspirationists. (Interestingly, the Mormons and Christian Scientists have solved this problem by simply adding some more reliable writings, one set of texts which exists — Mrs. Eddy's — and one set of which doesn't exist [the golden plates of the Book of Mormon]). And, most terrifying, for Christians, at any rate, there might be some other, as yet unknown, works. That is the issue behind canonicity. Even as "conservative" a scholar as Karl Barth has insisted that the canon isn't closed. He reminds us that conceivably there could be "lost," authentic books, or that a contemporary writing could be canonized (just as saints are), such as Martin Luther King, Jr.'s *Letter from the Birmingham Jail.*[14]

That these considerations are not exactly frivolous or irrelevant today is well attested as we watch our political society agonize over the authoritative role of the Supreme Court vis-à-vis our Constitution, and as we watch even such a venerable institution as the Anglican Communion and its so-called "American Branch," the Episcopal Church, being rent asunder by the claim, "The Bible says." Such an argument rests on a thoroughly pagan assumption that the Bible is not the community's book, but an oracle. And oracles have always been known for their ability to say whatever their consulters and protectors want them to say. Need I say that in today's culture, with the Bible being so regarded, the Bible's community is itself in great danger, especially if factions within that community think and behave in the same way?

But if the Bible is not an oracle, then how is it to be "received" by its community? Notice that I do not say "read" or "heard." That just adds another layer of variables and presuppositions, a methodology which, in fact, a lectionary might seem to assume with its dependence on written texts and either silent or spoken transmission.

14. Martin Luther King, Jr., *Letter from the Birmingham Jail* (San Francisco: HarperSanFrancisco, 1994).

In short, without surveying all the many ways the church has devised to deal with its Scriptures, I am proposing that there is a *modus* or manner of receiving Scripture that has not for some time been considered normative (or even important), and that *modus* or manner is the way in which the Bible shapes the liturgy and the ways in which the liturgy shapes — interprets — the Bible. This is probably the ancient presumption which links the "episcopal" office, that is, the community's liturgist, to the teaching office. Thus, to this day, in the Roman liturgy for the ordination of a bishop, the open book of the Gospels is laid on the back of the prostrate ordinand.

In an earlier time, the Old Testament people of God required the presence of a liturgical assembly of at least ten Jewish men, the *minyan,* for reading and praying Torah. And our Lord himself apparently reduced this number to its absolute numerical minimum, namely *two:* "Where two or three of you assemble in my name . . ." (Matt. 18:20). Such a principle also would seem to underlie the sixteenth-century reformers' opposition to the practice of a private mass. In the church's theological tradition, the corporate, liturgical linkage appears in the fifth-century Vincentian Canon *(Quod ubique, quod simper, quo ab omnibus),* and in the liturgical affirmation of Prosper of Acquitaine, also fifth century, *lex orandi, lex credendi.*

An interesting suggestion of this intimate connection between faith and worship, in both Protestant and Catholic circles, is the deep pastoral strife that ensues even when lawful ecclesial authority proposes changing liturgical patterns, language, furniture, gestures, service books, or hymnals. The local people of God regard "their" liturgy as being on a similar — and, I would say, related — level as their relation to "their" Bible.

Bible and liturgy: for centuries these two pillars of Christian faith and piety have somehow drifted apart. At the time of the sixteenth century in the West, it could be said that one side had lost the Bible from the liturgy, and the other, recovering the Bible, lost the liturgy. Is this an oversimplification? Perhaps it is. But today we seem to be remedying that sad bifurcation. That, at least, was the rationale of the ecumenical effort which has produced a rich biblical content for an almost lost liturgy — The Daily Office, the CCT's Daily Readings.

But, to what end? Who, in today's frantic world, says daily prayers with Bible readings (outside of monastery walls)? Yes, many clergy from the so-called liturgical churches do so, but in private. But what of the ordinary, lay people of God, most of whom love the Bible but do not know it, so that even where there are pew Bibles, page numbers must be given? This is an appeal for our churches to get over the fatal distinction between Word and liturgy that came close to losing both. That is the "end" or *"telos"* of the Daily Readings. As we ponder how to connect the Lord's Day with the rest of the week, our answer is found in a common lectionary or daily readings. This will also help to restore the Lord's Day as the preeminent day of celebration in the Christian community, and the other days as reflection and celebration.

CHAPTER EIGHT

Theological Significance of the Lord's Day for the Formation of the Missional Church

Darrell Guder

I would like us to think about the Sabbath in relation to the idea of a *missional* church.[1] The term "missional church" has emerged out of a longer conversation initially shaped and guided by Lesslie Newbigin, one of the great missional thinkers and ecumenical leaders of the last century. Bishop Newbigin, a Church of Scotland missionary to India for many years, was one of the founding strategists of the Church of South India and the only non-Indian elected by that church to be a bishop when it was founded just after World War II. Bishop Newbigin returned to Europe, and to Britain, in the 1970s after a lifelong ministry in India. It was in Britain that he discovered that what had been a "Christendom culture" when he had left years earlier for India was now no longer in place. Europe, and specifically the United Kingdom, had become a new mission field.

Western Christendom as a Mission Field

Newbigin began to ask the question, "If in fact we now live in the context of a mission field, how does the church located in that context become a missionary church?" How does this Western church, which has been privileged for a long time but now has been largely marginalized, readjust to a

---

1. See Darrell L. Guder et al., eds., *Missional Church: A Vision for the Sending of the Church in North America*, The Gospel and Our Culture Series (Grand Rapids: Eerdmans, 1998).

This essay is based upon a lecture given at the Lord's Day Alliance meeting at Princeton, September 13-14, 2005.

sense of "exile" within its own boundaries? After the loss of prestige, power, and the trappings of the authority of cultural occupation, this was the burning question before the church of the West, as Newbigin discerned it. It needs to be our question as well. It is an inquiry that arises out of the theological process surrounding the emergence of the ecumenical movement, going back to its formative event, the Edinburgh World Mission Conference of 1910.

This theological discussion has been gradually coming to terms with the fact that the seventeen-century project of what has been called Western "Christian culture," or "Christendom," or "the Constantinian church," was ending. As Kenneth Scott Latourette was writing his massive seven-volume work on the expansion of Christianity in the 1930s, he spoke about the disintegration of Western Christianity.[2] Many scholars of religion have picked up this theme in the century since 1910. Philip Jenkins summarized the process for the secular reading public in the West. His study of the "next Christendom" explores the significance of the massive demographic shifts in World Christianity as a movement that is increasingly more southern and Asian than northern and European or American.[3]

The North Atlantic cultures, which once formed the majority of Christendom, are now a minority of world Christianity, constituting about 35 percent of the world's Christian population. This demographic movement has engendered a complex, but fascinating and important discussion within the churches of the West about who we are and what our purpose might be. As a part of this process, it is increasingly recognized that to do a theology of the church that focuses only upon the church itself is very problematic. John's Gospel does not say that "God so loved those who have become card-carrying Protestants that He sent his only begotten Son"! Rather, the text says, "God so loved the world" — and it is *the world* which is the focus of the biblical witness. God's love for the world must not be reduced by translating that love merely into the preservation of particular institutions, traditions, or cultures. One of the missiologically significant things about the Pentecostal movement is that it reaches back to the book of the Acts of the Apostles, arguing that the gospel is to be translated into every culture and into every tongue, and that the Holy Spirit is given to the

---

2. Kenneth Scott Latourette, *A History of the Expansion of Christianity,* 7 vols. (New York: Harper & Brothers, 1945).

3. Philip Jenkins, *The Next Christendom: The Coming of Global Christianity,* rev. ed. (New York: Oxford University Press, 2007).

church to empower that translating witness. This is emphasized both in the Great Commission (Matt. 28:16-20) given by Jesus to his disciples and in the Pentecost experience of the earliest church (Acts 2). The followers of Jesus were to go into the world in order to disciple the "ethnicities." The gospel was to be brought to the distinctive cultural realities which are described as the "nations" — and we must be careful to avoid Christendom's distortion of the meaning of that term.

This rethinking of the gospel and the manner of its transmission has generated a shift away from a theology that focuses on the paradigm of a church as an end in itself to one that focuses on God's healing purposes for the world. In this way the church reclaims its proper task as God's chosen instrument, intimately related to the call of God upon Israel, for the healing intended for the whole world. We read that "God was reconciling the world to Himself in Christ" (2 Cor. 5:19), a reconciliation both between God and humanity and among the peoples in all of their ethnicities. This shift away from "ecclesiocentric mission" has been framed for many in the expanding discourse about the theology of the mission of God, the *missio Dei,* or "the sending of God."[4] The phrase, with its long and complex history, generally represents this shift away from church-centered theology and mission to gospel-centered theology and mission in which the church is God's called and chosen instrument for the accomplishment of God's saving purposes for the world.

Discussion among missiological students of Christianity in the West, particularly those under the influence of Newbigin, has coalesced in what is often described as the "Gospel and Culture" debate. It found concrete expression in North America beginning in 1988 with the formation of the Gospel and Our Culture Network. Lesslie Newbigin challenged a group of North American missiologists to engage the challenge of the gospel in the rapidly changing cultures of North America. They were encouraged to ask the question, "What are you going to do in North America about the fact

4. Mission, in this sense, is understood as being derived from the very nature of God. "God is by his very nature missionary" is a common way of putting it. The term, which began to emerge in (especially) the German missiological discussion from the 1930s onward, gained broad acceptance after the Willingen conference of the International Missionary Council in 1952. The idea that it can be traced back to Karl Barth (in his address to the Brandenburg Mission Conference of 1932) has been corrected by John Flett, who has shown that the language of the *missio Dei* from the 1950s on was an anti-Barthian interpretation of mission. See John G. Flett, *The Witness of God: The Trinity,* Missio Dei, *Karl Barth, and the Nature of Christian Community* (Grand Rapids: Eerdmans, 2010).

that America has become a mission field?"[5] The question has resonated in many contexts, including the Boston Theological Institute. Although the discussion takes place primarily at the level of fundamental theology, it clearly relates importantly to institutional and organizational factors such as the dramatic loss of members now common to all mainline churches. While church membership statistics may be superficial, they are important indicators of the changing character of our North American mission field. The Gospel and Culture questions have developed into a vibrant process moving now around the world. The World Council of Churches has been deeply involved in such issues, which are reshaping the understanding of mission in our world today.

Very instructive for this process is the growing concern in non-Western churches about the ways they engage their own cultures. While acknowledging their debt to the often self-sacrificial work of Western missionaries, they are challenging the cultural assumptions that often accompanied those mission efforts. As a particularly instructive example of ongoing contextualization, the African indigenous churches are translating the gospel and the church's missional vocation to be its witness into their own cultures in highly creative ways — and not without risks. An especially important protagonist of this process was the late Ghanaian theologian Kwame Bediako, who read the church fathers and drew them into the contemporary African experience without taking the detour through almost two millennia of Western Christianity. He noted how much closer the ancient patristic and modern African traditions are to each other than to the traditions of the churches of the North Atlantic world, or to those of Western Christendom.[6] Through those lenses, Western Christians are helped to recognize their own cultural captivity and, at the same time, to appreciate the essentially multicultural character of apostolic Christianity from the very beginning.

Within the North Atlantic community, the Gospel and Culture debate challenges the legacy of Christendom that has so profoundly shaped the Christian movement in the West today. Certainly the practice of Sunday as the Lord's Day is powerfully shaped by this history. A key emphasis in the

5. For the ongoing discussion within the Gospel and Our Culture Network, especially in its newsletters, see www.gocn.org. See also the *Gospel and Our Culture* volumes published as a series by Eerdmans Publishing Company.

6. Kwame Bediako, *Christianity in Africa: The Renewal of Non-Western Religion* (Maryknoll: Orbis Books, 1996); Bediako, *Theology and Identity: The Impact of Culture upon Christian Thought in the Second Century and in Modern Africa* (Oxford: Regnum Books, 1992).

Gospel and Culture discussion is to recognize how pervasive is the formative legacy of Christendom, and to do so both gratefully and critically. But we do so, knowing that we cannot address the missional challenge before us today as though there were no Christendom legacy. Nor can we pretend that this legacy is now or is rapidly becoming a closed chapter behind us. Although we now designate our years with the initials C.E. (for Christian Era), we do so knowing that for centuries we counted them *Anno Domini.*

Our approach to the Western Christian legacy must, therefore, be dialectical, neither a simplistic "yes" or "no." Christendom must be engaged in terms of its own ambivalence. It is a contradictory mixture of the divine and the human. Certainly Christians can neither claim nor act as though God had been absent from this history. Rather, we must testify that God has been faithful, regardless of how unfaithful we have been. We read our history in analogy to the long story of the children of Israel and their kings in the Old Testament, few of whom performed well in the eyes of the Lord. But if God was not served on the throne, his voice was heard through the prophets.

One of the most significant themes of this critical interaction with the Christendom legacy has to do with the theological place and importance of mission within Western theology. When we survey the history of theology through the centuries of Christendom, we are compelled to acknowledge that for over fifteen centuries we have done theologies of the church that never mention mission. Mission disappears from the theological language of Christendom at an early point. The reasons are complex, but it certainly had to do with the so-called "Christianization" of Europe, which generated the attitude that the task of mission had been completed. Everyone born within hearing range of church bells was, by virtue of birth and rearing, Christian. In that context, the central New Testament emphasis on mission largely disappeared from our theology. If we leap up to the nineteenth century at Princeton, we note that generation upon generation of Presbyterian graduates went out to the mission field, prepared to serve the gospel cause. Princeton's great theologian, Charles Hodge, was devoted to mission. He preached about mission in Miller Chapel. His sons went into foreign missions. Yet he wrote a three-volume systematic theology, which was a textbook at Princeton for years, in which the word "mission" never occurs. In this aspect, this three-volume systematic theology may be taken to represent the whole legacy of Western theological thought.

This is what we have to grapple with as we rethink and relearn a theology of mission that defines the very nature of the church, rather than at best one of its various functions. We have been so shaped by the mindset of Christendom, with its partnership of church and state and its assumption that our cultures were basically Christian, that we end up with a reductionistic understanding of the church's essence and purpose. Linked with that is an understanding of evangelism as church member recruiting. There is still a misconception at work in our churches that Christian identity is largely and effectively shaped in us by the cultural conditioning of our culture, so that evangelization is primarily about accepting Jesus and joining a church. God's mission is, of course, focused upon response to Christ's call to follow him as part of his people. But that call is about so much more than institutional identity and cultural cooperation. How the celebration of Sunday actually works in this cultural legacy is an instructive indicator of the missional reductionism which we inherit. If the church is truly "missionary by its very nature" (Vatican II), then our Sunday must be much more than a remnant of cultural Christianity.

Emerging Theology of the Ecumenical Missional Church

Out of this whole process is emerging a theology of the missional church. It is building upon the theology which was beginning to find its voice at the International Missionary Conference at Willingen in 1952, and which was also expressed in the doctrinal definitions of the Second Vatican Council. The brief Willingen declaration affirms mission as a movement generated and defined by the Triune God and centered upon the gracious reconciliation of all things to God's self. This is a theology of mission that is Christocentric and at the same time Trinitarian as it affirms the totality of God's reconciling work as Father, Son, and Holy Spirit.[7] The reforming council of the Roman Catholic Church, Vatican II (1962-1965), built its ecclesiology upon the basic conviction that "The pilgrim Church is missionary by her very nature."[8] Since Vatican II, the Roman Catholic Church has generated some of the most important missiological thinking among the Christian churches. This emerging theology of the missional church stresses, then, that the congregation, the particular community of believers in any particular place, is there because God has called and gathered it in

---

7. William Richebächer, "Willingen 1952–Willingen 2002: The Origin and Contents of This Edition of IRM," *International Review of Mission* 92, no. 367 (October 2003): 463-67.
8. *Decree on the Missionary Activity of the Church (Ad gentes)*, no. 2.

that place to be God's missional presence. This way of thinking about the church directly confronts attitudes and assumptions that are an obstacle to missional faithfulness. The congregation cannot be understood as the organizational result of people's drive to find an institution that will meet their religious needs. It cannot see itself as the franchise operation ensuring that there is a Presbyterian, Episcopal, Methodist, or Baptist voice in town. The congregation is evidence that God is faithful to God's purpose for all of creation, and that God calls into being the church as a called-out people to serve God's purpose in any given place.

Vatican II also makes it clear that the congregation is the primary unit of God's mission; it is the instrument and agent of God's Spirit for witness to God's love. This fundamental missional purpose of the congregation has enormous implications for the church and its practices, as well as for theological education for service in the church. Linked with this rethinking of the fundamental missional purpose of the congregation is the concentration upon the role of Scripture in such a community. How do we understand Scripture in relation to the missional calling of the church? How do we read Scripture properly if its Spirit-empowered task is to "equip the saints for the work of ministry" (Eph. 4:11)? What does it mean for our scriptural discipline today that the New Testament congregations understood themselves as missionary by their very nature? It was not the purpose or strategy of the first apostles to form congregations in particular places such as Corinth, Philippi, or Thessalonica, as secret societies to focus upon the salvation of their members and enjoy its benefits together. Paul went into Corinth or Philippi looking for the people God had prepared to become the community of witness to the gospel; and in response to their acknowledgment of Jesus Christ as Lord and Savior, he continued their formation to be such witnessing communities. And for this reason, he wrote to them: to continue the formation of such communities of witness so that they could be faithful to their missional calling.

When we start reading Scripture this way, using what we call a missional hermeneutic, fascinating things happen. In a course called "Missional Hermeneutics in Philippians," co-taught by my New Testament colleague, Ross Wagner, and me, we explore the missional reading of this Pauline epistle. Working with the Greek text, we ask, "How did this text, in Paul's mind and in the experience of that community, equip the Philippians to continue their faithful witness in Philippi? What did this text intend then? And how does it do that in our midst today?" How does any twenty-first-century congregation in North America encounter the apostolic word forming it for faithful witness as it engages the text? We experience, as we practice this hermeneutic, that indeed the purpose of the biblical text is the ongoing formation of the congregation toward its faithfulness to its missional vocation.

This missional conviction affects everything we do. Because we begin with missional vocation, everything that follows is profoundly reoriented. If evangelism has been member recruitment at best, and more often viewed as the "e-word" modern Protestants have difficulty saying, then we now understand that evangelization is the invitation to discipleship for the purpose of the apostolate. Evangelization is the invitation to respond to Jesus' own invitation to "follow me" (John 1:43) and "come and see" (John 1:46). It is not the goal but the initiation of the congregation's calling. Like Andrew and Philip in John's Gospel, those who are called immediately become those who are sent, as they reach out to Simon Peter and Nathanael. For the students in a seminary, this means that they should realize that they are not merely preparing for ministry but are already engaged in it. All discipleship must flow into apostolate, if missional vocation is properly understood and practiced.

It should be obvious that such a missional approach to the theology of the church and its practice will have consequences for the patterns of thought and conduct inherited from Christendom. That reductionism or even removal of mission must be contested. Simplistic equations of cultural identity and Christian vocation must be corrected. One is not a Christian because of the geography of one's birth! To be attentive to Christian works is not to labor away at works that will save us, but to carry out the vocation of witness: "You shall be my witnesses" (Acts 1:8) means that we shall be about doing as well as saying witness. The false dichotomy between the enjoyment of the benefits of knowing and following Christ and the calling to serve him as his witnesses will have to be rejected. In the early Christian churches of the first four or five centuries, becoming a follower of Jesus Christ meant going to school, after the patterns of Jesus' disciples who became his students. It was called catechesis, and it lasted one, two, three years, concluding with the celebration of baptism. This did not imply that the catechumen was not a Christian until she or he was baptized. Rather, it was understood that God was already working in a person's life long before one responded, and that response needed to take the form of disciplined catechetical formation leading to baptism. Baptism meant that one was incorporated into the Eucharistic Community, gathered around Jesus in order to be prepared and sent by Jesus as his witnesses in the world. All of this was rooted in the recognition that vocation costs something. It could mean that a person did not quite fit into her or his culture anymore. It could mean the risking of life: the word "witness" means, after all, "martyr."

Clearly, we have a complex fabric of cultural compromises that have shaped us over the years with which we must now deal. We have to engage our cultural presuppositions in order to understand both the faithfulness of God and our wandering ways which require continuing conversion. At this point I am much influenced by the theologian Karl Barth, who reminds us that it is necessary to be modest in the way in which we go about doing our theology. We have been persuaded for so long in the West that our theology is normative theology and that the rest of the world ought to follow our example. However, we are gradually learning that we, like all others, are very conditioned by our own cultural process. We have been wearing our own blinders, and we have some deeply rooted misunderstandings.

To put it in theological terms, we need a profoundly eschatological understanding of who we are and what we are doing. This is the place in which we find ourselves, but we are not simply standing in this place. We are moving along a pathway, a pilgrimage, and the entire event is defined by the outcome, which, because of God's promises, is certain. The story is not over yet: "He who has begun a good work in you will complete it in the day of Jesus Christ" (Phil. 1:6). Therefore our life and our ministry are characterized by our waiting upon the Lord, by growing and often tested faithfulness, by perseverance, and by patience. This is not a repristinization of early Christianity. It is not my understanding of the challenge we face that we should return to the situation, structures, or conditions of the early church. We cannot retreat to a pre-Constantinian refuge.

I am not arguing for a return to anything. In fact, I have become a little bit suspicious of that little prefix "re": re-newal, re-turn, re-born, etc. There is a suggestion in these terms that we need to go back to something. I do not think that in terms of the New Testament we ever go "back" to anything. What I am saying is that we must hear again, and we must lay claim to, the missional vocation and self-understanding of the early church. There are many obstacles to doing so because of all the intervening layers of practice, attitudes, and conformities that the Constantinian project has engendered, all of it suffused with our sense of being privileged in the world's order because we are Christians. We have to lay claim to this fundamental missional understanding of every congregation, that each congregation is called to be light and leaven and salt. Every congregation is described by Paul's words to the Corinthians, "You are Christ's letter to the world" (2 Cor. 3:1-3).

It is to this calling that every congregation is summoned. Each community is to live its life worthy of the calling with which it is called — an overarching theme of the Pauline epistles (e.g., Eph. 4:1). Missional theology is discovering in patristic theology, in early Christian catecheses, in the struggles of the early church with the religious pluralism of its day, resources for what we face in the West today. What kind of a world was the first-century church living in? What kinds of claims were they making in that world? Religious pluralism is not a novelty for the apostolic church! The fact that we now have temples and mosques down the street is simply putting us into a situation very like that of early Christians trying to decide how to live the life of faith amidst many challenges. Missional thinking is not a novelty so much as a call to the earliest understanding of the church's purpose and the practices that form it for that purpose.

Missional Thinking and the Practice of the Lord's Day

How we apply missional thinking to the Sabbath as the Lord's Day is of vital importance. The Lord's Day is a primary test case for the church's missional vocation. Let me illustrate this with a few comments about the significance of missional theology for the theology and practice of the Lord's Day.

The biblical discipline of reserving one-seventh of our time for Sabbath purposes is a fundamental pattern, discerned throughout the Jewish and Christian Scriptures, for the formation of God's people for their calling. There is a profound missional functionalism in the discipline of the seventh day. Its import can be seen in diverse ways. The fact that Christians gather is certainly a form of public witness. The gathered Christian community is not a secret society, not a devotee of arcane practices closed off from the surrounding world. It is to be light that is not set under a bushel. It is, to repeat a point made by Paul in 2 Corinthians, to be Christ's letter to the world. This can be illustrated today in much of the non-Western church. There are wonderful accounts about churches being formed in villages in Africa. The Christian community gathers in a public place in the village, where it sets up a simple roofed shelter — a framework of branches and poles, and a roof of palm leaves. The Christians gather in a church without walls, fully visible to anyone who chooses to watch. And many do gather and watch. This visible and audible witness results in a gradual movement of observers into participants, as villagers come under the roof to become a part of this publicly worshiping community. The act of public worship is an event with evangelistic impact.

Complementary to the understanding of gathered worship as public witness is the formative importance of the Sabbath for our vocation and mission. Building on the pervasive Old Testament emphasis upon Israel's vocation as witness, and expounding the New Testament's emphasis upon the expansion of that witness to the whole world, we can recognize that the observance of the seventh day is God's gift for our formation for our missional vocation on the other six days. We cannot be about our mission if we are not in a process of discipline and formation. Discipleship is a way of talking about how we are formed together to serve Christ's calling, and the model for this is in the synoptic Gospels, Matthew, Mark, and Luke. Jesus calls disciples. Disciples are those who go to school with Jesus, originally according to the model of rabbinic formation in first-century Palestine. In fact, in the New Testament world of the rabbi, disciples lived with their rabbi twenty-four hours a day; they memorized everything he said, and they watched everything he did, and they learned him and his message.

Jesus' disciples are immediately engaged in his vocation. He sends them out. Throughout the Gospels we find stories of Jesus sending out the disciples to test their vocation. Discipleship is a biblical way of talking about the gathering of the church; it defines what we are for and what we are to do when we gather. In Mark 3:13 we read the account of the calling of the Twelve, where the Gospel writer notes that Jesus also defined the Twelve as apostles. This is an important missional gloss. Discipleship was not an end in itself; the disciples were not drawn to Jesus to meet their own religious needs. Their formation was for their mission: they were discipled in order to be sent out, that is, to be apostles. This fundamental movement from discipleship to apostolate defines the significance of the seventh day for the missional community. The seventh day is the necessary time of public and disciplined practice of being with Jesus so that we can be sent by him. As the gathered community encountering Christ in our midst, we are enabled to embark upon and engage in the apostolate which is our purpose. Gathered worship is rightly the central and orienting focus of the congregation, not as an end in itself, but as God's divine enabling for the missional vocation which is the purpose of the Christian life, both corporately and personally. It is God's way of continuing our formation, week by week, for mission.

The early church understood that. Why did the early church adopt the practice of a Gospel text for every Sunday — a practice continued in many liturgical traditions? The church must be evangelized every Sunday to be sent out. The ancient liturgy ended with the priest's charge: *Ita, missa est.* "Go, thou art sent." As we think through the character and the meaning of the seventh day, we might also find it helpful, building on Reformed understandings of the Lord's Supper, to understand the table sacrament as Christ's encounter with his people to equip them for his mission.

Sacramental theology and practice can truly be developed in terms of missional formation. In the language of *Baptism, Eucharist and Ministry,* our baptism is our general ordination to Christ's service.[9] Baptism is the church's celebration of God's faithfulness in building his community to continue its witness, one by one. By grounding baptism in this missional understanding, we see in a fresh way why baptisms take place in the gathered community and on the Lord's Day. They must be a part of Sabbath because they reconfirm constantly our common vocation. Baptism defines the missional vocation of the community, and the encounter with the Risen Lord at his table continually implements that calling through his giving of himself, the equipping power of his word proclaimed, and the hearing and responding of the community to his apostolic charge.

It is, then, a particular and difficult challenge to pursue this missional thinking with regard to the theology and practice of *ordered ministry.* From a missional perspective, one of the most problematic outcomes of the complex history of Christendom is the clergy/lay distinction — my Reformed convictions become very visible at this point. We Presbyterians in North America have, I think, lost something important by replacing the term "teaching elder" to define ordained or ordered ministry with the phrase "minister of word and sacrament." It is encouraging to note that there is a growing discussion about this theme within our confessional family. We need to address the Ephesian emphasis (4:11ff.) that certain "ministers of the word" ("apostle, prophets, evangelists, teaching-pastors") are Christ's gift to the church "to equip the saints for the work of ministry."

In the understanding of missional vocation, the priority is placed upon the whole community; for that purpose there are to be apostolic,

9. World Council of Churches, *Baptism, Eucharist and Ministry* (Geneva: WCC Publications, 1982).

prophetic, evangelistic, pastoral, and teaching ministers of the Word — all of whom together are needed to equip the saints for the work of ministry. It is intriguing that one cannot find in Karl Barth's massive *Church Dogmatics* a fully developed theology of ordained office. There is discussion of the "ordering of the community," and clearly there is a concern for qualified and responsible proclamation and teaching. At one very interesting point he discusses the importance of mentors and models, where he is reclaiming the rabbinic formation that characterized Jesus' own life and ministry.

As we continue working with missional theology, we will need to focus more and more on a missional redefinition of ministry. This might imply that the test of any congregation's missional faithfulness is the way in which all of its members leave every Sabbath day knowing that they are bearing one of those little "Pentecost" flames on their head; that every one is an apostolic witness. The lay apostolate is the test of our gathered Sabbath practice. If we understand a seventh of our time as God's gift for our formation, so that we can be sent out in the world to practice the life of witness and return to our gathering for ongoing formation for our sending, then we may be moving closer to our true calling of discipleship and apostolate. In that Pentecostal rhythm the Lord's Day will play the central and defining role.

Social Integrity

Readers will have recognized that the authors who have written on Sabbath/Sunday are not limited by their subject matter to some historical events whose passing we might rue or regret. No, Sunday observance is a theme that has many contemporary connections with the pressing problems of our day: How do we organize our lives together (with emphasis on "together") in ways that are healthy and hopeful? Where does Sabbath rest fit in with the contemporary pace of life? How do we incorporate respect for the environment into a way of life that sustains us as we try to sustain the environment? Can the American imagination find place for a common rhythm of rest and work or are we doomed to fragmented and isolated contacts with each other?

Certain ideas or themes come up again and again as writers examine American culture and the Sabbath rest: common good; social integration; common day of rest; not an individualistic matter, but a shared social good. In this last section of the book, the authors explore contemporary ideas about how extensive the influence of Sabbath/Sunday is in our culture and propose further ways to show how rest and responsibility can be expanded. Alexis McCrossen challenges the overly individualized and commercialized Sunday as it is practiced in the United States and proposes a "remaking" of Sunday, one that helps us "escape the limits of selfish individualism and market capitalism." In a similar way, Thomas Massaro argues for a greater respect for Sabbath to sensitize Americans to the dangers of overwork and its consequences.

Ruy Costa asks whether there is an alternative future for the Sabbath. He argues that Sabbath keeping represents an alternative way of life, which does not chime in with the dominant values of the culture. Starting with the biblical tradition of Sabbath, Costa demonstrates how such an alternative is not merely opting for cultural oddity, but embracing a profound change of perspective, at once personal and communal, that will itself change the culture. Aida Spencer reinforces this line of thinking by providing direction, for both the individual and the community, taken from Jesus' reformulation of Sabbath regulations as they appear in the New Testament.

Finally, Donald Conroy shows how the different faith traditions can come together to address environmental issues in global society, an idea connected with Sabbath, or Sunday as Sabbath, that has practical consequences but may not be immediately obvious to all. Reprising some ideas from Pope John Paul II's *Dies Domini,* he offers practical considerations for cooperation of the churches in protecting the environment.

The conversation continues. Many more voices are here to be heard.

CHAPTER NINE

"That Sunday Feeling":
Sundays in the United States

Alexis McCrossen

In 1891 the New York publishing house Charles Scribner's Sons released *The Sabbath in Puritan New England*. In this book Alice Morse Earle lovingly describes the Puritan Sabbath. She begins with the sounding of horns and drums to announce Sabbath-morning meetings. Then she pictures hordes of Puritans who took loaded guns with them to church each Sunday, intent on killing Indians or wolves should either interfere with worship. Several chapters depict entire communities seated on hard, backless church benches in "icy cold meeting houses." In one of these chapters Earle quotes a Puritan magistrate's (Judge Sewall) observation about administering the Lord's Supper one winter Sunday: "The communion bread was frozen pretty hard and rattled sadly into the plates."[1] A chapter titled "The Length of the Service" tells us that it was unending. Earle delighted in what she called "the most grotesque, the most extraordinary, the most highly colored figure in the dull New England church-life, the tithingman."[2] His job was to rouse parishioners who dozed off, punish rowdy boys, chase away dogs who wandered into the sanctuary, and enforce the blue laws at all times.

After describing the tithingman, the deacon, and the minister at some length, Earle decries the reports of atrocious singing by Puritan congregations, who did not have the benefit of hymnals, music directors, or professional choirs and therefore, according to her account at least, could not carry a tune. Earle's tribute to the Puritan Sabbath ends with a charge to her contemporaries:

1. Alice Morse Earle, *The Sabbath in Puritan New England* (New York: Charles Scribner's Sons, 1891), p. 85.
2. Earle, *The Sabbath in Puritan New England*, p. 60.

Patient, frugal, God-fearing, and industrious, cruel and intolerant sometimes, but never cowardly, sternly obeying the word of God in the spirit and the letter, but erring sometimes in the interpretation thereof, — surely they had no traits to shame us, to keep us from thrilling with pride at the drop of their blood which runs in our backsliding veins. Nothing can more plainly show their distinguishing characteristics, nothing is so fully typical of the motive, the spirit of their lives, as their reverent observance of the Lord's day.[3]

This reverence for the Sabbath, and the accompanying nostalgia for earlier, simpler times, also inspired the founders of the Lord's Day Alliance (LDA) several years earlier.[4]

When the LDA formed in 1888, there was extensive conflict over the meaning and observance of Sunday. Defenders of the Sunday-Sabbath — or the Puritan Sabbath as it was known — called for federal troops to protect the day from desecration. Politicians won and lost elections based on their position on the "Sunday question." Waves of immigrants populating American cities brought their own brands of Sunday observance, which included drinking beer, playing baseball, and reading sports pages. Entertainment impresarios opened their venues, thus transforming Sunday from a day of rest into a day of profit.[5] As contemporaries noted with shame, the dollar mark had been irrevocably imprinted upon Sunday. Unlike Earle's idealized vision of Puritan New England, Sabbath had become but one of the many meanings for Sunday.

The LDA and other Sabbatarian organizations believed the Sunday-Sabbath symbolized civilization. They hoped that Sunday observance would cultivate and protect liberty and other conditions necessary for democracy. It provided time for people to renew themselves, tend to the virtues necessary for good citizenship, and reaffirm membership in families and churches. A healthy nation needed its citizens to attend to each of these duties. Prominent among those who sought to remind Americans of their duty to observe Sunday as the Sabbath were Sabbatarians. Despite losing some political battles (in particular one concerning the transportation and delivery of mail on Sunday), these self-proclaimed protectors of

---

3. Earle, *The Sabbath in Puritan New England*, p. 327.

4. I point to the nostalgic impulses of Sabbatarians in *Holy Day, Holiday: The American Sunday* (Ithaca, NY: Cornell University Press, 2000), pp. 34-37.

5. McCrossen, *Holy Day, Holiday*, pp. 93-110.

the Sunday-Sabbath faced little opposition throughout most of the century.[6] However, by the 1890s approaches to Sunday varied dramatically. Many American held fast to Sunday, for it was the day of rest, mandated by both law and custom, and much needed after six long days of mostly arduous work. But blue laws were under assault, and what it meant to rest itself was under revision. Most Americans wanted to keep Sunday separate from the workweek, but they desired the liberty to do with it what they would.

And so, within this context, Earle's *The Sabbath in Puritan New England* was more than a history of Sunday in an earlier time. It was a missive, a political tract, and a call to action. It sided with those who would fashion the American Sunday into a day for church, and more church, a day of tithingmen and tuneless psalm singing, and little else. As should now be clear more than a century later, Earle and her allies, including the LDA, failed in their mission. They could not stem the tide of change. They could not prevent the opening up of Sunday to secular forces. Nor could they fashion one definition of rest that would have suited all the citizens across the nation. None could have, for the nation itself was undergoing rampant and unprecedented economic, social, and political transformation. It would become industrialized, urbanized, and atomized by the 1920s, despite the resistance of millions of Americans, motivated by a wide array of commitments.

A nation as diverse as the United States is held together by shared economic activities — work, consumption, even taxes. For several centuries common respite from marketplace pressures in the form of Sunday rest also held families, communities, and the nation together. Nevertheless, there was often a great deal of conflict over styles of Sunday observance: one man's form of rest was another man's vision of blasphemy. Because of

6. About Sabbatarianism in the United States during the nineteenth century see Alexis McCrossen, "Sabbatarianism: The Intersection of Church and State in the Orchestration of Everyday Life in Nineteenth-Century America," in *Religious and Secular Reform in America: Ideas, Beliefs and Social Change,* ed. David K. Adams and Cornelis A. Van Minnen (Edinburgh: Edinburgh University Press, 1999). For a history of Sabbatarianism that includes references to instances of it outside of the United States, see Alexis McCrossen, "Sabbatarianism," in *Encyclopedia of Protestantism,* ed. Hans Hillebrand (New York: Routledge Press, 2003). Concerning the Sunday mails conflict, see Richard John, "Taking Sabbatarianism Seriously: The Postal System, the Sabbath, and the Transformation of American Political Culture," *Journal of the Early Republic* 10 (1990): 517-67; James Rohrer, "Sunday Mails and the Church-State Theme in Jacksonian America," *Journal of the Early Republic* 7 (1987): 54-74; and Bertram Wyatt-Brown, "Prelude to Abolitionism: Sabbatarian Politics and the Rise of the Second Party System," *Journal of American History* 58 (1971): 316-40.

the investment Americans had in the differentiation of time between *work* and *rest* — and because of a deep-seated fear of *idleness* — they fought endlessly in public and private over Sunday. That idleness threatened the health of the nation was a very old theme. Work was at the heart of efforts to "redeem the time": many believed that Sunday was the only day when it was safe to cease working, since its attendant religious duties precluded idleness.

Until the mid-twentieth century, most agreed that Sunday ought to be set aside from work, reserved for worship, rest, and recreation. This provision for Sunday as a unique and privileged day in the weekly calendar was written into civil law. However (as with all laws concerning values), religious, ethnic, and individual practices shaped the interpretation and enforcement of the blue laws. Neither in the seventeenth century nor today in our own time have all members of the American community assented to "blue laws."[7] Differences of opinion about how best to spend Sunday eventually undermined consensus about the day. A wide variety of groups entered into these debates — above all, Protestants, Catholics, and Jews. In doing so, they expressed beliefs about the right use of time. During the twentieth century, Sunday's status as a common day of rest was sacrificed to the market and to democratic individualism. Many Americans came to find their rest in the rides and games of Coney Island, in the world of spectator sports, and in countless other activities that were above and beyond the mundane, but neither sacred nor profane.

Today, Sunday is a hybrid of religiosity, recreation, and recovery from the night before. Many Americans work on Sundays; supermarkets are open; trains run; and 1-800 operators are standing by. Yet for most of us, the day still *feels* different from the rest of the week. For some it is a day of pressed clothes and fine hats; for others it is the only day of the week they don't shave. Sadly, for many Americans Sunday is, as F. Scott Fitzgerald put it some time ago, "not a day — but rather a gap between two other days."[8] This essay sketches out how Sunday has come to feel as it does in contemporary American life. It is animated by concerns about the organization of daily life, about the apparent dominance of an unhealthy work ethic, and about the disintegration of community. A great variety of conditions

7. Winton Solberg's history of Sunday in the colonial period makes this point evident: *Redeem the Time: The Puritan Sabbath in Early America* (Cambridge: Harvard University Press, 1977).

8. F. Scott Fitzgerald, "Crazy Sunday," reprinted in *Babylon Revisited and Other Stories* (New York: Charles Scribner's Sons, 1960). The story was originally published in 1932.

prompted the changing nature of Sunday observance, but this essay addresses three key developments: the changing relationship between work, rest, and leisure; the rise of individualism; and the obsession with play, especially in the form of organized sporting events. The commercialization of everyday life and of the meaning of life itself is at the root of each condition, as it is at the root of Sunday's transformation during the twentieth century. Ironically, however, it at once has enabled Sunday to remain a vibrant and special day for many Americans and at the same time has caused the diminishment of many aspects of Sunday which earlier generations of Americans cherished.

Work, Rest, and Leisure

The shortening of workweeks and workdays provided other times to rest than Sunday. Sunday thus lost its privileged status as *the day of rest*. "Leisure" replaced "rest" as the opposite of "work."[9] There was a time, not so long ago to have slipped from living memory, when each Sunday most restaurants were closed, students did not do their homework, and businessmen put their ledgers away. If we move a little deeper into history, into the antebellum era, we see that most domestic servants refused to work on Sunday, that fields lay untended, and that even slaves were given a day of rest. After the Civil War, legal, religious, and social bans against Sunday labor began to fade, victim to the logic of continuous manufacture, rising standards of living, and increased disaffection between capital and labor.[10] Even today Sunday labor is often privileged: those who work for wages are promised double-overtime for Sunday shifts, and salaried workers, while not monetarily compensated, do get "points" for showing up on Sunday. Despite our overwhelming sense that we are working too hard, it is un-

9. Concerning the shortening of the length of the workweek and workday, see David R. Roediger and Philip S. Foner, *Our Own Time: A History of American Labor and the Working Day* (New York: Verso, 1989); Benjamin Kline Hunnicutt, *Work without End: Abandoning Shorter Hours for the Right to Work* (Philadelphia: Temple University Press, 1988); Benjamin Kline Hunnicutt, *Kellogg's Six-Hour Day* (Philadelphia: Temple University Press, 1996). Concerning the relationship between work, rest, and leisure, see McCrossen, *Holy Day, Holiday,* pp. 8-20, 137-51.

10. One of the central purposes of *Holy Day, Holiday* is to address the rising tide of paid labor on Sunday. See especially chapters 1, 7, and 9, each of which details changing attitudes and needs for Sunday work.

likely that Americans could return to Sunday as a day of rest, even if they wanted to do so.

Let's take Sunday travel as an example of the disintegration of bans against Sunday work, and of the difficulty of returning to an earlier time when Sunday work was performed infrequently. Today, with an almost mandatory Saturday-night layover on most domestic flights, a good number of Americans travel on Sunday. There was a time when Sunday travel was nearly impossible, and avoided if at all possible. It was believed that God would punish the Sunday traveler with a gruesome accident, and American courts often upheld this theory by refusing judgments in favor of passengers (or their families) who were injured while traveling in steamboats or on trains on Sunday.[11] But, as Americans became more and more geographically mobile, bans against Sunday travel began to disintegrate.

The westward movement provides an excellent set of examples and stories. The historian Winton Solberg has detailed the observance of the Sabbath on the Overland Trail. He divided pioneers into three groups — those who wanted to, but did not, stop traveling each Sunday; those who did not want to stop each Sunday; and those who did stop each Sunday in an effort to observe the Sabbath. Many pioneers "regretted the necessity of traveling" on Sunday, but could find no alternative, since more than two thousand miles had to be crossed by wooden-wheeled wagons before the snows fell on the Sierra Nevada mountain range. Their diaries are replete with descriptions of efforts to observe the Sabbath, disagreements within caravans over the question of Sunday travel, and, as the trail became more and more arduous, the gradual breakdown of regard for Sunday.[12]

Visitors and settlers who went west by sea faced interminable months of voyage, during which they had to negotiate with the others on board about how to observe Sunday. Some sailors wrote in their diaries, "today is

---

11. McCrossen, *Holy Day, Holiday,* pp. 36-37, 86. For details about American case law which upheld judgments against passengers injured while traveling on Sunday, see George E. Harris, *A Treatise on Sunday Laws* (Rochester, NY: The Lawyers' Co-operative, 1892), pp. 185, 188, 193-99.

12. For historical accounts about westward migration and the observance of Sunday, see Winton Solberg, "The Sabbath on the Overland Trail to California," *Church History* 59 (1990): 340-55; McCrossen, *Holy Day, Holiday,* pp. 39-41. Diaries that include accounts concerning Sunday travel on the Overland Trail include the diary of Mary Parkhurst Warner, 1864 (Bancroft Library, University of California at Berkeley); the diary of P. F. Castleman, 1849 (Bancroft Library, University of California at Berkeley); and the diary of E. A. Spooner, 1849 (Kansas State Historical Society).

the day of rest," and kept it as such. Others took the opportunity to carouse or continued to work apace. Not all passengers found themselves on ships where Sunday was "known by the improved appearance of all on board." Some found Sunday at sea dismal for the lack of divine services and the excess of noise. Many passengers, faced with unending days of rest during the voyage, sought to sanctify the day in sartorial, ritual, and gastronomic gestures.[13]

By the time the railroad took visitors and settlers west, it had been agreed that trains would run on Sunday. A great deal of resistance and debate preceded this consensus. A variety of railroad companies voluntarily shut down on Sundays. Others ran regular schedules, taking more passengers on excursions on Sundays than on any other day of the week. During the 1890s, controversy migrated to the issue of running streetcars on Sunday.[14] By the twentieth century, some localities attempted to prevent automobile travel by preventing gas stations from opening on Sundays, but these efforts were soon abandoned.[15] The individual freedom that the automobile granted practically eradicated biases against Sunday travel. So, as should be clear from this brief history of the disintegration of a variety of bans against Sunday travel, the territorial, economic, and technological growth of the United States was inescapable, even within the realm of what was considered "sacred."

In the decades after the Civil War, state legislatures and courts responded to these pressures on the community and on Sunday by amending state laws to accommodate the recreation and rest needs of the community. Blue laws had remarkable staying power. But by World War II, state legislatures and local boards began to repeal, amend, and ignore blue laws altogether. The late-1950s saw a revival of interest in Sunday laws, such that scores of storeowners and others who had violated them for decades were arrested and faced trial. In 1961, Supreme Court Justice Felix Frankfurter cogently and thoroughly traced the origin of Sunday laws to religious roots. He held that these laws evolved to serve a range of community needs, and therefore should stand. Frankfurter argued that Sunday was

13. The diary of Gilbert Patten Allen (Bancroft Library, University of California at Berkeley), entry dated Sunday, April 10, 1864; the diary of Anne W. Booth (Bancroft Library, University of California at Berkeley), entry dated Sunday, April 28, 1849. About Sunday observance aboard ships, see Alexis McCrossen, "Sunday: Marker of Time, Setting of Memory," *Time and Society* 14 (March 2005): 25-38.

14. McCrossen, *Holy Day, Holiday*, pp. 80-87.

15. McCrossen, *Holy Day, Holiday*, pp. 90-92.

necessary for strengthening the home, which was at the core of communal health. Ultimately, using almost mystical language, he referred to the "special things" that Sunday rest provides, suggesting that twenty-four-hour rest provisions could only supplement Sunday laws, not replace them. With one exception, the other Supreme Court justices agreed with Frankfurter, upholding the constitutionality of Sunday laws in a landmark decision on a series of cases grouped under *McGowan v. Maryland*.[16] Despite this finding, most states allowed their blue laws to lapse during the last third of the twentieth century.

Individualism

Since the seventeenth century, Americans have tried to set Sunday apart from everyday experiences. Contemporary Americans express few opinions about what the day should feel like, yet in our practices we express an inaudible and indelible desire for a day set aside from the market and from selfish individualism. Our efforts, and those of our predecessors, have involved a complicated set of individual, institutional, and community initiatives. As we have seen, what Sunday should feel like has been under constant revision in the hands of theologians and lawmakers. Cultural and commercial institutions have also influenced our approach to Sunday, offering "special" attractions, such as matinee performances of operas and ballets and all-day Super Bowl coverage. We define Sunday today largely in individual terms, thinking about what we as individuals would like to "get out" of the day.

Such individualism did not always characterize Sunday. During the colonial period the entire community was included in church services, an inclusion that was often coerced by fines, tithingmen, and other forms of social control. Moving into the nineteenth and twentieth centuries, Sunday services of some of the frontier churches, most African-American churches, street-front churches, and televised churches all sought to form and hold together communities. Religious services provided a common focus and purpose for the day, giving men, women, and children an opportunity to put on their "Sunday best," see and be seen, and participate in a potentially affirming set of rituals in a holy space.

16. *McGowan v. Maryland*, 366 U.S. 420 (1961). About this case, see McCrossen, *Holy Day, Holiday*, pp. 107-8; Alexis McCrossen, "Neither Holy Day nor Holiday: Sunday in the 1960s," *Southwest Review* 82 (1997): 366-81.

The modern ideal of Sunday as a day to be passed, partially at least, in the home has its roots in the nineteenth century's reorganization of time, work, and domestic relations. For many Americans, Sunday in the home involved a cold dinner, stern parental demeanors, and restless children. In between three church services and Sunday school, the home was simply a place to rest, to take Scripture to heart, and to anticipate six more days of labor. During the Victorian era, Sunday came to be divided between devotions to God and family. The "domestic Sabbath" emerged as an alternative and a supplement to Sunday in the pew.[17]

To further illustrate the development of the domestic Sabbath, we should consider two prominent Victorian American families' home Sundays. The Beechers and Bancrofts each spent Sunday in different ways. Yet each family's approach to and internal conflict over the day stands for some of the larger trends in the development of the domestic Sabbath.

Lyman Beecher, one of the first Sabbatarian leaders and a powerful figure in American Protestantism, was the patriarch of a New England family that included Catherine Beecher (of *American Woman's Home* fame), Harriet Beecher Stowe (literary spokeswoman for sentimental Protestantism), and Henry Ward Beecher (libertine and liberalizer of Protestantism). Lyman maintained a strict Sunday centered on the church and the church alone.[18] His children, however, envisioned Sunday as a time for

17. About Sunday in the home, see McCrossen, *Holy Day, Holiday,* pp. 111-36. For more about domesticity and religion in the nineteenth century, see Colleen McDannell, *The Christian Home in Victorian America, 1840-1900* (Bloomington: Indiana University Press, 1986, 1994); Ann Taves, *The Household of Faith* (Notre Dame: University of Notre Dame Press, 1986); and James H. Smylie, "'Of Secret and Family Worship': Historical Meditations, 1875-1975," *Journal of Presbyterian History* 58 (1980): 95-115. Concerning family amusements and recreations, see Donna R. Braden, "'The Family That Plays Together Stays Together': Family Pastimes and Indoor Amusements, 1890-1930," in *American Home Life, 1880-1930,* ed. Jessica H. Foy and Thomas J. Schlereth (Knoxville: University of Tennessee Press, 1992), pp. 145-61.

18. Lyman Beecher played an important role in the antebellum conflict over the delivery of the mails on Sunday, publishing two pieces meant to sway opinion against such an activity. Lyman Beecher, "Pre-Eminent Importance of the Christian Sabbath," *The National Preacher* 3 (1829): 155-60; Lyman Beecher, "Mr. Johnson's Report on Sabbath Mails," *The Spirit of the Pilgrims* 2 (1829): 143-44. The literature about Lyman Beecher and his family is extensive and includes the following: Milton Rugoff, *The Beechers: An American Family in the Nineteenth Century* (New York: Harper and Row, 1981); Vincent Harding, *A Certain Magnificence: Lyman Beecher and the Transformation of American Protestantism, 1775-1863* (Brooklyn, NY: Carlson, 1991); Stephen H. Snyder, *Lyman Beecher and His Children: The Transformation of a Religious Tradition* (Brooklyn, NY: Carlson, 1991); and James W. Fraser,

the reaffirmation and strengthening of domestic ties. Harriet popularized special Sunday toys, liberating children from straight-backed chairs and unending silence.[19] Henry Ward Beecher advocated that parks, libraries, reading rooms, and museums be opened on Sundays so as to spread the gospel of culture.[20] The Beechers' story highlights the cross-generational tensions that erupted as Sundays spent outside of the confines of the church and the family came into vogue.

Across the continent, another prominent nineteenth-century American family negotiated the tensions encircling Sunday. Henry Howe Bancroft, an entrepreneur living in California after the Civil War, used Sunday to catch up on business matters, ride, hunt, water his orange trees, and carouse with friends. He did not think much of Sunday one way or the other. His wife, Matilda, on the other hand, firmly believed in a Sunday spent in church, at Sunday school, around the dinner table, and then in pious reading. Their differences deeply influenced their four children, who kept diaries during their childhood. The three sons resented their mother's efforts to impose a "New England Sabbath" on them. They preferred a California sort of Sunday, complete with swimming and scouting. The only daughter, Lucy, shared her brothers' irreverence for the day. She dreaded the times when the family left its farm near San Diego for San Francisco and settled into a routine of Sunday school, church services, and family repose. The Bancrofts rejected a religiously oriented Sunday in favor of a recreational Sunday, much to their mother's distress.[21]

Pedagogue for God's Kingdom: Lyman Beecher and the Second Great Awakening (Lanham, MD: University Press of America, 1985).

19. Harriet Beecher Stowe wrote a great many sketches and short stories concerning Sunday, including the following: "The Sabbath: Sketches from the Note-Book of an Elderly Gentleman" (1843), reprinted in volume 15 of *The Writings of Harriet Beecher Stowe* (New York: AMS Press, 1967); "The Old Meeting-House" (1843), reprinted in volume 15 of *The Writings of Harriet Beecher Stowe;* "Home Religion" (1865), reprinted in volume 1 of *The Writings of Harriet Beecher Stowe; Oldtown Folks,* vol. 1 (1869), reprinted in volume 9 of *The Writings of Harriet Beecher Stowe.*

20. Henry Ward Beecher, *Libraries and Public Reading Rooms: Should They Be Opened on Sunday?* (New York: J. B. Ford, 1872). About Henry Ward Beecher and liberal Protestantism, see Clifford E. Clark, *Henry Ward Beecher: Spokesman for a Middle-Class America* (Urbana: University of Illinois Press, 1978); William G. McLoughlin, *The Meaning of Henry Ward Beecher: An Essay on the Shifting Values of Mid-Victorian America* (New York: Knopf, 1970).

21. The diaries of the Bancroft family are kept in the Hubert Howe Bancroft Collection at the Bancroft Library, University of California at Berkeley. Hubert Howe Bancroft's memoirs

Americans Learn How to Play

It was the Bancrofts rather than the Beechers who set the pattern for Sunday that the majority of Americans have followed. To be sure, Americans attend church, some joyfully, others resentfully, most simply dutifully. But our delight is in recreation, the outdoors, and organized sports. Sunday, however, has not always been a sporting day. In fact until the 1930s the bans were quite strong against Sunday sport, especially professional sport. Nevertheless, during the late part of the nineteenth century a broad group of reformers determined that recreation provided a more meaningful and lasting kind of rest than simple repose. The devoted Christians among them promoted what was called "muscular Christianity." Some Protestants discovered that one could commune with God in the outdoors, while at play, on a bicycle, or even at the putting green. The only limit they placed on Sunday sports was that they remain within the world of the amateur. Even during their time this was largely an idealistic and unrealistic vision.[22]

This dramatic change in attitude toward sport, the body, and play was made possible in part by the blurring of stark differences between holy and profane that had animated Protestantism for centuries. Undergoing a process that historians have labeled "sacralization," activities, such as dancing or reading fiction, which had once been condemned as sinful gained new legitimacy. It is important to caution, however, that mutation does not mean destruction: going to church on Sunday certainly persevered.[23]

---

are instructive; see *Retrospection, Political and Personal* (New York: The Bancroft Company, 1912), and *Literary Industries: A Memoir* (New York: Harper & Brothers, 1891). The only biography of Bancroft was written more than half a century ago; see John W. Caughey, *Hubert Howe Bancroft, Historian of the West* (Berkeley, CA: University of California Press, 1946).

22. McCrossen, *Holy Day, Holiday*, pp. 100-105. About "muscular Christianity" see Clifford Putney, *Muscular Christianity: Manhood and Sports in Protestant America, 1880-1920* (Cambridge: Harvard University Press, 2001).

23. Concerning the history of liberal Protestantism and the process of sacralization, see Kenneth Cauthen, *The Impact of American Religious Liberalism* (Lanham, MD: University Press of America, 1962); Richard W. Fox, "The Discipline of Amusement," in *Inventing Times Square*, ed. William R. Taylor (New York: Russell Sage, 1991), pp. 83-98; Richard W. Fox, "The Culture of Liberal Protestant Progressivism, 1875-1925," *Journal of Interdisciplinary History* 23 (1993): 639-60; Jean-Christophe Agnew, "Times Square: Secularization and Sacralization," in Taylor, ed., *Inventing Times Square*, pp. 2-13; and Glenn Uminowicz, "Recreation in a Christian America: Ocean Grove and Asbury Park, New Jersey, 1869-1914," in *Hard at Play: Leisure in America, 1840-1940*, ed. Kathryn Grover (Amherst, MA: University of Massachusetts Press; Rochester, NY: The Strong Museum, 1992), pp. 8-38.

Mainline Protestant clergy, editors of prominent periodicals, and popular authors embraced liberal Protestantism, which was responsible for reshaping the relationship between Christians and "the world."

Furthermore, millions of immigrants, representing more than two dozen different European nationalities, brought to the United States new Sunday customs and beliefs, which also contributed to the vogue for recreation and play. They were willing to fight for their right to drink beer on Sunday, attend theatrical productions, or witness sporting events. Many of these immigrants were devoted to traditions associated with high culture — such as symphonic music — and opened the way for the inclusion of what was considered "Culture" in the list of acceptable Sunday activity. It has been argued that immigrants, especially those of German extraction, taught native-born Americans how to play.[24] I would argue that it is to their credit that more than three-quarters of Americans today claim Sunday as their favorite day of the week.

Sunday and sport came to be deeply associated, in large part because competitive sports create new communities of fans and spectators. Many aspects of sporting Sundays have enhanced community ties, but the dominance of televised and commercialized sports have kept too many American indoors and glued to their television sets. Alone on the couch, they only vicariously belong to communities of fans and spectators, disconnected from their families, their friends, and their communities. Today there is a widespread feeling that sports have in some ways replaced the ritualistic aspects of religion. Our star athletes demonstrate the miracle of faith in their exploits on the court and field. Game day activities, from tailgate parties to parades, heighten anticipation and provide structured ways to participate in an event. Sports provide a way for Americans to transcend ethnicity, race, class, and political and religious identities and become fans. Being a fan of a sport or of a team takes time, and it is on Sunday that Americans have the time to indulge in double-headers, traffic jams near stadiums, and the like. So, as long as Americans remain obsessed with sports, the relationship between Sunday and sport is likely to continue to flourish.

24. David A. Gerber, "'The Germans Take Care of Our Celebrations': Middle-Class Americans Appropriate German Ethnic Culture in Buffalo in the 1850s," in Grover, ed., *Hard at Play,* pp. 39-60.

Conclusion

It is clear that Americans like Sunday. But too many like it because it is a day when we can hibernate, absorbed in our favorite pastime, whether it is the crossword puzzle, a football game, or a long nap.[25] Many different groups, including the Lord's Day Alliance, wish to meet the challenges of an overly individualized and commercialized Sunday. It may be that the solution lies not simply in refashioning Sunday. Nor does it lie in refashioning Americans so that they can better appreciate Sunday. Rather, it lies in remaking the United States of America so that both its citizens and its Sundays can escape the limitations of selfish individualism and market capitalism. And in that way, "that Sunday feeling" may be recaptured and spread.

25. A poll conducted in 1998 by the Gallup Organization for MCI showed that 79 percent of Americans preferred Sunday to all other days of the week. Results published in *MCI Tracker I* (June 1998).

CHAPTER TEN

Sabbath and the Common Good

Thomas Massaro, S.J.

The notion of the common good serves as the master concept of Catholic social teaching. The tradition of reflection on the common good extends back to the patristic era and medieval Scholasticism, but the most succinct summary of the term is found in the 1961 papal encyclical *Mater et Magistra*, where Pope John XXIII defines common good as "the sum total of those conditions of social living whereby people are enabled more fully and more readily to achieve their own perfection."[1] Four years later, the Second Vatican Council reaffirmed and expanded this definition, as have the recent popes Paul VI and John Paul II. Catholic social ethics holds that the key human goods we seek to accomplish are not achievements that can be measured or enjoyed primarily on the level of the individual. There is a fundamentally shared nature to our lives, so that social well-being is always more than the arithmetical sum of private enjoyments, which are transcended by the social dimension. Items such as a sound educational system, a pollution-free environment, reliable provisions for public safety, universal access to health care, and income security — all of these are key elements of the common good. A corollary of this definition is the observation that all members of society have an obligation to promote the common good, in order to provide for their needy neighbors as well as for future generations.

I propose the thesis that it is helpful to think of the practice of a common Sabbath as a matter of common good. The establishment or preservation of a time of universal rest, relaxation, and reflection surely advances

---

1. Pope John XXIII's 1961 encyclical *Mater et Magistra* (par. 65). Nearly identical language is used in the 1965 Vatican II document *Gaudium et Spes* (par. 26).

the conditions of human flourishing, opening up the possibility of clearing out time for all people to appreciate the beauty of creation, to find opportunities to celebrate life together, and to be receptive to the truths and promptings of God, including the call and duty to worship our Creator. Sabbath time is precious because it is a different type of time, when attention is devoted to things of intrinsic worth, valuable for their own sake and not for any instrumental or practical purpose. It is a distinctive time simply for "being," not necessarily for "doing." Marking such singular time is our way of saying as a human race that our existence has a transcendent meaning, impervious to any crass reductionism. The benefits of this type of leisure resist any sort of quantification, just as we would surely be foolish to try to place a dollar sign on conditions that promote the common good.

Nevertheless, to emphasize the transcendent and immeasurable value of Sabbath is not to deny the practical benefits that a time dedicated to rest and worship would bring to our society. America is a land of frenetic pace and over-taxed lives. If ever a culture needed a reaffirmation of principles of rest and recollection, it is ours today. Just think of the potential health benefits alone of a reduction in stress, as work-related stress is tightly correlated with illnesses, especially coronary disease. Further, confessing myself to be something of a "news junkie," my own experience of making annual eight-day retreats cut off from TV and print media suggests that many of us would benefit from a "media fast" which could be incorporated into an expanded view of the practices and customs that constitute the Sabbath. We simply concentrate better when we are not concentrating all the time, at least not in the familiar left-brain way.

One extremely obvious benefit of Sabbath is the respite it provides from commercialism. Juliet Schor's ground-breaking research has revealed the destructiveness of the "work and spend" cycle in which so many of us find ourselves trapped into longer work hours in a vicious circle of rising material expectations. As much as we justify more work time as necessary to support our families, many Americans find themselves in the ironic situation of sacrificing to the workplace the very precious time they would prefer to spend with their family members. Nobody should have to choose between these two goals, but somehow we have crawled inside this gilded cage of a prosperity we have no time to enjoy. Schor stands on the shoulders of the great father of modern sociology Max Weber in pointing out the irrationalities of the one-dimensional logic of the market. Her research is greatly encouraging to those of us who seek a counter-weight to the lure of commercialism and round-the-clock moneymaking.

Historically, of course, it has been the Christian churches that have most prominently championed the cause of publicly marking the Sabbath. Religious voices have performed this role for a variety of motivations, some of them particularistic and confessional in nature, others more humanistic and universal in their appeal. In the nineteenth and early twentieth centuries, the struggle for a shorter workweek found many supporters, including organized labor and other social movements, and I am proud to point to European and North American social Catholicism as one of the voices that spoke out for the well-being of exploited and overworked laborers in the new industrial order. The very first of the modern social encyclicals, Pope Leo XIII's 1891 document *Rerum Novarum,* called firmly for respect for the workers' rights to forgo labor on Sundays and Holy Days.

What types of arguments do Christian voices propose in support of the Sabbath? Most directly, they recognize keeping the Sabbath as a divine command, spelled out in Exodus 20:8 and Deuteronomy 5:12-15. The Sabbath is seen as a moral obligation, a duty to God as well as a principle of proper social order. Setting aside time for God and worship relativizes work and the ordinary routines of life, reminding us of our finiteness and offering an implicit critique of the status quo. The Sabbath is thus not a burden, but a divine gift, an act of divine mercy to us overtaxed mortals. It is also a reminder that, to cite Matthew 4:4, we do not live by bread alone, for our lives have more significance than the material dimension.

When the Sabbath comes up in the Gospel accounts, it is usually in the context of conflict, as in the controversy stories that pit Jesus against the scribes and Pharisees. So it is today: when Christian voices propose the common Sabbath as a counter to the 24/7 world of commercial transactions, controversy immediately arises. Herein lies the second point I wish to offer in my comments today: the need for caution in forging a strategy to propose a uniform observance of a common day of rest as a matter of public policy in a pluralistic society like ours.

As much as the arguments rehearsed above lead me to the conclusion that mandatory Sunday closings would go a long way in restoring the balance of labor and leisure America has lost, I am nevertheless left with unresolved questions about the wisdom of pursuing such a strategy. As I ponder the advisability of seeking legislation to enforce a common day of rest, I cannot help but think that an ambitious pursuit of legal sanctions to codify our common, faith-based desire commits the mistake of overreaching amidst the pluralism of twenty-first century America. I fear asking too much of our lawmakers, who must represent the interests of broad constituencies that lack consensus on the fundamental values discussed above. As a religiously diverse polity, America finds itself without universal agreement on the existence of God, much less the qualities of God (that is, a God who champions rest for God's people) that would support a universally mandated Sabbath. To work vigorously for such a species of legally enforced common Sabbath in good conscience, we would have to assume spiritual and cultural values now regrettably dormant in the United States. This is no reason to give up the fight, but merely a warrant to demonstrate restraint on the legal front until the requisite cultural conditions are in place.

The Catholic tradition of social ethics has long recognized a crucial distinction between what is moral (i.e., congruent with the fullness of the will of God) and what is legal (i.e., prudent measures to be incorporated into civil laws and appropriately enforced by secular authorities). It is no mere craven copout to invoke this distinction in this case. There are plenty of reasons to advocate Sunday as a day of rest, plenty of grounds upon which to address this argument to individuals who serve as employees or employers, plenty of merits to the argument that we would all be better off if the Lord's Day were treated as such. Yet an ambitious campaign to enforce Sunday closings risks running roughshod over the consciences of dissenters. It raises the uninviting prospect of asking lawmakers to distinguish somewhat arbitrarily between emergency and nonessential services, of enforcing unpopular restrictions and splitting hairs regarding different types of businesses whose functions are difficult to compare and evaluate in an objective way.

Those caveats having been uttered, I immediately find myself returning to my initial sympathy for the arguments of those who seek greater respect for the Sabbath. Would it not be wonderful if an educational campaign to sensitize Americans to the dangers of overwork and materialism succeeded in persuading millions to question the dominance of commercial values? Would it not be a great advance if a collective awareness of alternatives to round-the-clock capitalism moved us not only to adjust our private spiritualities and individual practices, but also to reform our public large-scale institutions, so that they too reflected and incarnated our values? In short, I am just as concerned about seeking too little as I am about demanding too much of Americans on this issue.

To summarize, in the first half of my comments I portrayed the reestablishment of a common Sabbath as a desirable development for our harried nation, indeed as one of the conditions of human flourishing that

Catholic social teaching would refer to as part of the pursuit of the common good. There are numerous reasons to support this initiative, some of them humanistic and non-objectionable to anyone of good will, others confessional and particularistic in nature. In the second part of my reflections, I shared concerns about the proper style and strategy by which such efforts should proceed, urging the restraint and prudence that the Catholic ethical tradition insists upon whenever it considers the process of translating desirable goals into civil laws. These caveats are more about the style than the substance of policy proposals. It is one thing to propose; it is another to seek to impose. Aware of the lessons of the past, such as the Prohibition interlude in the early part of the last century, the wise activist or reformer avoids all appearances of paternalism, but instead prefers and emphasizes the spirit of dialogue and mutuality.

I will rejoice if religious voices succeed in making a persuasive case for a common Sabbath. I have confidence that carefully crafted appeals to the common good may yet demonstrate how the religious community continues to be a vital force in our society, one capable not only of scolding and disciplining reluctant participants, but also of advocating for our common interests and even incorporating shared values into enlightened public laws.

CHAPTER ELEVEN

The Weekend: Labor and Leisure in America

Ruy Costa

Without sports there would be no next year
Without sports, weekends would be like weekdays
Without sports, who would we follow?

ESPN ADVERTISEMENT ON
BOSTON SUBWAY CAR

The Sabbath has been equated to a sanctuary in time in Jewish culture. The Sabbath survived the Christian switch from observance on Saturday to Sunday almost two thousand years ago. Yet, it is quickly disappearing from most communities at the beginning of the twenty-first century. Does the Sabbath hide in the complexity of its meanings a secret for its preservation for the future? If it does, it is because the Sabbath represents an alternative way of life. What follows is an argument that the Sabbath represents alterity in a time when a one-dimensional culture of production and consumption is becoming global.

Alterity

Think of alterity as a methodological affirmation of otherness in philosophy and ethics. Enrique Dussel, a Latin American philosopher and ethicist, articulates three moments of alterity as three face-to-face encounters that transcend the tyranny of sameness in Western dialectics: he begins with the erotic face to face; then he moves to the pedagogical face to face; and he concludes with the political face to face.[1] The Hegelian movement from the individual to the social is obvious: one individual meets another in the erotic face to face, then parents meet the child as another distinct from themselves in the pedagogical face to face, and finally, brothers and sisters meet each other in the social-political face to face.

The Sabbath in Scripture

Theologians have identified various themes in the references to Sabbath in Scripture. Some of these themes are especially relevant for our argument.

An Act of Worship

The most radical view of the Sabbath in the Hebrew Scriptures is articulated most clearly by the Deuteronomist writer, in Deuteronomy 5, where we find the call to Israel to hear the terms of the covenant. The call, "Hear O, Israel," articulates one of the most fundamental insights in Hebrew theology: that at the center of Israel's cultus is a conviction that revelation happens in history and that the heart of Jewish history is the memory of the Exodus.[2] The reason Israel should worship God is that God delivered Israel from slavery in Egypt. The claim places the Exodus at the genesis of this theological tradition. For the Deuteronomist, the Exodus is the great historical event upon which a theology of history is built. The call frames the Ten Commandments with YHWH's self-disclosure as the God "who brought Israel out of the land of Egypt, out of the house of slavery" (Deut. 5:6). The first commandment is against idolatry: "you shall have no other gods before me" (v. 7). The first and most repeated lesson in Hebrew theology is that the God whom Israel should worship is the God of the Exodus, the God who delivers slaves from their oppressors.

How is Israel expected to worship God? By keeping the Sabbath. The worship that God demands from former slaves is a weekly day off from work:

1. Enrique Dussel, *Método para una filosofía de la liberación* (Salamanca: Ediciones Sígueme, 1974), pp. 181-83.
2. Gerhard von Rad, "Das theologische Problem des alttestamentlichen Schöpfungslaubes," in *Werden und wesen des Alten Testaments*, Zeitschrift für die alttestamentliche Wissenschaft, vol. 66 (1963), pp. 138-47.

> Observe the sabbath day and keep it holy, as the LORD your God com-
> manded you. Six days you shall labor and do all your work. But the sev-
> enth day is a sabbath to the LORD your God; you shall not do any work
> — you, or your son or your daughter, or your male or female slave, or
> your ox or your donkey, or any of your livestock, or the resident alien in
> your towns, so that your male and female slave may rest as well as you.
> Remember that you were a slave in the land of Egypt, and the LORD your
> God brought you out from there with a mighty hand and an out-
> stretched arm; therefore the LORD your God commanded you to keep
> the Sabbath day. (vv. 12-15, NRSV)

The weekly Sabbath is a perennial reminder that the Israelites were
slaves whom God delivered at one particular historical moment. So, the
Sabbath is a weekly gift intended to remind Israel of that extraordinary
historical gift, the Exodus. The intention of Sabbath rest is to cultivate a
collective memory, a memory sacred as the center of the biblical culture, a
memory of YHWH as the God who delivers the poor and oppressed from
their chains.

The Sabbath, therefore, is intended for the whole community. There
are no exceptions. That is why in biblical Israel the Sabbath is to be observed by everybody together, at the same time; heads of households, their
children, servants, and so on, "so that your male and female slave may rest
as well as you" (v. 14). Community rest is the only worship acceptable to a
God who delivers slaves from slavery. YHWH wants to be known as the
God of rest, and in that rest all are equal. Anywhere people are oppressed
by socio-economic and political structures, this biblical memory of
YHWH as a God who delivers the poor and oppressed is a subversive
memory.

An Economic Model

Leviticus and Numbers articulate even further the communitarian implications of the Sabbath. As the weekly day of rest is a time for collective renewal, so the economy of biblical Israel includes the concepts of a sabbatical year and the year of the Jubilee, the year after a week of sabbatical years,
that is, after forty-nine years, when prisoners should be set free, creation
should rest (including humans and animals), and the economic resources
of the nation should be redistributed among its inhabitants:

You shall have the trumpet sounded throughout all your land. And you shall hallow the fiftieth year and you shall proclaim liberty throughout the land to all its inhabitants. It shall be a jubilee for you: You shall return, every one of you, to your property and every one of you to your family. That fiftieth year shall be jubilee for you: you shall not sow, or reap the aftergrowth, or harvest the unpruned vines. For it is a jubilee; it shall be holy to you: you shall eat only what the field itself produces. (Lev. 25:9-12)

Two foundations of Sabbatical theology are reaffirmed here: (a) the year of the Jubilee, the crown of sabbatical celebrations, weaves together forgiveness of offenders, rest from labor, rest for the land, and redistribution of economic resources; and (b) the celebration of this periodic rest/renewal of society and creation is declared by the sacred text as "holy" — "it shall be holy to you." The principles of the Sabbatical year and the year of Jubilee were intended as a periodic renewal of the community when everybody has a chance to start anew. The observance of these principles is not only good practice or prudential advice but belongs in the realm of the cultus; they are set apart as holy.

A New Work Ethic

In Exodus 16 the Israelites are given distinct instructions regarding provisions for food in the desert and the observance of the Sabbath. Their instructions were simple: (a) each person should gather enough food each day for all those in their own tents (Exod. 16:16); (b) they should not gather for more than one day, and those who did found their leftovers spoiled next morning (v. 20); (c) in preparation for the Sabbath, however, they should gather enough for the next day — and it would not spoil! (vv. 22-26). Some disobeyed that instruction and worked on the Sabbath. They were punished. In Numbers 15 a man is stoned to death for collecting sticks on the Sabbath. The two narratives suggest a struggle to impress in the minds of the people the need to observe the Sabbath as an act of trust in God in contrast to trusting one's own resources or ingenuity. As a freed nation, called to be witnesses of YHWH's grace, Israel had to be liberated also from the spiritual oppression of the Egyptian work ethic. As a people liberated from Egypt, Israel was called to celebrate the fact that their liberation was the result, not of their work, but of God's. In fact, in Egypt, the more they worked, the stronger their oppressor became. The Sabbath was such a celebration. To stop productive activity is a confession of faith in God's providence. The opposite confession is the confession of faith in work: "we have to gather manna seven days a week or else it won't be there." That is the work ethic of Egypt. Exodus 16 condemns excessive accumulation and excessive work. Both are antithetical to the spirit of Sabbath. The celebration of the Sabbath is an invitation to enjoy life more with less.

A Memorial of Creation

Another theological interpretation of the Sabbath appears in Genesis 2:1-3 and parallel references to creation. The main claim of the reference to God's rest in the seventh day is that all things created were created by God in the preceding six days; that is, that after six periods of time, the seventh is a time when the creator does not need to create anything because everything that needs to be created already exists. In Genesis 2:2 the Sabbath is the crown of creation.

> The Sabbath is the true hallmark of every biblical, every Jewish and also every Christian doctrine of creation. The completion of creation through the peace of the Sabbath distinguishes the view of the world as creation from the view of the world as nature; for nature is unremittingly fruitful and, though it has seasons and rhythms, knows no Sabbath. It is the Sabbath which blesses, sanctifies and reveals the world as God's creation.[3]

In the Jewish tradition this celebration of creation takes place in the sacred ceasing of all labor activity and the sacred entering into a time of blissful rest and joy.

The rest granted to the land in the year of the Jubilee and in the Sabbatical year, and the rest granted to the animals together with humans each week, are all reminders of the importance of creation in the theology of the Sabbath. Much remains to be learned about the implications of the ancient Sabbatical prescriptions for the preservation and restoration of the earth's threatened eco-system.

3. Jürgen Moltmann, *God in Creation: A New Theology of Creation and the Spirit of God* (San Francisco: Harper and Row, 1985), p. 6.

A Cultural Paradigm

The Sabbath as a memorial of creation is an intentional step. As such, the Sabbath is a cultural activity, distinct from nature's ongoing rhythm of production and reproduction. The intentional separation of one day in seven for the celebration of life represents cooperation between the human race and God in the realm of culture.

Rabbi Abraham Heschel in *The Sabbath: Its Meaning for Modern Man*, refers to this distinction between sacred and profane time as the Jewish "architecture of time":

> Judaism teaches us to be attached to holiness in time, to be attached to sacred events, to learn how to consecrate sanctuaries that emerge from the magnificent stream of a year. The Sabbaths are our great cathedrals; and our *Holy of Holies is a shrine that neither the Romans nor the Germans were able to burn.*[4]

Rabbi Heschel's image of the "architecture of time" is a cultural model: what we do with our time tells who we are, which gods we worship, what our lives are made of, or what we make of our lives.

God's creation in Genesis includes the human race made in God's "image and likeness." In the image and likeness of their creator, humans are creative, that is, creatures capable of innovative and intentional action. An intentional pause in the regular cycles of nature elevates the time of the pause from the realm of event to the realm of cultural meaning.

A Pious Conspiracy

The Sabbath as a pious conspiracy is most obvious in the Gospels. Most references to the Sabbath in the New Testament are framed by "conflict stories," that is, stories which tell of Jesus in confrontation with religious and political authorities of the day. In Mark these stories appear in chapter 2 and 3:1-6, and each includes such Sabbath conflicts. At the end of chapter 2 Jesus is challenged by the Pharisees because his disciples are plucking heads of grain on the Sabbath day. Jesus responds in the rabbini-

---

4. Abraham J. Heschel, *The Sabbath: Its Meaning for Modern Man* (New York: Farrar, Straus & Young, 1951), p. 8.

cal style, with a counter question that sets a broader frame of reference for the discussion of what is or is not lawful. His conclusion is twofold: he said to them that (a) "the Sabbath was made for humankind and not humankind for the Sabbath"; and (b) "the Son of Man is Lord even of the Sabbath" (Mark 2:27 and 28, NRSV).

By the time the fourth Gospel was written, at the end of the first century A.D., church and synagogue were already separated from each other by the confession that Jesus is the Lord of the Sabbath.[5]

The pious conspiracy of the Gospels identifies the Sabbath with resurrection: the restoration of body and soul. The conflict between Jesus and the authorities was, on the one hand, about the healing of the body on the holy day; on the other hand, however, it was also about the healing of the spirit. With his actions and with his words, Jesus was inviting the people to re-create, re-define, re-imagine the Sabbath as a memorial of creation and liberation, a memorial "for humankind."

The End of the Weekend

The erosion of the Sabbath in Western societies is the result of a process of elimination of religious and civic holidays that started with the rationalization of time during the industrial revolution.

The case of the British railroad system illustrates how time management changed radically with the emergence of modernity. Since European cities and towns were all equipped with solar clocks, their time zones were determined by their own geographical locations. So, when a train departed from London at 12:00 noon, it was not 12:00 noon in nearby towns and villages, and that natural "disorder" caused the railroads enormous confusion in the scheduling of their times of arrival and departure. They resolved the confusion by establishing time zones large enough for their traveling range and thus synchronized their clocks.[6] Obviously, when it is 12:00 noon in London it is not solar high noon everywhere in the London

5. Eduard Lohse, in *Theological Dictionary of the New Testament*, ed. Gerhard Friedrich, vol. 7 (Grand Rapids: Eerdmans, 1964), p. 28.

6. Niegel Thrift, "A Capitalist Time Consciousness," in *The Sociology of Time*, ed. John Hassard (New York: St. Martin's Press, 1990), p. 122. See also John de Graaf, ed., *Take Back Your Time: Fighting Overwork and Time Poverty in America* (San Francisco: Berrett-Koehler Publishers, 2003).

time zone. Natural time was replaced by conventional time to meet the needs of the emerging transportation industry.

Today, cities and villages around the world are bombarded by real time news and commercial transactions taking place anywhere in the globe; the global clock connects financial centers from Tokyo to London to New York, and local rhythms of life are impacted by the presence of innumerous external times. The compounded times, the fact that we live under various clocks all running simultaneously, generates what some sociologists now call "compressed time," that is, an experience of time in which a lot more happens at the same time all the time. The train never stops. Non-marketable events need to be accommodated as intrusions in a system designed to be productive 24/7.

The phenomenon of the rationalization of time was first named by Max Weber.[7] Rationalization, in Weber's analysis, is characterized by four variables: (a) efficiency, (b) quantification, (c) predictability, and (d) control.[8] The emergence of rationalized systems marked a paradigm shift from previous systems, in that rationalized systems — because of their efficiency and capacity for control — impose themselves on society. Weber was so alarmed about this that at the end of *The Protestant Ethic and the Spirit of Capitalism* he called this an "iron cage."[9] Weber also cautioned that "rationalized" is not the same as rational. Systems that are efficient, quantifiable, predictable, and controlling can also be totally insensitive to human needs and agency.

The "iron cage" is a reference to the rigors of modernity, such as rational accounting, quantification, predictability, and control, that gain and increase their grip on society precisely because of their economic efficiency. In Weber's words, "the Puritan wanted to work on a calling; we are forced to do so."[10]

The rationalization of time illustrates Weber's iron cage precisely: the Protestant tradition in which Weber finds a culture that values hard work and savings, the spirit of capitalism, also values the practice of the Sabbath,

7. Max Weber, *The Protestant Ethic and the Spirit of Capitalism* (New York: Charles Scribner's Sons, 1958); *General Economic History* (Glencoe: The Free Press, 1972); Max Weber, *From Max Weber: Essays in Sociology,* ed. and with an introduction by H. H. Gerth and C. W. Mills (New York: Oxford University Press, 1964). See also Ruy O. Costa, *Globalization and Culture* (Louisville: ACSWP, Presbyterian Church [USA], 2003).

8. Max Weber, *Economy and Society* (Totowa, NJ: Bedminster, 1921, 1986).

9. Weber, *The Protestant Ethic,* p. 181.

10. Weber, *The Protestant Ethic,* p. 181.

the observance of the Day of the Lord. In the Protestant system analyzed by Weber, Sabbath keeping was at the center of time budgeting. Yet, as the religious foundations of the Protestant ethic fade away, the rational spirit that legitimates the rationalization of time renders the religious observance of the Sabbath obsolete. "To-day the spirit of religious asceticism . . . has escaped from the cage. But, victorious capitalism, since it rests on mechanical foundations, needs its support no longer."[11] When time is reduced to money, the Sabbath becomes unaffordable. That was precisely the argument used by the agents of corporations lobbying the states' legislatures at the end of the twentieth century when the last Sunday closing laws were finally defeated.[12]

The pressure for always-increasing productivity and the impact of that pressure on the lives of the American people have been well demonstrated by economist Juliet Schor. In *The Overworked American,* Schor documents the rise in working hours in the United States since the 1960s. The main variables in her research are "an increase in the number of people who hold paying jobs; a rise in weekly hours and in weeks worked each year; and reductions in paid time off, sick leave, and absences from work."[13] She argues that given the increase in productivity of the U.S. worker in the last half century, "we could now produce our 1948 standard of living (measured in terms of marketed goods and services) in less than half the time it took that year."[14] Instead, what has happened is that we have embraced a pattern of greater consumption, or what she calls "the work-and-spend cycle." This pattern represents a collective choice of money over time even though the distribution of the monetary rewards of the pattern is grossly weighted in favor of the moneyed classes. Schor's analysis was challenged by other economists using different metrics to demonstrate that in fact work time is diminishing in the USA. One such approach is to look at work hours per occupation versus per worker. In a subsequent publication Schor demonstrates that in a market where people hold two or more jobs such data is incomplete.[15] Volunteer organizations, such as churches, have felt the impact of "time starvation" on their membership as fewer and fewer people can afford to volunteer for non-paid work. Political scientist Robert Putnam looks at the impact of

11. Weber, *The Protestant Ethic,* p. 181.

12. Archives of the Massachusetts Council of Churches.

13. Juliet Schor, *The Overworked American* (New York: Basic Books, 1991), p. 24.

14. Schor, *The Overworked American,* p. 2.

15. See Juliet Schor, "The (Even More) Overworked American," in *Take Back Your Time: Fighting Overwork and Time Poverty in America,* ed. John de Graaf (San Francisco: Berrett-Koehler Publishers, 2003).

time starvation on political engagement. In *Bowling Alone* he measures the relationship between time to socialize (like bowling together) and time for other social activities, such as engagement in political campaigns, etc. And he concludes with alarm that in our culture more and more people are "bowling alone" because of the pressures of the market.[16]

The erosion of a common day of rest, the Lord's Day or the Sabbath, is only one more concrete outcome of the unfolding of the logic of what Juliet Schor calls the "work-and-spend cycle." If people are not working on weekends they are most likely shopping. Thinking of different times as distinct entities, it is reasonable to say that Sabbath time has become a marginalized entity in our times.

Sabbath Keeping as an Alternative Way of Life

Erotic Alterity: Body and Soul

The erotic moment of alterity is its paradigmatic moment; that is, in the erotic encounter the self is faced with its equal, the one that is not the self and whom the self very much needs. The erotic moment is the first face-to-face (no masks, vulnerable, authentic) moment of alterity. It is also that moment that injects life energy into life. Freud's appropriation of Greek mythology helps illustrate this: Freud argues that humans are driven by the tension between Eros and Thanatos, Thanatos representing the instinct of death and Eros the instinct of life. Eros represents the life energy that brings us to our feet, that makes us walk erect, that makes us live in fullness of life versus those things that drag us down and lead to death (technically, back to matter from whence we come). In *Civilization and Its Discontents,* Freud argues that as a society becomes more complex people need to repress their instincts in order to function in that society.[17] Max Weber also looked at industrialization and the development of mechanical reproduction as a process that transformed Western culture from one governed by the natural cycles of nature to one governed by the artificial rhythms of the machine. Others have documented this movement from a

16. Robert Putman, *Bowling Alone: The Collapse and Revival of American Community* (New York: Simon and Schuster, 2000).

17. Sigmund Freud, *Civilization and Its Discontents* (New York: W. W. Norton and Company, reissued ed., 1989); see also *Complete Psychological Works of Sigmund Freud,* ed. J. Strachey (London: Hogarth Press, 1967).

culture governed by the rhythms of the body to a culture where the body is governed by the rhythms of the clock. If rationalization of time and repression of the instincts go hand in hand, Sabbath keeping in the midst of compressed time provides an oasis for erotic alterity.

The celebration of the traditional Jewish Sabbath begins with a dinner that incorporates a feast for the senses with a feast for the soul. Good food, good wine, a table decorated with candles and flowers, plus prayers, blessings, remembrance, and thanksgiving. People dress up for a party, at home, week after week. It is a time set aside for joy.

The celebration begins with anticipation — like the satisfaction of any drive that intensifies with a period of necessary waiting. Prior to the arrival of the evening, preparations are made, often culminating in a last-minute rush as the sun drops in the sky toward twilight and the sacred moment approaches. Before the Sabbath arrives, as a much-expected date, all work needs to be finished, including the work of getting oneself groomed for the occasion. Then eighteen minutes prior to sunset, the candles are lit, the seats are taken, and the transition from everyday time to Sabbath time begins with the first prayer: *Barukh ata Adonai Eloheinu melekh ha-olam, asher kid'shanu b'mitzvotav v'tzivanu l'haldlik ner shel Shabbat*: "Blessed are You, LORD, our God, King of the universe, who have sanctified us with Your commandments and commanded us to light the Shabbat candle."[18] During the Sabbath one ought to abstain from anything unpleasant, from fasting to stressful conversation. The Jewish tradition associates Sabbath with *Menuha*, the state wherein all lie still, "wherein the wicked cease from troubling and the weary are at rest . . . the state in which there is no strife and no fighting, no fear and no distrust."[19] A Midrash on Genesis teaches that on the Sabbath "even the ungodly in Gehenna may rest from their torment."[20] The list of forbidden activities in traditional observation includes various sets of efforts, related to various types of labor. On the other hand, the activities encouraged on the Sabbath, like the Sabbath dinner, are celebrations of life in community and the goodness of created human nature, such as being with one's immediate family, attending synagogue for prayers, visiting family and friends within walking distance, hosting

18. For a complete collection of Sabbath prayers, blessings, and readings see *The Authorized Prayer Book*, ed. Joseph Hertz, the late Chief Rabbi of the British Empire, rev. ed. (New York: Bloch Publishing Company, 1955).

19. Heschel, *The Sabbath*, p. 23.

20. Midrash on Genesis, "Sanhedrin," in the Babylonian Talmud; summarized by Lohse, in *Theological Dictionary of the New Testament*, vol. 7, p. 8.

guests, singing special songs for the Sabbath meal, reading, studying and discussing Torah and commentaries, and enjoying marital relations, particularly on Friday night.

Erotic alterity? Yes. A time set aside for the celebration of life. *L'chai-im.*

Pedagogical Alterity: Worship

Pedagogical alterity is the affirmation of the other in education. Dussel names oppressive education as the effort of parents to reproduce themselves in the child, who, in this relationship, is the dominated other. (Dussel, by the way, refers specifically to the father's desire to reproduce himself in the child.) In a face-to-face pedagogical encounter, the parent needs to see the child in her own integrity. This does not mean that no teaching takes place. It means that the teaching that takes place does not reduce the child to a copy of the parent. While oppressive education is designed to reproduce the sameness of today tomorrow, the pedagogical moment of alterity opens tomorrow for a distinct future. Tomorrow should not be a copy of today. Oppressive education reduces all distinctions to sameness; pedagogical alterity affirms distinction: it wants to foster face-to-face encounters that generate conversation and empower the silent voices. In Jewish tradition, the Sabbath is a silent witness to the age to come, a foretaste of the Messianic Kingdom.[21]

The last blessing in the Jewish Shabbat is a thanksgiving for God's separation of the holy from the profane: *Barukh ata Adonai Eloheinu melek ha-olam, ha-mavdil bein kodesh l'hol, bein or l'hoshekh, bein yisra'el la-amim, bein yom ha-sh'vi'i l'sheshet y'mei ha-ma'a'se. Barukh ata Adonai, ha-mavdil bein kodesh l'hol:* "Blessed are You, LORD, our God, King of the universe, who distinguish between the sacred and the secular, between light and dark, between Israel and the nations, between the seventh day and the six days of labor. Blessed are You, LORD, who distinguish between the sacred and the secular."

In a postmodern society that disdains boundaries and is offended by people who dare to claim a distinct identity (their otherness in distinction to the sameness of the totality), a prayer that praises God for distinguishing between "the sacred and the secular, between light and dark, between Israel and the nations" will inevitably offend many. Yet, lest pluralism degenerates

---

21. Lohse, *Theological Dictionary of the New Testament*, vol. 7, p. 8.

into homogeneity and hegemony, the contribution of distinct voices needs to be not only permitted but also promoted. And the ancient practice of Sabbath keeping provides a time-tested frame for communities to engage in reflection and build culture. The contribution of the biblical cultures of Sabbath keeping to these restless times may be precisely the invitation to stop and think. The ancient Greeks thought that society needs a leisure class to develop its culture. In Scripture, on the other hand, it is not just a segment of society that has the privilege of developing culture; rather, the whole community is called to save a segment of time for the cultivation of the spirit. And when Jesus reminded his audience that "The Sabbath was made for humankind and not humankind for the Sabbath," in response to rigid and oppressive practices and beliefs, he was inviting his people to be creative in relationship to the Sabbath. The early Christian communities understood Jesus' invitation and reinvented their weekly Sabbath.

The Sabbath, a day distinct from other days, is a pedagogical invitation to cultural alterity.

Political Alterity: The Economics of Time

And then we come to political alterity. Dussel deals with political alterity as the affirmation of socio-political diversity and the empowerment of marginalized communities in the face of growing domination of the centers of power. While Dussel's approach draws primarily on the history of Latin America as a region that was exploited and marginalized by the North Atlantic nations, it may be more relevant for us to look at political alterity within the North Atlantic totality and its internal power dynamics. In *The One Dimensional Man*, Herbert Marcuse looks at the value system of Western societies that reduces life to economics.[22] This one-dimensional view of reality emerges from what Marcuse and others have called the commodification of life, that is, the inversion of non-economic variables into economic valuables. We talk about "saving" time and "spending" time, and we, in the United States at least, say that "time is money." These are economic words. When time is reduced to an economic variable in our language, are we not confessing that money has become the center of a cult which defines the value of everything else?

22. Herbert Marcuse, *The One Dimensional Man* (London: Routledge and Kegan Paul, 1964).

Heschel's imagery of the architecture of time is a socio-political, cultural, and theological construct. Our collective definition of time structures makes time a temple, a bank, a garden, or a jail.

When the sacred rhythm of work and rest is replaced by a restless 24/7 culture of production and consumption, society has made a choice to build its time as a materialistic castle, or, to use Weber's image, an iron cage. No wonder that such a society does not know "whom to follow." No wonder that for such a society, without sports, "weekends are just like weekdays." No wonder that the experts in the worldview of such a society, the marketing gurus, interpret its eschatology as a hopeless, nihilistic, empty cynicism for which the only expectation for next year is another round of sports events: no future possible. Why? Because, whether or not one calls it religion, those values that structure our time shape our souls, and a society that has opted to ignore a rhythm of work and rest/reflection/recreation has opted for a way of life in which time is flat and one day, indeed, is no different from the other. Here the Jewish Sabbath prayer, "Blessed are You, LORD, our God, King of the universe, who distinguishes . . . between the seventh day and the six days of labor," becomes a pious protest. Given that the engine erasing the distinction of one day from another is an advanced economy that demands more and more time to be sacrificed on the altar of the market, theologically speaking, one cannot escape the prophetic charge that the absence of Sabbath in our time is an expression of idolatry.

Another critical issue related to the politics of the Sabbath is the fact that secular societies are not governed by religious prescriptions and in a pluralistic society no one religious tradition should prevail over all. So, which day should be the collective Sabbath?

Retrieving the Sabbath as a pedagogical moment of alterity, or Sabbath keeping as an invitation to reinvent culture, one is confronted with the radical invitation to reinvent the Sabbath itself. (And wasn't this precisely what Jesus did when he healed on the Sabbath day and explained why?) So, Sabbath keeping is, on the one hand, a practice that confronts the larger, materialistic culture with an invitation to stop the treadmill and rethink things (critique *ad extra*); and, on the other hand, Sabbath keeping is an invitation to a face-to-face conversation about the traditional Sabbath itself (critique *ad intra*). In the spirit of re-creating the Sabbath as an expression of spiritual renewal, an alternative may emerge: an alterity both to the abolition of Sabbath and to the privilege of one Sabbath day over the others. Communities of faith who invest time in the reflection over their praxis may consider whether in a post-industrial economy a practical solution for the implementation of a common day of rest may not call for the practice of alternative common days of rest for the different communities.

Two antitheses present themselves immediately: (a) the privatization of Sabbath with the dispensation of disconnected and uncoordinated "days off," and (b) the loss of certain benefits of collective times of rest, such as the benefits to the environment, etc. Private days off from work do not meet the communitarian meaning of the Sabbath and even undermine it: when a mother has her day off on Tuesdays and a father his days off on Saturday and/or Sunday, they do not have family time off together. In order to preserve the Sabbatical character of days off from work, those days need to be acknowledged together by a given community. Perhaps a consensus is viable whereby Fridays, Saturdays, and Sundays would be allowed as choice Sabbaths for the communities that observe it. As far as other Sabbatical implications, such as rest for the environment, Sabbath-keeping communities should continue to invite the wider society to consider the potential benefits of collective Sabbath keeping. A compromise honoring cultural diversity in a secular society would be better than the current situation, when all communities that want to practice a day of rest and renewal find themselves collectively losing their options. As alterity in time, the Sabbath bears in its structure of meaning the logic of its own self-transcendence and the secret of its own survival.

Political alterity, then, as it is applied to time, is an invitation to affirm that not all time is money or that not all time should be money. Some time should be alternative time. Some time should be a break away from economic activity. Some time should be Sabbath time.

Conclusions

In a time of global economic restlessness, our culture generates symbols such as the neologism "24/7" and a secular cult that elevates 24/7 economic activity to a value. In such a context, Sabbath keeping, as an observance of a regular day of collective rest and renewal, represents an alternative way of life, a way of life dissonant from the dominant values of the culture. This alternative way of life is consistent with various expressions of the Sabbath in Scripture (such as Sabbath keeping as a memorial of creation, as worship, as an alternative ethic of work and rest, etc.), and as such, Sabbath keeping is an expression of "alterity": a philosophical and ethical concept conceived at the margins of modernity as a tool of reflection on its totality. "24/7" is the new time totality. Sabbath keeping is its alterity.

As alterity in time, Sabbath time is a celebration of three face-to-face encounters: the erotic, the pedagogical, and the political. First, Sabbath time is eros time for the body as an alternative to work and for the spirit as time for worship. Second, it is pedagogical time in the sense that Sabbath is a time intended for the renewal of the mind. And third, it is political time because rest for the body, renewal for the mind, and worship of a God who frees the slaves from their chains are an alternative (alterity) from the primary demand of the economic system: time for production and consumption.

CHAPTER TWELVE

Seven Principles for the Seventh Day

Aída Besançon Spencer

If you do a word study on "Sabbath" in the Bible, certain principles emerge which serve as a summary of the basic themes of Sabbath observance. The Old Testament references may be grouped into seven, which is appropriate for the seventh day instituted by a holy God (seven being also a symbol of holiness). And Jesus' critique of the misuse of the Sabbath laws may also be grouped into seven principles for a balanced presentation.

Old Testament	New Testament
1. Finish Work (Gen. 2:2)	1. Have Mercy (Matt. 12:7)
2. Rest (Gen. 2:2-3; Exod. 20:9-11)	2. Serve (Mark 2:27)
3. Be Holy (Gen. 2:3)	3. Do Good (Luke 6:9)
4. Praise (Lev. 23:2-44)	4. Liberate (Luke 13:11-16)
5. Have Faith (Exod. 16:16-30)	5. Heal (Luke 14:3-5)
6. Remember the Sign (Exod. 31:13-17)	6. God Works (John 5:17)
7. Liberate (Deut. 5:12-15)	7. Worship Jesus (John 9:5-38)

Some Pharisees who desired to practice rigorously God's commands in the Old Testament were understandably confused and incensed when they saw Jesus teach, heal, and also allow his disciples to do things that appeared to be unlawful or not permitted by God's laws on the Sabbath. Today, as well, we might ask, if Jesus is indeed God incarnate, why would He disregard His own revelation? This apparent discordance may be resolved when we understand that Jesus first looked at the intention of the Old Testament laws or principles and then kept in mind a whole package of principles for the Sabbath that He applied appropriately for each individual case. Thus, sometimes focusing on an individual law or principle without observing the individual situation or person and the full context of principles can result in a misapplication which may end up disagreeing with God's original intention.

Seven Sabbath Principles (Old Testament)

The Sabbath rest is mentioned as early as Genesis 2:2-3. After the six days of creation, Genesis tells us: "And God finished by the seventh day His work which He had done and He rested in the seventh day from all His work which He had done. And God blessed the seventh day and He declared it holy because in it He rested from all His work which God in creating accomplished" (my literal translation). Four key main verbs may be highlighted here: *finish, rest, bless,* and *declare holy.* Thus, the Sabbath involves the finishing or completion of work, the resting from all one's work, God blessing the day, and the day therefore becoming holy.

1. Finish Work

The sacred Scripture says that when God works, He finishes work. As recounted in Genesis, God had finished the work of creation, including making man and woman in His own image. The idea of finishing or completing indicates that the creation is good as it comes from the hand of God; nothing needs to be added. After God finishes the work of creation and rests, God blesses the day, and therefore the day becomes holy. What is implied is that to work and to finish work is good. In the New Testament Jesus picks up this idea and repeats it when He says: "My Father is still working, and I also am working" (John 5:17).[1] You cannot rest if you have not worked.

2. Rest

God's rest becomes a model for all human beings and animals as well. It is a command that extends to all: Hebrews, Gentiles, men and women, employer and employee — even the land from which humans were created!

1. All Bible quotations are from the NRSV unless otherwise noted.

Exodus 20:10 directs: "You shall not do any work — you, your son or your daughter, your male or female slave, your livestock, or the alien resident in your towns." Even the injunction to subdue the land and name all the animals must have a pause. The land received rest from farming every seven years and every fifty years (Lev. 25:2-12). If the Hebrews had not "rested" the land, God would make sure it rested when the people were punished for not having given the land rest (Lev. 26:34-35, 43; 2 Chron. 36:21). The verb *shabath* means "to desist, cease, rest, or come to an end,"[2] and this is what God did in creation; so too His creatures must imitate the Creator in stopping work, which includes sowing and planting and harvesting and trading and cooking.[3]

3. Be Holy

Third, the word study brings up "bless" and "declare holy." Blessing and consecration of the seventh day result in the distinction to be made between the holy and the common. The common is the good work of six days. In comparison, the seventh day becomes "holy," the day which is "selected" or set aside. The third principle of Sabbath can seem to be in tension with the second principle, because the priests and the Levites and the gatekeepers "work" on the seventh day. The priests handle the ritual sacrifices, while the Levites guard the temple and later lead in the praise of God.[4]

4. Praise

But is this not the task of blessing, this praise of God or "bending the knee"?[5] God's rest is not idleness, because He blesses all creation by His Sabbath. In response, the priests and Levites and gatekeepers are to main-

---

2. Karl Feyerabend, *Langenscheidt Pocket Hebrew Dictionary to the Old Testament* (New York: McGraw-Hill, 1969), p. 341; Francis Brown, S. R. Driver, and Charles A. Briggs, *A Hebrew and English Lexicon of the Old Testament* (Oxford: Clarendon, 1968), pp. 991-92.

3. Exod. 34:21, agricultural work; Neh. 10:31; Jer. 17:21-27, trading; Exod. 16:22-23; 35:3, cooking (Shab. 1:10).

4. Lev. 24:8; 16:19-34; 2 Kings 11:5-9; Neh. 13:22; 2 Chron. 8:14; 23:4-6; Ezek. 22:26; 44:15-27 (also they teach and judge).

5. Feyerabend, *Langenscheidt*, 48; Brown, Driver, and Briggs, *A Hebrew and English Lexicon of the Old Testament*, p. 138.

tain and lead praise and thanksgiving. Their role is necessary, because the Sabbath Day and festivals are set aside for convocations of praise. Weekly seventh-day convocations and yearly celebrations, such as Passover, Unleavened Bread, Weeks (or Pentecost), Firstfruits, Trumpets, Tabernacles (or Booths), Day of Atonement, and Purim festivals mark an important aspect of the day of rest (Lev. 23:2-44; Esther 9:18-32). The Bible records Psalm 92 as "A Song for the Sabbath Day," a praise song, whereby the singer remembers that "It is good to give thanks to the Lord" (v. 1a). The New Testament appropriates this aspect of Sabbath praise and holiness by describing the Sabbath as a time of silence (Luke 23:56), a quality of life all Christians should have (1 Tim. 2:2).

5. Have Faith

What follows is that ceasing from work necessitates faith or trust in God that God is able to provide the necessities for living despite humans taking the time for rest. This is especially a lesson given to the Hebrews in the wilderness — the bread from heaven on the sixth day would last two days (Exod. 16:16-30). The sixth-year harvest would last through the seventh year (Lev. 25:21). And in numerous Old Testament references one notes that the Sabbath is closely connected with not having idols (Lev. 19:3-4; 26:1-2; Ezek. 20:16, 24; 23:38-39), since faith in a living God is a necessary aspect of desisting from work. An idol cannot provide food when one rests. The author of Hebrews also highlights this aspect of the Sabbath: "We who have believed" enter into God's rest (Heb. 4:3). Testing God and unfaithfulness are therefore contrary to entering God's rest (Heb. 3:17-19; 4:11; Ps. 127:1-2). The opposite of faith in God is, then, the pursuing of one's own self-interests (Isa. 58:13-14).

6. Remember the Sign

Godly rest is also a testimony or a sign of God's having made the world in six days. Thus, it may be seen as evangelistic, as well as a ritual, a reminder, or a covenantal sign. Rest is even a faith statement about the creation of the world and God's sanctifying work in a community's life (Exod. 31:13-17; Ezek. 20:12-13; Isa. 56:6). The breaking of this covenant has serious ramifications: excommunication and even death.

7. Liberate

As a holy and blessed day, the Sabbath is also intended as pleasing to God, a reminder that God is holy and good to all. Thus, God cannot endure impressive convocations that exist together with evil (Isa. 1:13). The Sabbath is a time to refrain from evil (Isa. 56:2). Because all are enjoined to rest, therefore, the Sabbath is a time for liberation, the time when the Hebrews remember that they had been slaves who were now liberated (Deut. 5:12-15). The fiftieth-year Sabbath required liberation and offered hope for all (Lev. 25:10).

Thus, Old Testament regulations about the Sabbath can be summarized in seven godly principles: finish work, rest, be holy, praise, have faith, remember the sign, and liberate.

Seven Sabbath Principles (New Testament)

Now the Gospel writers record six incidents revolving around the Sabbath that appear to undermine what the Old Testament teaches but, when further studied, actually nuance Old Testament teaching. And these six incidents are: the eating of the grains (Matt. 12:1-8; Mark 2:23-28; Luke 6:1-5), the healings of the man with the withered hand (Matt. 12:9-14; Mark 3:1-6; Luke 6:6-11), the bent-over woman (Luke 13:10-17), the man with dropsy (Luke 14:1-6), the man ill for thirty-eight years (John 5:1-18; 7:21-24), and the man born blind (John 9:1-40). From these six occasions, we can derive Jesus' seven principles for the seventh day.

1. Have Mercy

When the disciples were plucking heads of grain, the Pharisees accused them of harvesting on the Sabbath (Matt. 12:2). Jesus responded by using the incident of David and his soldiers eating what was not lawful for non-priests, the bread of the Temple, to reveal the larger principle that mercy or steadfast love is more important than the literal fulfillment of regulations (Matt. 12:7; Hos. 6:6). He also established that, as the Son of God, He had ultimate authority over all Sabbath regulations.

2. Serve

Condemning people is not primarily what the Sabbath is all about. Mark records an additional explanation from Jesus at the eating of the grains: "The sabbath was made for humankind, and not humankind for the sabbath" (Mark 2:27). In other words, the goal of the Sabbath was to serve humans. Resting certainly is a blessing for humans. When David was fleeing King Saul's attempt to kill him, because he and his men had kept themselves ritually pure Ahimelek the priest offered to give them the consecrated bread of the Presence from the holy place in the temple (1 Sam. 21:3-6). Satisfying the hunger of unjustly persecuted men would be a compassionate service to them.

3. Do Good

Next, the harvesting on the Sabbath is followed in all synoptic Gospels by the issue of healing on the Sabbath. Healing is not clearly called "work" in the Old Testament, but it is in the rabbinic oral laws of the Mishnah: "They may not straighten a [deformed] child's body or set a broken limb" (Shab. 22:6). Again, Jesus is concerned with the intent of the Sabbath law. He asks: "Is it lawful to do good or to do harm on the sabbath, to save life or to destroy it?" (Luke 6:9). In the first incident (Luke 6:1-2), the Pharisees accuse Jesus' disciples, and when Jesus defends the disciples the Pharisees turn their attention to Jesus to accuse Him (Luke 6:7). They cannot find any refutation for his claim that the Sabbath is for doing good and giving life. But they are furious because they think Jesus is flaunting God's command not to work (Old Testament principle two).

4. Liberate

It is only Luke who records the next incident, in which the conflict between Jesus' understanding of the Old Testament and that of his contemporaries is most evident. When a bent-over woman is healed on the Sabbath, the ruler of the synagogue closely paraphrases the Old Testament: "There are six days on which work ought to be done" (Luke 13:14; cf. Exod. 20:9). This incident highlights the potential conflict inherent in setting aside one day a week in which not to work. Can we do this consistently? If the Sabbath is a day for freeing and taking care of people as well as resting from work, then the Old Testament command to rest must be lived alongside a deeper meaning of liberation. Jesus reminds His listeners that the Sabbath is a day for liberation (Old Testament principle seven), and Jesus sees the healing of the woman as freedom from Satan's bondage in Luke 13:16. Moreover, after Jesus heals the woman who was bent over for eighteen years, the woman and the crowd rejoice at all that Jesus is doing (Luke 13:13, 17), and that reminds us of the Sabbath principle of praise (Old Testament principle four). A healing in this case is called liberation. Thus, even though the healing of this Jewish woman appears to contradict the Old Testament principle of rest (Old Testament principle two), yet it, as well as the New Testament principles of having mercy, serving humanity, and doing good (New Testament principles one, two, and three), is in agreement with the Old Testament principle of liberation (seven).

5. Heal

The next incident is also unique to Luke. By this time the Pharisees are observing Jesus even before He does what to them appears questionable on the Sabbath. Jesus asks of the lawyers and Pharisees whether the Sabbath is a day of healing or not (Luke 14:3). Then Jesus heals the man who has dropsy. Jesus compares His healing to emergency help. Emergency help takes precedence over the injunction not to work. According to the Mishnah, animals could be led by a chain or driven to a pen on the Sabbath (Shab. 5:1; 13:5). If animals and children could be pulled out of a well, was not this a type of "healing," a precedent for healing an adult?

6. God Works

The Gospel of John records two more incidents. In the first, a man who has been ill for thirty-eight years is cured and then caught in a dilemma. In order to demonstrate his faith to Jesus, he has to arise, take up his mat, and walk (John 5:8). The man is cured and follows Jesus' command to arise, take up his mat, and walk (5:9). The religious leaders, however, tell him he cannot carry his mat on the Sabbath; that is work, and such work (carrying a burden) is not allowed on the Sabbath (5:10). Later, Jesus responds to the Jewish leaders' attacks on His healing on the Sabbath by explaining: "My Father is still working, and I also am working" (5:17). So Jesus' defense appears to undermine the basic core principle of the Sabbath: God rested; therefore, humans should rest too (Old Testament principle two). However, if the first Old Testament principle is to finish work, the implication is that work itself is good. Jesus, as the Son of God, is always at work (5:17-18).

Later, during the celebration of the Festival of Booths, Jesus explains how fulfilling one law might appear to break another law, as when a child must be circumcised on the eighth day, even if this is a Sabbath Day (John 7:22-23; see Shab. 18:3; 19:2). So, the principle here, according to Jesus, is not to judge by the outward appearance or superficial criteria, but rather to judge by righteous judgment (John 7:24). Possibly, we may conclude that, even though God stopped creating on the seventh day, God did not stop sustaining and directing the world (as Col. 1:17 says about Jesus). So God's work is to heal, hearkening back to the first Old Testament Sabbath principle: finish one's work. God finishes His work.

7. Worship Jesus

The final incident in the Gospel of John that relates to the Sabbath is the healing of the man born blind. Jesus reiterates the need to do God's work while it is still possible (John 9:4). Jesus here breaks the Sabbath rule of not working not only by healing the blind man but also by making mud and spreading it on the blind man's eyes (9:6, 14-16). The focus in this event is on the nature of Jesus: His power to heal reveals that He is not a sinner but the Messiah. He is the Lord God, whom the seeing man worships (John 9:22, 31-38). So, here Jesus has highlighted the Sabbath as a day of faith (the fifth Old Testament Sabbath principle).

In summary, we learn from the Old Testament that work, though common, is good. Holy rest, or ceasing from work, is good, too. The Sabbath is intended for praise. It necessitates faith, pursuing God's interests, not one's own interests. Sabbath-keeping is part of our covenant with God, a sign to all. The Sabbath is a time for liberation. Jesus does not attack those who abide by these principles. However, He makes it quite clear that simply condemning people is not what the Sabbath is all about (see also Col. 2:16-17). Rather, these incidents from the New Testament remind us today that we should never allow the literal fulfillment of the Sabbath principles to undermine its foundational intentions: mercy, service, doing good, liberation, and healing. Our rest should not blind us to God's never-ending work. Another way to understand what Jesus did is to recognize that, even though Jesus had to re-clarify the misuse of rest (the second Old Testament principle of the Sabbath), he elevated the Old Testament principles of liberation (the seventh principle), work as good (the first principle), praise (the fourth principle), and having faith (the fifth principle).

Therefore, we, too, should recognize the difficulty of maintaining all seven Old Testament principles of the Sabbath. We can best actualize them by remembering Jesus' seven principles as wholesome correctives of Sabbath misuse, keeping foremost in our mind the intentions and underlying principles of the Sabbath regulations.

CHAPTER THIRTEEN

Sabbath in an Age of Ecology within an Emerging Global Society

Donald B. Conroy

Introduction: Setting the Context

In our age the environmental crisis has become so urgent that it impinges on the very existence of the created order of nature which sustains all life. To a significant extent we humans are culpable for having created a variety of ecological crises facing the human family and the global community. Necessity now compels us to look to an age of ecological regeneration as well as conservation. This is no small challenge.

Centuries of mainly utilitarian ethics and denial of the problem have now been joined by the "postmodern" rejection of earlier systems of meaning. Is there anything in the history of the human family that could help redeem us from the trap of ceaseless productivity and guiltless consumption of resources that threaten the continued ability of the planet to sustain life?

The gift and treasure of the Sabbath tradition can have profound meaning and real impact on the quality of life in this new era of global awareness. After all, the Sabbath tradition itself was developed over long periods of time in the context of many cultural crises and influences in the ancient world. The Mediterranean basin and Fertile Crescent areas were crossroads for commercial and cultural exchange.

The exchange often was violent as political, cultural, and religious worldviews clashed. Yet the ancient Israelites came to understand the ori-

---

For research and major input to this chapter the author is deeply indebted to Peggy Dutch, Ph.D. candidate, Duquesne University, Pittsburgh.

gin and ordering of the cosmos, and their place in it, in relation to an all-powerful, loving, compassionate Creator God who was and remains intimately interested and involved in human history. This Creator God invites mere humans to share both in the work of creation and in the divine rest which follows.

The Sabbath tradition teaches the intrinsic value of a rhythm of creative activity and accomplishment followed by periods of withdrawal and repose. This cyclical rhythm sets limits on human exploitation of the gifts of creation. It also provides time and opportunity for reflection on how best to utilize and appreciate God-given natural resources for the common good of all.

Humans have lost that rhythm and the valuable lesson of *voluntary self-restraint* that such a rhythm teaches. In trying to recapture or re-envision such rhythm and balance, care must be taken to respect local cultures and the particularity of diverse customs, including religious and theological. This is one of the major challenges facing the human family as the impact of globalization is increasingly felt in all sectors.

The highly industrialized and technologically developed societies are facing both the choice and the necessity of reflecting on the lack of harmony with the created order. This lack of harmony is clear from the experience of everyday life and from the increasingly mounting evidence of the sciences as they examine the biological and sociological patterns now emerging.[1]

Today, in the United States, we have a unique opportunity to explore how Sabbath keeping can be a way of achieving a new ecological balance for the global community. The opportunity of exploring the relevance of biblical Sabbath for today's world is ours partly because of our constitution's insistence on the freedom of religious expression as well as the protection of the value of religious liberty for all, and partly because we contribute significantly to the ecological imbalance threatening the survival of the earth and its inhabitants.

By drawing on the tradition of Sabbath we can discover ways in which the new global cultures and emerging economies can meet the challenges of this new era. While no one particular religious worldview will ever be mandated for citizens or guests of this nation, we also are free to explore

---

1. Cf. Donald B. Conroy and Rodney L. Petersen, *Earth at Risk* (New York: Prometheus Press, 2000), and the latest reports of the Worldwatch Institute, *State of the World*, 2008-2009.

new ways of looking at old practices and to ask new questions in light of the emerging challenges. In finding a common set of needed values in the practice of Sabbath keeping, we can offer this amazing practice to our society as a gift, newly adapted to our own times.

Arguably, many, if not most, contemporary Americans would be quite bewildered by, or subtly opposed to, the suggestion that ancient understandings of biblical Sabbath might have something important to offer today's world. First of all, some might contend that this practice is "old" or obsolete. Second, it has been replaced by newer social practices and cultural perspectives. Third, there is a legacy of subtle, and sometimes blatant, anti-Jewish or "anti-Judaizing" tendencies left over from the earliest Christian writers.

The New Testament writers and early church fathers had little or no choice but to use categories of ancient Greek philosophical thought and the idiom of Greek language. This extensive culture was the major worldview of their day in the Mediterranean basin. They had to use Greek language and thought patterns as they tried to express the Oneness of the Creator God and the belief that this One God became incarnate in human flesh and yet remains both Divine and One.

Without having a grasp of the ancient Hebrew world to bridge the chasm between Hebraic thought and the Hellenic linguistic and cultural patterns, these early Christian writers set out to articulate new theological insights which clashed with previous ways of understanding the Creator God. Unfortunately, this inevitably led to a certain degree of antipathy toward the roots of the parent faith tradition, Judaism, and one of its main cornerstones, the Sabbath.

This antipathy toward Judaism and its seventh-day Sabbath persisted for centuries throughout the medieval period. It became further complicated during, and subsequent to, the sixteenth-century difficulties between the Protestant reformers and the Church of Rome, and even among the reformers and their followers. Polemical positions hardened. The disparity between Jewish and Christian understandings of Sabbath grew and became set with time. Furthermore, as the centuries passed, the disparity in various Christian understandings and practices of a day set apart from the labors and chores of the workweek increased among the many denominations of Christianity. This led to many different Sabbath or Sunday customs within Christianity itself.

Basically, there are three traditional approaches that have been used in the history of Christianity in interpreting the Sabbath commandment.

One approach, always representing the minority, asserts that Saturday is the Sabbath, and Christians are bound by the biblical command to observe the original day of Sabbath. A second approach is that observance of the Sabbath has been transferred to the first day of the week for Christians. They are bound by the biblical command to observe Sunday (the Lord's Day) as a day of both rest and worship with the faith community. The third approach is quite ancient, having begun in the early church and continued throughout the patristic and medieval periods right up to the present. This last approach posits that Christians are freed from the "ceremonial" observance of the biblical commandment, but they either choose, or are required, to worship together on Sunday, the Lord's Day, based on their specific denomination.

The question of ceasing productive activities and precisely what constitutes "work" or "servile work" is still open for discussion. Many Christian writers have become bogged down in such definitions. Once legal or canonical definitions are identified, often the next step is to find creative moral exemptions or "loopholes" in the restrictions in order to excuse oneself or one's group from following the biblical command. This in turn has led to wide variations in practices and regulations among Christian denominations as to preferred methods of Sabbath observance.

At times in our nation's history, strict "Sunday Blue Laws" were enforced rigidly albeit with very different interpretations and practices among Christian groups. Such laws were intended to protect workers, families, and other factors contributing to the stability of the social fabric of the nation, including the free exercise of religion. Many times the goals underpinning the "Sunday Blue Laws" were quite noble. Unfortunately, the civic laws inadvertently brought negative attitudes as well. Many did not understand Sabbath observance. Also, specifically Sunday legislation was considered by some to be an unjust imposition on those for whom Sunday has no religious importance, as in the case of followers of religions beyond the pale of the Hebrew or Christian Bible.

Yet from a secular viewpoint the state holds that all people are entitled to the benefits of a day of withdrawal from their labors for the purposes of repose and refreshment as well as of worship or meditation. We commonly acknowledge in our modern society that worship of any type cannot be forced or coerced. However, since coercion violates both human dignity and religious liberty, this free observance provides an opportunity to the nation and wider world society for sharing the blessings and benefits embedded in Sabbath keeping.

In addition, another significant factor to consider is the arrival on the world stage of a third form of monotheism which traces its heritage back to the biblical patriarch Abraham through his elder son, Ishmael. This younger branch of the Abrahamic faith tradition brings both additional and different understandings of the need to set apart time for worship. In addition to special times of prayer each day of the week, Friday is a day of special significance in Islamic tradition. However, neither Saturday nor Sunday is of special religious significance for adherents of this faith.

While notions surrounding the differentiation of the sacred and the secular or profane aspects of human life can be very different among these three forms of monotheism, there is real common ground. Each of these three monotheistic faiths posits a belief in a Creator God who is vitally interested and involved in human history. Each recognizes the human need to set aside time from human labors. Each agrees that time with family as well as time for worship of the Creator are important values to be defended and practiced in visible and tangible ways. These are profoundly important social values.

The instinct to observe times of withdrawal from human labors, however, is not limited to monotheistic worldviews by any means. Ancient and contemporary religions of both East and West include both doctrine and practices concerning withdrawal and repose.[2] The "active not-doing," *wu-wei*, of the *Tao* is one example from Chinese traditions. The *dharma*, *bhakti*, *maya*, and *moksha* (duty/obligation, love/devotion, illusory quality of worldly things, and liberation from bondage to illusion and suffering) of Hinduism are compatible with the instinct of withdrawal and repose.[3] Moreover, in both the Hindu and Buddhist traditions, the days of the new moon and full moon are observed as times for fasting and self-sacrifice.[4]

Aboriginal, African, and Native American traditions also have teachings and practices concerning the balance between work and withdrawal from work as well as the need for repose both for humans and the rest of nature. So the instinct to balance work and repose need not be limited to a particular religious worldview to the exclusion of others. Finally, Ringwald points out the obvious fact that, while "the Sabbath" is not legislated by either state or federal statutes, it is protected and it provides the

2. Christopher D. Ringwald, *A Day Apart: How Jews, Christians, and Muslims Find Faith, Freedom, and Joy on the Sabbath* (Oxford: Oxford University Press, 2007), p. 166.

3. Denise Lardner Carmody and John Tully Carmody, *Ways to the Center: An Introduction to World Religions,* 4th ed. (Belmont, CA: Thomson Wadsworth, 1993), pp. 74, 105, 115-16.

4. Ringwald, *A Day Apart,* p. 166.

anchor for an institution beloved universally in the United States, namely, the weekend.[5]

However, in *Dies Domini* Pope John Paul II warns against simply letting the Sabbath blend in with the contemporary weekend when secular society looks exclusively to leisure, sports, and other profane activities and neglects to observe the sacred nature of the Sabbath. Leisure and recreational activities are healthy for the human psyche; that is a given. But self-centered pleasure-seeking activities which ignore the human impact on others and on the environment at large can clearly contribute to the degradation of other persons, societies, and the delicate ecosystems which sustain life.

The world community is now witnessing and is caught up in cultural, philosophical, religious, and socio-political clashes on a scale which our forebears and our ancestors in multiple faiths could not have imagined. Modern technological achievements have brought the "pre-modern," "modern," and "post-modern" philosophical systems into intimate proximity and face-to-face confrontation. There is mutual incomprehensibility, often resulting in mistrust of "the other."

Since the treasure and gift of *Shabbat* was presented to the ancient descendents of Abraham, Isaac, and Jacob in the context of cultural and religious diversity, maybe there is something in the Creator's design that we have not yet examined or perceived. The biblical accounts present Sabbath as the great equalizer among inhabitants of the land. The "rest" was meant for all, including the king, the children of Israel, their domestic help, and other laborers, as well as the alien who lived in their midst. The "rest" was even extended to the animals, as beasts of burden, and to the land itself. The observance of a cyclically recurring day of ceasing from labors, a day of delight and gladness, became an important visible outward sign of the covenant with the benevolent Creator of all.

We have seen already that the instinct to observe times of withdrawal from human labors is a common thread among various religions and religious worldviews. Even the secular world reveres the weekend, an institution anchored by the Sabbath. There is a great deal of common ground to work with in relation to stopping human productivity and consumption of the world's resources on a cyclical basis. The cyclically recurring day(s) do not necessarily have to be the same, nor must they have the same significance for everyone, everywhere. But the need for regular periods of withdrawal and repose is a given part of the human condition whether one ac-

5. Ringwald, *A Day Apart*, p. 157.

cepts the Creator/creation motif or not. Yet, owing to the social nature of humans and the need for a shared sense of time and place to build up the human condition to emulate worthwhile values, an agreed upon day of rest or series of days, such as the weekend, by means of shared Sabbath experience and observance greatly contributes to the well-being of society as well as to the communal witness coming from the faith community.

Such beliefs, values, and witness are seen in the following biblical themes:

1. Servitude vs. Freedom

Taking just one book from the Pentateuch as an example, it is quite obvious that the major part of the book of Exodus is about liberation from that which enslaves or oppresses. The whole book is an epic narrative about divine intervention to release the people from enslavement to Pharaoh's anti-creational agenda. Both Jewish and Christian traditions celebrate the events and make them come alive in the present through liturgical celebrations.

Considering that the first four commandments of the Decalogue (three in the Catholic tradition) are tied to liturgical celebrations of the historical deliverance of the people from Egypt, Walter Harrelson has suggested strongly that the Ten Commandments not be categorized as "law" at all. Rather, the Decalogue should be seen as a "great charter of freedom," something which liberates rather than enslaves.[6] Such a theme can contribute to an ongoing sense in contemporary society of the need for liberation of enslaved peoples in marginal immigrant populations and also raise consciousness in our own times of the importance of social justice and environmental values that liberate all of creation, as Saint Paul says in Romans 8.

2. Everlasting Covenant and Torah

As Christians continue to study the Scriptures in relation to the whole canon, without the presuppositions imposed by Greek philosophical lenses, and instead look to the particular milieu out of which each of the books emerged, new light will be shed on these ancient yet living texts.

6. Walter J. Harrelson, *The Ten Commandments for Today* (Louisville: Westminster John Knox, 2006), pp. 15-18.

This kind of study, "higher criticism," has been happening in gradually increasing depth and frequency since about the middle of the last century to the recent Synod on the Word of God held in the fall of 2008. It is worth noting, too, that the polemics of the sixteenth-century Reformation period seem to be softening somewhat as scholars and church leaders come together in a spirit of both ecumenical and inter-faith dialogue.

The permanence of God's commitment and the everlasting nature of Divine love, justice, and mercy become through Sabbath observance a continual process of deepening within our personal and social consciousness.

3. Evolving Understandings of Covenant: Particular and Universal

Admittedly, the term *covenant* is a biblical term with profound meaning within Judaism and increasing significance for Christianity. Still, it is not devoid of meaning for people of other traditions. In the theology of the Old (or First) Testament, observant Jews were to follow the teachings of *Torah,* keep the covenantal relationship with YHWH alive, and observe Sabbath in visible ways so that others might see and recognize the wisdom of this practice.

By expanding on the theme of covenant and using Sabbath as the weekly renewal of our sense of covenant (and the effort on our part to keep it), we have a means of a more profound understanding and appreciation as we go thorough the seasons of the year and the cycles of our lives. As families, communities, and nations we can experience the manifestations of the Divine covenant in particular ways as well as in our universal humanity. The Psalms and the Wisdom literature in general can greatly help in approaching the ways this reality applies to our particular life circumstances and to our common human condition.

4. Presence: Awareness of and Access to the Divine

Most theistic worldviews have some sense of the presence of the numinous and spiritual order in which the Invisible God comes to relate to our lives and our world. This human accessibility to the Divine is abundantly manifest in the way we continue to set aside an entire day for Sabbath. In Christian parlance, God is all-knowing, all-powerful, and ever-present. This idea of presence at all times and everywhere is something that catechisms have stressed for the last five hundred years. Yet, many of us find it difficult to live in the awareness of God's presence in the activities of daily living. Hence we establish rituals and rhythms; identify certain moments, people, places, and objects as holy; and set them apart for special religious or spiritual signification of God's presence with us and our accessibility to God and the spiritual realm. Biblical Sabbath provides an added dimension in which to experience God's presence, namely, the dimension of time.

In these four themes the biblical tradition helps us to understand God's ways, which transcend our world but touch our lives. Through the medium of Sabbath keeping we are given a deeper understanding to form our lives and impact our world. But as we explore these general themes we also have the great creation story in Genesis and the earliest traces of God's blessing and commitment to the human race and its welfare.

In the poetic style of the first story of creation, we read that the Creator paused after each of the first five days' work and found it to be "good." On the "sixth day" humankind was created. We are told that God paused and found everything that had been wrought to be "very good." Yet the Divine role in creation was not completed yet. Nothing had been blessed or made holy — that is, set apart and consecrated by covenant. Everything was good, in fact very good. But nothing and no one species had been blessed, made holy, set apart for the special purpose of the Creator. Time, the "seventh day," is set apart from the others and made holy. It is only later in the story line that people are especially blessed and made holy, as Noah, Abraham, and their descendents are given a special or chosen relationship through covenant living and Sabbath keeping. Moreover, they are sanctified as they "remember" and "observe" (keep/guard) the Sabbath as a *sign* of the continuing presence of the Divine in the midst of human history and human endeavors.[7]

The Need to Address the Emerging Global Reality

Considering the emerging global society that is more and more interdependent, we have passed from the era of isolated faith practices to a time in history where most people are becoming aware of very different beliefs, ei-

---

7. Cf. D. A. Carson, ed., *From Sabbath to Lord's Day: A Biblical, Historical, and Theological Investigation* (Grand Rapids: Baker, 1982; Eugene, OR: Wipf and Stock, 1999).

ther through social means of communication, such as television and the Internet, or by meeting people in the public square with very diverse religious backgrounds. In the middle of this diversity, Sabbath keeping and sanctifying the weekend can relate without explanation to the present and coming generations of believers and their everyday companions in school or colleagues at the office. It becomes more and more obvious that we need to discover ways to preserve key values in our faith tradition but open doors of cooperation and understanding to others unacquainted with our beliefs, values, and rituals.

As we look at the practice of Sabbath keeping, we see from the biblical tradition a rich tapestry of such important ways of knowing and experiencing God's invisible presence in the creation. Moreover, because of the intimate and profound connection with Torah and covenant, as Jews and Christians we have a way of approaching God's providential presence and saving concern for us.

First of all, we can consider covenant as a way of seeing our common access to God's presence and his bond with us through creation. We see in the great saving events of the Exodus through the biblical vision a way of approaching the deeper mysteries of our own existence. We also begin to see the challenges of our common humanity and the "covenantal" nature of the web of all life that we commonly refer to as the natural environment and with which we are so interconnected and on which we are dependent in body and soul.

The covenant that was made by God with the Hebrews, that beleaguered group of ex-slaves who became God's chosen people, formed the key to their existence and to ours. Once they experienced the Exodus event and the unforgettable theophany when God made the covenant with Moses as prophet and mediator, they began to see things differently, even though there was much back-sliding. They emerged through a long journey in the environmental solitude of the Sinai, coming to see themselves, their God, and their future in a new way. From the time they received the Decalogue they had a unique experience of a God who gave them the exceptional gift of a weekly reminder of their liberation from slavery and God's invisible presence. This Sabbath reminder visibly and tangibly signifies God's presence and providence on a weekly basis through the events of history and elements of nature.

We are also reminded by the historian Thomas Cahill that, in addition to the "innovation of speaking the unspoken moral law" through the Decalogue (the key to keeping the covenant and understanding its wisdom through the Torah), we should take note of the innovation which got its start in the Jewish Sabbath. Cahill notes that no ancient society before the Jews had a weekly day of rest for joyful reasons. (Other societies, however, did observe *tabu* days when no work was to be done. These days were experienced as days of curse and fear.) For the Israelites, the God who made all things and then "ceased" on the seventh day bade them to do the same. God, of course, didn't need to "rest," but through Moses and the command of the Decalogue he asked the Israelites to stop their hard work and reflect on the goodness of his presence and his glory in creation around them as they gave praise to the One who would continue to be with them in their journey to the land of promise and forever into the future.[8]

As this people of God thought more about this present covenant, they carried out the Sabbath keeping in their lives as a nation, especially chosen, but, as Isaiah proclaims, one to become a "light to the nations." At that point they reflected back on the story of this God of gods, who called their ancestors Abraham, Isaac, and Jacob many centuries before. But they didn't stop there, as their weekly Sabbath reminded them. In fact, as they heard mythologies from the neighboring cultures, they came to borrow and revise some parts and make the story of creation uniquely their own. They began to tell their story anew with a much greater sense of how their God not only superseded the pagan gods but was the only God who existed. They realized that these so-called gods were in fact no-gods. They did not really exist.

Yet what did exist, the world around them, was made out of nothing (see the later inter-testamental writings), and their God YHWH, whom Moses perceived on the mountain in the burning bush, was the one and only God who made everything by his Word *(dabar)*. Taking the great creation story, they retold it with their God, who made it in six days and made it "good." Then, much to their wonder, YHWH ceased and "rested" in their anthropomorphic analogy on the seventh day. This is a sign to them that they too must "rest" each week and honor God and respect his handiwork, not their own.

However, as they reflected back, they didn't stop there. They realized that YHWH not only made all things, visible and invisible, but that this Lord God was with their ancestors and the human race from time immemorial. In spite of the fall and the wickedness of the human race, the

8. Thomas Cahill, *The Gifts of the Jews: How a Tribe of Desert Nomads Changed the Way Everyone Thinks and Feels* (New York: Nan A. Talese, 1998), p. 44.

Lord God (YHWH) didn't give up on humans and creation. They then recalled the time of the Great Flood or floods (possibly the end of the great Ice Age) when all humans were wiped out except for Noah and his family and all the animals he was commanded by the Lord God to save in the Ark.

This fantastic story, as mythical as it sounds to modern ears, not only has a kernel of everlasting truth, but it embodies implications for the whole of humanity and creation, as the book of Genesis reveals.

The story is dramatically told in Genesis:

> God blessed Noah and his sons and said to them: "Be fertile and multi-ply and fill the earth. Dread fear of you shall come upon all the animals of the earth and all the birds of the air, upon all the creatures that move about on the ground and all the fishes of the sea; into your power they are delivered. Every creature that is alive shall be yours to eat; I give them all to you as I did the green plants." (Gen. 9:1-3)

Then a breakthrough in their awareness of what the covenant between Israel and the Lord God really implies gradually emerged in their consciousness. The Creator then said to Noah and his family: "See, I am now establishing my covenant with you and your descendants after you and with every living creature that was with you: all the birds, and the various tame and wild animals that came with you out of the ark" (Gen. 9:8-10).

The sacred text proceeds in the next seven verses to make the point that the covenant is not with humankind alone but with all creation; it does this by repeating in several ways that the Lord God's pact is not only with the human race but with all living things and the whole web of life. God then points to the "rainbow" in the sky and adds: "This is the sign that I am giving for all ages to come, of the covenant between me and you and every living creature with you." And verse 17 repeats this *universal* covenant: "God told Noah: 'This is the sign of the covenant I have established between me and all mortal creatures that are on earth."

We have now a fuller picture or understanding of what the Sabbath and the covenant with which it is inextricably bound implies: *We humans are also to be responsible for and respect all living things and all creation.* This builds on what Adam was commanded to care for in the garden and now what Noah and his descendants are bound by covenant to respect.

The Torah expands in various ways upon this responsibility. Also, the Psalms and other Wisdom literature bring out the significance of this universal covenant. Now that in our time we have scientific evidence that humans have in the past and continue in the present to impact negatively the creation — that is, the natural environment of the air, water, land, fish, and animal realms — we must acknowledge in the present our collective and personal violations of God's covenant.

Herein we have an opportunity to come to our senses. But this new awareness is possible only if we do not mindlessly continue to construct (like the Tower of Babel) a planetary civilization supported by an economy and a culture that work continuously (24/7) and voraciously consume beyond our needs.

In this way we can see an opportunity to change — a God-given solution — if we are willing to consider the actual facts surrounding our lifestyle and culture. It can begin with realizing that Sabbath keeping leads to our acting more responsibly as earth stewards and caretakers of creation. This Sabbath keeping not only gives rest for ourselves and the economy but gives us time to reflect and have the leisure time to be regenerative through God's Spirit by taking the Sabbath rest seriously.

A very helpful development in the consideration of Sabbath observance and the implications for church and society comes in Pope John Paul II's apostolic letter "Observing and Celebrating the Day of the Lord" *(Dies Domini)*, published in 1998. In this little-known apostolic teaching, addressed to the whole church, the late pope calls upon all Christians to observe Sunday in a way analogous to the Jewish Sabbath. This papal teaching has not received a lot of attention, but, if read thoughtfully in light of ecumenical developments and pastoral concerns, this is a very timely treatise.

The pope was able to come to his suggestions in this letter only after years of prayer and study in attempting to improve relations between Judaism and Catholicism. On November 17, 1980, the pope addressed the Jewish Community in Mainz, West Germany. In this address, he referred to contemporary Jews as "the people of God of the Old Covenant, never revoked by God, the present-day people of the covenant concluded with Moses." This was a major development.

This represents a change in thinking, or doctrinal development, from the earliest centuries of Christianity. Recall that the early and medieval church fathers consistently and deliberately wanted to place distance between Christianity and Judaism. Considering the historical, cultural, political, social, economic, and religious climate at the time, their blatant antipathy toward Judaism is not surprising *for that time.* However, those same exigencies no longer exist today. This was noted already at the Second Vatican Council (1962-65).

While a total review of the lengthy *Dies Domini* cannot be given here, several highlights and implications have great relevance to the theme of this chapter. In particular, these might be noted:

- By looking anew at the practice of Sabbath keeping, Christians can take a fresh look at their own roots and those of their Jewish brothers and sisters.
- This possibility arises from a new rapport between Christianity and Judaism established in recent times in the work of Vatican II.
- This relates to the renewal of Christian faith but also to the organization of civic society and how our lives are impacted by observing the weekend.
- The process can be undertaken in a biblical and theological rediscovery that has implications pastorally, ecumenically, and inter-religiously.
- Sabbath keeping touches many aspects of our contemporary existence: work and leisure; home and family life; cultural development; economic use of natural resources; and respect for creation.

These five highlights or implications gleaned from *Dies Domini* and set forth in light of present issues lead us to what might be considered practical customs and practices which can reflect and build on this process of recovery and development of Sabbath. In particular, there are three areas we can emphasize and underscore as we look at the future of an increasingly global and secularized society and try to bring a fresh awareness of the Divine presence and God's role in human history today:

1. Through the presence of God in the family — often called the basic cell of society and church — awareness of the Divine can be fostered in taking time not only for explicit worship in church, synagogue, or mosque but also in the home as a household of faith with rituals, shared meals, and time together in recreation in parks and out-of-doors in natural settings.
2. The awareness of the Divine presence in congregations can be enhanced and further developed through creation-centered or ecologically sensitive dimensions of worship and ritual already found and now recovered and implicated in Sabbath worship as well as in religious education and ecumenical interaction.

3. The implications of the Creator's presence as seen and experienced in the created order and harmony can be manifest in a wide variety of weekend activities and events undertaken to heal, sustain, and regenerate the natural ecology. At the same time this brings about new awareness of the spiritual dimensions of life for the future of society and continuance of life on our planet.

In this way Sabbath keeping gives focus and energy to a new religious and ecumenical effort to look into raising our awareness through thought and scholarship to see how this activity can energize and renew collaboration of various faith traditions. This results in a call to action for a much deeper and wider consciousness of the importance of Sabbath keeping for mission and eco-ministry. Thus, by keeping the Sabbath, we experience the covenant promise in a profound way *in time* by its weekly re-occurrence and symbolized *in space* by the rainbow — both given for all time as signs to Israel and all our ancestors who have believed in the living God who is ever present with us.

CHAPTER FOURTEEN

The American Sunday and the Formative Work of Jonathan Edwards

Louis J. Mitchell

Jonathan Edwards was arguably America's greatest philosopher theologian, and he was very connected to the topic of Sabbath and the Lord's Day. He was the College of New Jersey's (Princeton University) third president, serving there in 1758 until his untimely death. He was primarily a preacher. We know him and study him in many different kinds of fields, but it was as a preacher addressing Sabbath concerns out of the context of Sabbath observance itself, preaching to God's people gathered on the Sabbath, that we encounter this theme: "the perpetuity and change of the Sabbath."

The Perpetuity and Change of the Sabbath is a sustained discourse comprised of three sermons or three preaching units. It was first preached, according to Mark Valeri, early in Edwards' pastorate in 1730 or very early 1731.[1] He preached it again at least once. We know this because of later inserted additions to the manuscript. It is an exegetical and theological defense of Sunday Sabbath observance. It was part of Edwards' defense of the Puritan practice of the Sabbath over and against the slightly different interpretations of Anglicans and Loyalists in the British context, the rationalists and skeptics who dismissed Sabbath observance as superstitious, and what Valeri calls "market-minded businessmen" who really just wanted to make money seven days a week. Additionally, in New England there were sectarian groups such as the Seventh Day Baptists in Rhode Island who practiced Seventh Day or Saturday Sabbath observance. In 1703

---

1. Mark Valeri, ed., *Sermons and Discourses, 1730-1733*, The Works of Jonathan Edwards Series, vol. 17 (New Haven: Yale University Press, 1999).

This reprise, compiled by Rodney L. Petersen, is based on an address by the Rev. Dr. Lou Mitchell in 2004 at a gathering of the Lord's Day Alliance, at Princeton Theological Seminary.

Jeremiah Dummer, of a prominent New England family, published a work that had some influence in which he questioned Sunday observance from both a scriptural and an historical standpoint. *The Perpetuity and Change of the Sabbath* was Edwards' answer to this challenge to the Puritan Sabbath/Sunday.

Edwards' text for this series is 1 Corinthians 16:1-2: "Now concerning the collection for the Saints upon the first day of the week where every one of you lays by him in store as God hath prospered him." In typical Puritan preaching fashion, after introducing the text Edwards gives a brief exposition of the text in its biblical context. This sets the stage for him to announce the doctrine of the sermon: "'Tis the Mind and Will of God that the first day of the week should be the day that should be especially set apart for religious exercises and duties amongst Christians."

After announcing the doctrine that the first day of the week should be the day especially set apart, Edwards declares that there are some who deny this. He says, "Some refuse to distinguish the Sabbath from any other day of the week. Some see it as a custom or tradition, by human appointment only but see no divine imperative in its observance. Others see the Jewish Sabbath as a perpetual obligation not abrogated but still in effect." For Edwards this is an important matter. He says these words to his congregation: "No Christian should rest until he has satisfactorily discovered the Mind of God in this matter. Should the Christian Sabbath be of divine institution it is doubtless a thing of great importance to religion whether it be well kept or no. Therefore every Christian should be well acquainted with the institution of it." Edwards continues, "I design now therefore by the help of God to show that it is sufficiently revealed in the Scriptures." That is his prime objective: to show that this is a scriptural doctrine, that the first day of the week is the mind and will of God, and that it should be distinguished in the Christian church from other days of the week as a Sabbath to be devoted to religious exercises.

The overall outline of the three-part sermon series promotes and elucidates that doctrine. He offers two broad propositions in the first two sermons; in the third sermon he outlines the application of those propositions. Proposition one is this: "'Tis sufficiently clear that 'tis the Mind and Will of God that one day of the week or one day in seven should be devoted to rest and religious exercises throughout all ages and nations but not only amongst the Israelites 'till Christ came, but even in these Gospel times and amongst all nations professing Christianity." In other words, in the first sermon Edwards demonstrates that it is God's will that one day in seven be set aside as the Sabbath. Proposition two argues: "That 'tis the Will of God" that this day — that is, the one-in-seven that he addressed in the first sermon — "shall be the First Day of the week." Under the Gospel dispensation, or in the Christian church, one day in seven, Sunday being the day, the first day of the week, is the day established as the Christian Sabbath. The third section is that of application and exhortation. Here there are two broad principles. First, he counsels thankfulness for the institution of the Christian Sabbath. Second, he exhorts the faithful to keep holy this day. This is a very typical Puritan sermon structure: text, doctrine, propositions with sub points, objections to be considered, followed by application and exhortation.

As Edwards develops the first sermon in the three-part series, he works to show that it is from God's mind and will that one day in seven be set aside for rest and religious exercises throughout all ages and for all nations, and that this was true for Old Testament Israel and for the New Testament church as well. He lays out his argument in six points. He notes that having such a day is "consonant with human reason." It is common sense that there must be specific periods for secular business to be conducted and there also must be a definite period for religious practice. Having one-sixth time, says Edwards, is better than having no sixth or particular time. He goes on to say that the best model for this is the pattern of work and rest established at creation. The Fourth Commandment makes God's mind in this matter quite clear, he argues. This commandment "is no doubt everlasting in a perpetual obligation"; this is a key phrase in that it is a perpetual obligation, "at least as to the substance of it as is intimated by its being engraven in tables of stone and 'tis not to be thought that Christ ever abolished any commandment of the Ten[;] there is the complete number ten yet and will be to the end of the world." The commandments are not abolished by Christ. They are not diminished in any way; but it is the substance of the commandment that continues into perpetuity. Edwards writes, "Some say that the Commandment is perpetual but not literally so, that is that one in seven is in a mystical sense, that now all time is holy, that there is no distinction between one day and the next"; but he absolutely rejects that mystical interpretation. Edwards is arguing for perpetuity in the commandment, that is, in the substance of it. The main rejection of such perpetuity is that the duty required is not a "moral" duty by the language of the day. Edwards recognizes a distinction between ceremonial laws, like many in the Old Testament, and what he calls moral laws. The latter, which includes the Sabbath, are established by God, but they also derive from "the nature of things and the general state and nature of mankind as well as God's revealed Will." Moral laws are established not only because God says so but because that is the way the world is. That is the way we are. That is consistent with reality.

The second sermon begins again with the biblical text, followed by Edwards' second proposition, that it is the will of God that this day, the one-in-seven, should be the first day of the week under the Gospel dispensation of the Christian church. He argues that the Fourth Commandment offers no objection against this being the day, that the perpetuity of the commandment is simply one day in seven, without identifying a particular day. This is an important point for Edwards. It is the substance of the commandment, one day in seven. The model of creation establishes the pattern: God worked six days in seven, and rested one day in seven. So the Sabbath pattern is to rest one day in seven, without necessarily identifying which day this should be. The Sabbath in the Old Testament commemorated God's work in the creation of the world, and this, he argues, is consonant with celebrating and commemorating the day of God's new creation work, that of redemption. In Genesis 1:1 we read that God created the heavens and the earth; thus the church of old commemorated the seventh day. Again, in Revelation 21:1, Edwards says, "God created a new heaven and a new earth and those who belong to the new creation commemorate that." Citing 2 Corinthians 5:17, he writes, behold everything passes away. Behold everything becomes new. And then from Hebrews 4:10 he writes that as Christ entered into his rest, so God did from his; Christ rested from his work when he rose from the dead. He finished the work of redemption; Christ's humiliation was at an end. He rested from his labors and was refreshed.

As the Jews were commanded to remember their deliverance from Egypt, writes Edwards, so Christians remember their freedom from sin. Exodus was a type of Christ's redemption. This example of Reformed typology illustrates the primary way by which Puritans interpreted the Scriptures, that is, that there are types that foreshadow later realities or fulfillments of the types. The Exodus and our spiritual redemption, says Edwards, have an exact identity of reason: one is the type, the other is the antitype. Quoting Psalm 118:22-24, which talks about the stone which the builders rejected becoming the head or cornerstone, Edwards writes, "This is the day which the Lord hath made and we will rejoice and be glad in it." He says the stone is Christ and the day of rejoicing is the day of Christ's resurrection. The day that was the Jewish Sabbath has now been supplanted by the Christian Sabbath for those of the new creation; Christ as the creator of the world did not rest on the seventh day but remained imprisoned by death. He took another day on which to rest. The Sabbath is to be a day of rejoicing, not of mourning. Christ chose the first day of the week on which to appear to his disciples and on which to pour out his Holy Spirit at Pentecost. In the New Testament this is the day of the public worship of the primitive Christian church by the direction of the Apostles, the first day of the week, called the Lord's Day in the New Testament. Tradition through the first three centuries of Christian history confirms what Scripture establishes as the practice of the church.

The last point Edwards makes in his second sermon is the suggestion that the practice of the Lord's Day is, perhaps, the subject of progressive or gradual revelation. In deference to the Jewish community, he suggests, it was purposely avoided as an explicit doctrine in the New Testament by the Holy Spirit; and "it was very possible that the Apostles themselves at first might not have had this change of the day of the Sabbath fully revealed to them." Edwards concludes the sermon by saying that the Spirit was "careful to bring in the observation of the Lord's Day by degrees," and that he leaves for everyone to judge whether there is sufficient evidence as to God's mind and will that the first day of the week should be kept by the Christian church as the Sabbath.

This brings us to the last sermon, "On Word of Application." In typical Puritan fashion Edwards restates the text, the doctrine, and the two general propositions; and he then proceeds to the application and exhortation. Through two exhortations he argues, first, that we should be thankful for the institution of the Christian Sabbath. It is to be a day of physical and spiritual rest and a day of rejoicing. He writes, "The Christian Sabbath is one of the most precious enjoyments of the visible church. Christ showed His love of His church in the instituting of it and it becomes the Christian church to be thankful to her Lord for the name of this day as the Lord's Day or Jesus' Day . . . as it intimates the special relation it has to Christ in the design of it which is the commemoration of our dear Savior in His love to His Church in the redeeming of it."

Second, Edwards exhorts the church to keep the day holy. He writes: "Seeing therefore that God has sufficiently declared His Mind in this take heed that you do according to it. God has given such evidences of this being His Mind that He will surely require it of you if you do not strictly and conscientiously observe it. If you do so you may have this comfort, that in the reflection upon it that you have not been superstitious in it but have done as God has revealed it to be His Mind and Will in His Word that you should do and that in so doing you are in the way of God's acceptance and reward." Edwards continues with five motives as to why this should be the case.

1. God is honored by Sabbath keeping. Edwards adds, if it were not for the Sabbath there would be but little public and visible appearance of serving, worshiping, and reverencing God. The Sabbath seems to have been appointed, in part, for the visibility of religion in the public realm.

2. The business of Sabbath practice is the greatest business of our lives, that is, the business of religion. We are made principally for serving and worshiping God.

3. Our time belongs to God. God can command us any way God chooses.

4. The Sabbath is a day wherein God especially confers God's grace and blessing. God also observes the Sabbath, Edwards argues. God has not only hallowed the Sabbath but has blessed it (citing Exod. 20:11). Edwards encourages us to read the Scriptures and attend the preaching of the Word, for it is "the likeliest time to have the Spirit accompanying of it."

5. There is a relationship between Sabbath keeping and the general state of religion. He writes that in those places where the Sabbath is kept well, religion in general will be most flourishing.

Edwards next offers some suggestions for how the Lord's Day, as Sabbath, should be kept. For example, we ought to be exceedingly careful to abstain from sin. The Sabbath being holy time, it is especially defiled by the commission of sin upon this day. Edwards writes, "We ought carefully to watch over our own hearts and to avoid all sinful thoughts on the Sabbath Day and we ought to maintain such a reverence for the Sabbath as to have a peculiar dread of sin such as shall awaken us to a very careful watch over ourselves." Next, we ought to abstain from worldly concerns. Our focus of concern on the Lord's Day should be upon Jesus Christ and his redemption. Third, we should spend time in religious exercises, looking upon such as rest and refreshment for the soul. Fourth, we are especially to meditate upon and celebrate the work of redemption. The Lord's Day is that day on which Christ rested and was refreshed after he had endured the labor of winning for us our salvation. This is the day, Edwards argues, following his typological exegesis of Scripture, of our deliverance out of Egypt. And, finally, this is a day for the work of mercy and charity, activities that are proper and acceptable to Christ on this day.

On the Lord's Day, as the Christian Sabbath, what better can be done, Edwards argues, than that we express our mercy and love to our fellow creatures and especially to fellow Christians. Christ loves to see us show our thankfulness in this manner. Therefore, Edwards argues, we find that the Holy Spirit was available that such work be performed on the first day of the week in the primitive church. For this reason, Edwards concludes, our text of 1 Corinthians 16:1-2 is especially appropriate. Contemporary theologian Robert Jenson writes, talking about the contribution and relevance of Edwards' thought, "Room is left for another kind of interpretation that evaluates Edwards' views not only by their originality or power or historical fruitfulness but by their intention of truth. One may ask not only why was Edwards great but was Edwards right?"[2] We can now add, one may ask not only *was* Edwards right, but *is* he?

---

2. Robert W. Jenson, *America's Theologian: A Recommendation of Jonathan Edwards* (New York: Oxford University Press, 1988).

Contributors

Horace T. Allen, Jr., Th.D., is Professor of Worship Emeritus, Boston University School of Theology; a minister of the Presbyterian Church, USA; and founding co-chair of the English Language Liturgical Consultation. He is author of numerous articles and handbooks on aspects of liturgy and worship.

Alkiviadis C. Calivas, Ph.D., is former president, dean, and Professor of Liturgics Emeritus at Holy Cross Greek Orthodox School of Theology; and a protopresbyter in the Greek Orthodox Church in America, a province of the Ecumenical Patriarchate. He is author of the three-volume *Essays in Theology and Liturgy* (Holy Cross Orthodox Press, 2002-3).

Donald B. Conroy, S.T.L., Ph.D., is a priest of the Catholic Diocese of Greensburg (PA); president of the International Consortium on Religion and Ecology; North American chaplain to the International Confederation of Christian Family Movements; and former member of the United Nations Advisory Committee on Environmental Sabbath/World Day of Rest. He is co-editor/author of *Earth at Risk: Advancing the Environmental Dialogue Between Religion and Science* (Humanity Books, 2000).

Ruy Costa, Ph.D., is Executive Director, The Episcopal City Mission, Boston; former Associate Director for Public Policy, Massachusetts Council of Churches; a minister in the Presbyterian Church, USA; principal author of "Globalization and Culture" for the PCUSA; and the editor/author of *One Faith, Many Cultures: Inculturation, Indigenization, and Contextualization* (Orbis/Boston Theological Institute, 1988).

Marva J. Dawn, Ph.D., author, musician, and educator, is associated with the parachurch organization Christians Equipped for Ministry in Vancouver, Washington. She also serves as Teaching Fellow in Spiritual Theology at Regent College in Vancouver, British Columbia; a Lutheran evangelical, she is the author of numerous works on Christian spirituality, including *The Sense of the Call: A Sabbath Way of Life for Those Who Serve God, the Church, and the World* (Eerdmans, 2006).

Darrell Guder, Ph.D., is Dean of Academic Affairs and Henry Winters Luce Professor of Missional and Ecumenical Theology, Princeton Theological Seminary; a minister in the Presbyterian Church, USA, he has served as president of the American Society of Missiology (ASM), 2007-8; and he is the author of numerous books in theology, including *The Continuing Conversion of the Church: Evangelization as the Heart of Ministry* (Eerdmans, 2000) and *Exhibition of the Kingdom of Heaven to the World* (Witherspoon Press, 2007).

Thomas Massaro, S.J., Ph.D., is Professor of Moral Theology and Director of the S.T.L. program at the School of Theology and Ministry at Boston College. He has authored a number of works on Catholic social teaching and the moral evaluation of public policies regarding domestic and international issues, including foreign policy, anti-poverty efforts, and globalization. His recent publications include *Living Justice: Catholic Social Teaching in Action* (Rowman & Littlefield, 2008).

Alexis McCrossen, Ph.D., is Associate Professor of History, Southern Methodist University. An author and frequent speaker on topics of Sabbath/Sunday and popular culture in the United States, she is the author of *Holy Day, Holiday: The American Sunday* (Cornell University Press, 2002) and is the editor/author of *Land of Necessity: Consumer Culture in the United States-Mexico Borderlands* (Duke University Press, 2009).

Timothy A. Norton, co-director of the Lord's Day Alliance of the U.S., has served the organization since 2000. A graduate of the University of Central Florida (B.A. in Organizational Communication) and Southwestern Baptist Theological Seminary (M.A. in Christian Education), Norton has been an associate pastor and development vice president, and is founder and principal consultant of his fundraising, marketing, and communications consulting firm, Crux Communication. He serves as associate editor of *Sunday* magazine.

Edward O'Flaherty, S.J., Ph.D., is Director of the Office of Ecumenical and Inter-religious Affairs of the Roman Catholic Archdiocese of Boston, and a member of several ecumenical organizations, including the Board of Directors of the Massachusetts Council of Churches and the Lutheran–Roman Catholic Dialogue of New England. He has served as president of Weston Jesuit School of Theology. He is the author of *Iglesia y Sociedad en Guatemala (1524-1563)* (Universidad de Sevilla, 1984) and has reviewed anthropological studies for theological journals.

Dennis T. Olson, Ph.D., is the Charles T. Haley Professor of Old Testament Theology and chair of the Biblical Studies Department, Princeton Theological Seminary. An ordained Lutheran minister, he has chaired the Convocation of Teaching Theologians for the Evangelical Lutheran Church in America. His research interests include the Pentateuch, the exegesis of Genesis and Exodus, Old Testament theology, and the relationship of biblical theology and the practice of ministry. He is a prolific author and is currently the Pentateuch general editor for a thirty-volume project titled *The Encyclopedia of the Bible and Its Reception* (Walter de Gruyter).

Rodney L. Petersen, Ph.D., is Executive Director, Boston Theological Institute, and teaches in its member schools; a minister in the Presbyterian Church, USA, he has served as pastor in Presbyterian and United Church of Christ churches and works with several voluntary organizations, including the Refugee Immigration Ministry (RIM), the Alternatives to Violence Program (AVP), and the Inter-Religious Center on Public Life (ICPL). He is the editor/author of numerous publications related to theological education, including *Theological Literacy for the Twenty-first Century* (Eerdmans, 2002), and *The Antioch Agenda* (ISPCK, 2007).

Aída Besançon Spencer, Ph.D., is Professor of New Testament, Gordon-Conwell Theological Seminary. Originally from the Dominican Republic, she has taught English and Spanish in the Caribbean and North America. Dr. Spencer has worked as a community organizer, social worker, minister, and educator in a wide variety of urban settings; an ordained minister in the Presbyterian Church, USA, she sits on several boards, including the boards of reference for the Network of Presbyterian Women in Leadership and for Christians for Biblical Equality. Her publications include, with William David Spencer, *Joy Through the Night: Biblical Resources for Suffering People* (Wipf & Stock, 2007) and *Ministering Together in the Church* (Wipf & Stock, 2008).

Gloria White-Hammond, M.D., is a staff pediatrician at the South End Community Health Center in Boston, Massachusetts. Together with her husband, Raymond Hammond, M.D., she is co-pastor at Bethel AME Church in Jamaica Plain, Massachusetts. In addition to her other responsibilities, she is the founder of and consultant to the church-based creative writing and mentoring ministry called Do the Right Thing, for high-risk black adolescent females. Dr. White-Hammond serves on the Executive Committee of the Boston Partners in Education and on the Children's Health Advisory Committee of the Harvard School of Public Health and the Women's Health Leadership Forum of Brigham and Women's Hospital. Additionally, she is founding director of My Sister's Keeper (Darfur Action).

Index of Subjects

Abraham, 30, 168, 172, 174
Adam, 175
alterity, 139; erotic, 148-50, 154; pedagogical, 150-51, 152, 154; political, 151-53, 154
American Academy of Religion, 30
Amish people, 27, 33-34
Anglicans, 102, 179
Annan, Kofi, 14
Athanasius, 62
attention deficit hyperactivity disorder (ADHD), 6
Augustine, 62, 84

B'Tselem, 16
Bancroft, Henry Howe, 130
Bancroft, Matilda, 130
baptism, 97, 112, 116
Baptism, Eucharist and Ministry, 116
Baptists, 63
Barth, Karl, 95, 102, 107n.4, 113, 117
Basil the Great, 73, 75, 88
Bediako, Kwame, 108
Beecher, Catherine, 129
Beecher, Henry Ward, 129-30
Beecher, Lyman, 129
Between Sundays (Ramshaw), 100
Blake, William, 10, 11
blue laws. *See* laws, governing the Sabbath

Boaz, 23, 26
Bobrinskoy, Boris, 74
Borgmann, Albert, 21
Boston Theological Institute, 108
Bowling Alone (Putnam), 148
Buddhist tradition, on rest, 168
busyness, 7-8, 10. *See also* time
Byzantine Rite, 69, 70

Cahill, Thomas, 173-74
Calivas, Fr., 87
Calvin, John, 63, 93n.1, 94
canonicity, 101-2
capitalism, and the Sabbath, 147
Catholicism: on importance of Sunday gathering, 88-90; social ethics of, 134, 136-38; and use of Scripture and lectionary systems, 98-99, 101, 103-4
Chariots of Fire, 10
Children's Defense Fund, 5
Chinese traditions, on rest, 168
Christ. *See* Jesus Christ
Christianity, shift in, 106, 108. *See also* church
Christmas, 94, 98
Chrysostom, John, 75
church: calendar, 93-98; early, x, 46, 53, 61-62, 71-72, 79, 80-81, 87-88, 93, 97, 100, 112-16, 166-67, 176; liturgy, 98-

Index of Scripture and Other Ancient Sources